OUTLAWS
OF THE WILD WEST

For the Treadwell family:
Toby, Sam, Rex and Bebe

OUTLAWS
OF THE WILD WEST

TERRY C. TREADWELL

FRONTLINE
BOOKS

OUTLAWS OF THE WILD WEST

First published in Great Britain in 2021 by

Frontline Books
An imprint of
Pen & Sword Books Ltd
Yorkshire - Philadelphia

ISBN 978 1 52678 237 3

A CIP catalogue record for this book is
available from the British Library

Typeset in 10.5/13 pt Palatino
by SJmagic DESIGN SERVICES, India.

Printed and bound by CPI Group (UK) Ltd, Croydon, CR0 4YY

Pen & Sword Books Ltd incorporates the Imprints of Aviation, Atlas,
Family History, Fiction, Maritime, Military, Discovery, Politics, History,
Archaeology, Select, Wharncliffe Local History, Wharncliffe True Crime,
Military Classics, Wharncliffe Transport, Leo Cooper, The Praetorian Press,
Remember When, Seaforth Publishing and Frontline Publishing.

For a complete list of Pen & Sword titles please contact

PEN & SWORD BOOKS LTD
47 Church Street, Barnsley, South Yorkshire, S70 2AS, England
E-mail: enquiries@pen-and-sword.co.uk
Website: www.pen-and-sword.co.uk

Or

PEN AND SWORD BOOKS
1950 Lawrence Rd, Havertown, PA 19083, USA
E-mail: Uspen-and-sword@casematepublishers.com
Website: www.penandswordbooks.com

Contents

Introduction

There is a popular misconception, created by writers and filmmakers, about the outlaws that roamed the American West in the period between 1850 and 1900. Some of them appear as colourful, romanticised, legendary characters, such as Frank and Jesse James, who had stepped outside the law due to the harshness of life after the Civil War, or under circumstances beyond their control. In some cases this was true, but in the vast majority of cases it was not. In the main they were dirty, hard-drinking layabouts who occasionally were forced to work through necessity.

With new settlers arriving with almost every boat, the surge into the West continued unabated and with these settlers came the misfits of society. Amongst them were gamblers, prostitutes, swindlers and fugitives from justice, convicted criminals, adventurers, deportees and indentured servants. The wilderness, into which the majority of these new settlers headed, was harsh beyond any comprehension they may have had, and it was the misfits who quickly tired of the arduous daily grind to keep enough food on the table. It was from this background that the majority of outlaws came. There were also a few educated ones who came from good families, who were just headstrong and looking for excitement, and then there were the ones that were the end product of the Civil War. The latter found themselves with nothing after the war, and to survive, some of them turned to a life of crime, but these were the exception rather than the rule.

The word outlaw usually struck fear into the hearts of law-abiding people in the West, but it was not a word that was unique to them. The word goes back to Anglo-Saxon times when the word outlaw meant just that: 'outside of the law'. Other names used at the time in the West, were 'Desperado', 'Road Agents' and 'Brigands'. The word 'Desperado' is an old Spanish word and 'Brigand' comes from the Italian 'Brigantes' or bandits of the Mediterranean mountains.

One of the first recorded outlaws arrived with the Pilgrim Fathers in 1620. He was a man by the name of John Billington who came from London. During the voyage to the New World, he had been disciplined by the captain of the *Mayflower* for using blasphemous language. During the next ten years or so Billington fought with the other colonists on a regular basis, then in 1630 he was convicted of the killing of a man by the name of John Newcombe, and was hanged. He became the first convicted murderer of the American colonialists.

The outlaw came into his own in the mid- to late nineteenth century. A few outlaws became household names, like the James brothers, Billy the Kid, Butch Cassidy and the Sundance Kid, and Henry Plummer, but the vast majorities were the nameless misfits of society. In 1877 the State Adjutant General of Texas, in that one year, posted wanted posters for some 5,000 outlaws and bandits in the Rio Grande district alone. He even went as far as asking Congress to approach the Mexican government and ask them to stop shielding American outlaws. Northern Texas and Kansas were deemed to be the wildest areas of America, and as one writer put it, 'Every small town had hundreds of saloons populated by depraved people who used whiskey'.

It was also very difficult to find anyone who was prepared to wear a badge and enforce the law. A perfect example of this is in the memoirs of a man called Bob Wright, one of the founders of Dodge City. He wrote that when Dodge City sprang up, the nearest law was over 90 miles to the north-west in Hays City. People in Dodge had to settle any disputes themselves – one way or another, with handgun, shotgun or rifle.

The outlaws, who were the scourge of the west for a number of years, were not, as some 'dime novelists' put it, the Robin Hoods of the West. Far from it: the majority were just a collection of vicious, violent, devious low-life, who showed a complete disregard for anyone or anything. They spent their ill-gotten gains on women, gambling and whiskey and displayed little or no respect for civilised behaviour, the law or compassion for their fellow man. The following stories are of just a few of the outlaws that terrorised the West in its formative years.

Chapter 1

William Clarke Quantrill

During the American Civil War a number of outlaws operated under the guise of guerrillas, fighting on the side of the Union or the Confederacy. Amongst the worst of these was a band led by William Clarke Quantrill, which came to be known as Quantrill's Raiders. They consisted of supporters of the Confederacy, and operated by harassing the Union Army and attacking their supply lines. Initially senior Confederate officers encouraged their raids on the enemy, but as time went on the 'raiders' became more and more barbaric, feeling they had the freedom to do whatever they wanted to, looting, raping and killing without reason, all under the flag of the Confederacy.

William Quantrill was born in Canal Dover, Ohio on 31 July 1837, the oldest of twelve children. His childhood was marred by an abusive father who died leaving the family destitute and with large debts. Quantrill became a schoolteacher at the age of 16 in order to help the family survive. After a year of teaching he left to take a job in a lumberyard in order to earn more money. It was whilst working in the lumberyard that he had his first encounter with the law, when he killed a man in a fight. He pleaded self-defence, and as there

A young William Clark Quantrill.

1

were no witnesses and the man was a complete stranger to the area, he was released without charge. The law, however, still unsure about the incident, advised him to leave the area and move on. Quantrill moved to Fort Wayne, Indiana and took up the post of schoolteacher. This job only lasted a year and he moved back to Canal Dover to live with his family.

In 1857 there was a move by many people from Ohio to relocate to Kansas in search of cheap land. Two local men, Henry Torrey and Harmon Beeson, were persuaded by Quantrill's mother to take her son William along with them. The two men agreed to pay for a parcel of land for the Quantrills in return for several months' work from William.

Torrey, Beeson and Quantrill settled in Marais de Cygnes, Kansas and purchased some land for the three of them. The promise given by William Quantrill to work for some land just faded away after a couple of months and he spent most of his time just wandering about the land with a rifle. Because of this Torrey and Beeson laid claim to the land they had purchased for Quantrill and, after a court case, were awarded compensation of which they only received a small part.

In the meantime Quantrill had taken up with some of his hometown friends who had started a settlement on Tuscarora Lake near Erieville, New York. This arrangement lasted for only a couple of months as Quantrill was caught stealing from some of the other settlers' cabins and he was thrown out of the settlement. In January 1858 Quantrill signed on as a teamster with the US Army expedition that was heading to Salt Lake City, Utah. Nothing more is known of him until one year later when he appeared in Lawrence, Kansas teaching school. The school closed the following year, leaving Quantrill unemployed.

He joined up with a band of outlaws who were rustling cattle and stealing horses and then discovered that they were capturing runaway slaves and selling them. This gave him the idea of using free black slaves as a kind of bait to lure in runaways and then return them to their owners for a reward. Finding this quite lucrative, he expanded this enterprise by raiding farms where he knew slaves were kept, and taking them under the pretence that he was an anti-slavery fighter. He then took the freed slaves, and some of the livestock he appropriated, and re-sold them to other farms. This former bible/school teacher from Utah, who had a sideline as a horse thief, soon found himself wanted for horse stealing, slave stealing and murder. The start of the Civil War was a godsend to Quantrill, as he could now carry on plying his vile trade under the umbrella of fighting for the Confederate cause.

In 1861 William Quantrill went to Texas with a Cherokee Indian and Confederate sympathiser by the name of Marcus Gill, who happened to be the war chief of the Cherokee Nation in Texas. He and Quantrill enlisted in the 1st Cherokee Regiment of the Confederate Army, serving under General Sterling Price. Whilst in the regiment, Quantrill became friendly with a man called Joel Mayers who taught him all about guerrilla warfare tactics. After fighting in two battles, Wilson's Creek and Lexington, Quantrill deserted and went to Blue Springs, Missouri, to set up his own guerrilla organisation.

Once set up with a small hard core of like-minded men, he offered his services to the Confederate Army and recruited a large number of criminals and misfits into his outfit, including a man by the name of Bill Anderson, who was later to become known as 'Bloody' Bill Anderson. Quantrill's Raiders, as the unit became known, had grown to over 400 men and had come to the attention of the leaders of the Confederate Army. They recognised the disruptive potential of the hit-and-run raids that Quantrill's Raiders were prepared to carry out, and although they did not agree with some of their methods, it was decided to unofficially commission them to carry out attacks against the Union Army and their strongholds. This in effect gave the Raiders unfettered permission to do whatever they wanted. They would operate behind enemy lines and harass Union troops

William Clark Quantrill in the early part of the Civil War.

'Bloody' Bill Anderson.

and interrupt their supply lines in a series of hit-and-run raids, taking no prisoners. Initially they only did this, but the majority of the raiders, being the killers and criminals that they were, also used this role to

3

Left: A later picture of William Clark Quantrill.

Below: Jesse and Frank James when riding with Quantrill's Raiders.

carry out raids on innocent people, killing and looting. Among some of those who rode with Quantrill, were Frank and Jesse James, Arch Clement, Dave Pool, Bill Hendricks, and Cole and Jim Younger.

One of their most notorious raids was carried out on a town called Lawrence, Kansas. In August 1863, 450 men rode into the town, and as they rode down the main street, they calmly and methodically started shooting all the men and boys they could see. As they did so, the womenfolk stood and watched helplessly as the merciless killings continued. Over 150 men and boys were slaughtered, along with a number of women who just happened to be in the way. The excuse given by Quantrill for the raid was that the town was being used as a Union Army supply centre and that his men had been fired on. The truth was more likely to be somewhere between that and that the raiders liked to kill. The raid lasted two hours, and after looting and torching much of the town, and leaving the dead sprawled all over the streets, the Raiders left. A second similar raid was carried out on Baxter Springs, Kansas two months later, but by now a large number of the 'Raiders' were seeing the raids for what they were – excuses to kill and loot. A large number of Quantrill's men decided that enough was enough and 'deserted'.

Amongst his Raiders was said to have been a woman fighter by the name of Sue Mundy, a specialist in artillery. She in fact was a He, a man by the name of Marcus Jerome Clark and had been

Three of Quantrill's most vicious raiders. L–R: Dave Poole, Arch Clement and Bill Hendricks.

One of Quantrill's Raiders.

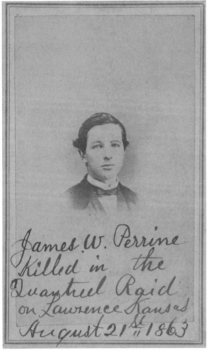

Above: Drawing of Quantrill's Raiders sacking the town of Lawrence, Kansas.

Left: Photograph of young James Perrine, killed in the raid on Lawrence, Kansas, by Quantrill's Raiders.

'Sue Mundy', said to be one of the few female members of Quantrill's Raiders but in fact a man by the name of Marcus Jerome Clark.

given the name 'Sue' because of his long hair and delicate appearance. He was with a group of renegades that was headed for Paris, Tennessee, when they came under fire from the local militia loyal to the Union. One of their gang was killed and a number wounded. The remnants of the group took shelter in a barn, but word had reached the Union Army garrison at Louisville who immediately sent a troop of soldiers to deal with them. They surrounded the barn and demanded their surrender. 'Sue' agreed on the condition that they would be treated as prisoners of war, which was assured. He and the others were hanged three days later.

The Confederate Army were both sickened and angered by Quantrill's Raiders and refused to acknowledge them. They even sent out troops to try and locate the Raiders in an effort to bring them to justice – as did the Union Army. With his force greatly depleted and troops from both armies looking for him, Quantrill, and with what was left of his Raiders, headed for Texas, where they carried out a series of robberies and murders. At the end of the war, Quantrill realised that the whole of the Union Army would soon be after them and decided to surrender, claiming that they were regular Confederate troops, a point that would be strongly argued against by the Confederacy.

But the days of Quantrill and his Raiders were numbered when on 10 May 1865, whilst trying to join up with General Robert E. Lee, Quantrill and some of his men were cornered at the James Wakefield farm near Smiley, Spencer County, Kentucky, all wearing Federal uniforms. They came under attack from a Union Ranger party and, in trying to escape, William Quantrill was badly wounded and two of the men with him killed. He was taken to the military prison, Louisville, Kentucky and given the barest of medical treatment. William Clarke Quantrill died on 6 June 1865.

However, 'Bloody' Bill Anderson had left Quantrill earlier, together with Arch Clement, Frank and Jesse James and their cousins Bob and Cole Younger, amongst a number of other outlaws. The gang attacked and looted the Union stores depot at Centralia, Missouri, and whilst in the process of doing this, a train arrived carrying twenty unsuspecting Union soldiers. Anderson ordered all the soldiers from the train and watched as Arch Clement shot them all dead – one by one.

Above left: Frank James after his release from prison.

Above right: The body of 'Bloody' Bill Anderson.

The gang went on the run, pursued by Union soldiers who were hell-bent on revenging their comrades. As the gang fled to the north of Missouri, the soldiers intercepted them and shot almost all of them down, including Bill Anderson and Arch Clement. The James Boys and Younger Brothers, however, escaped, and headed for the family ranch, where they laid low for a couple of years.

The James/Younger Gang.

Chapter 2

Sarah Catherine Quantrill

Although Sarah Quantrill was never an outlaw inasmuch as she never robbed or killed anyone, she was the wife of William Clarke Quantrill and accompanied him on a number of his murderous raids and enjoyed the spoils from the subsequent robberies and looting that took place.

Sarah Catherine Quantrill (née King) first met William Clarke Quantrill at her father's farm near Blue Springs, Missouri, in the winter of 1861. She was just 13 years old and Quantrill was 23. Quantrill, and more than a hundred of his men had set up camp around Robert King's farm. Sarah King arrived home from school to find her father and Quantrill discussing the progress of the Civil War, and was instantly attracted to the young charming Confederate officer. He was handsome, had blue eyes, was well built, and carried himself with an air of arrogance and self-assuredness. Despite the age difference William Quantrill was immediately attracted to Sarah. Neighbours who knew her remembered that she was very pretty and looked much older than she was.

Sarah Quantrill.

Sarah had been raised on the farm, spending most of her time outdoors. She had been riding since she was old enough to hold a rein. William Quantrill started to make frequent visits to the King farm after his introduction to Sarah. He regularly dined with her and her family, and the two of them took long horseback rides together. It didn't take long before Sarah's mother and father became concerned about the relationship that was developing and the age difference between the two of them. In an effort to put an end to it, Sarah's parents made it clear to both Quantrill and Sarah that they were concerned about what they considered to be an inappropriate relationship and wanted it to end and forbade Sarah to see William Quantrill again. But the strong-willed Sarah had other ideas and the arrogant William Quantrill refused to obey and they continued their relationship in secret. Sarah would sneak out the house to meet Quantrill and the pair continued to spend time talking about their lives and possibilities for the future.

William Quantrill was very open with Sarah about his difficult upbringing and trouble with authorities. His family came from Hagerstown, Maryland and he was born at Canal Dover, Ohio, on 31 July 1837. He told Sarah that he was a quiet, reserved boy, but would fight if drawn into a brawl and was obliged to defend himself. He said that in his early years he had wanted to become a teacher and potential landowner. He told her about some neighbours buying a piece of land on his behalf, because he was too young to enter into an agreement with a bank to purchase the property. Quantrill said that later when he asked for the deeds they refuse to give them to him saying that the property was theirs. Angered by this, he stole some of their livestock and was arrested for the theft. Whether this was true or not is not known.

Shortly after this he moved to Kansas where he became a schoolteacher. When asked about the war William Quantrill told Sarah that he had been friends with John Brown and that the two disagreed with slavery. They made midnight raids across the border into Missouri and stole slaves away from their owners and sent them into freedom. This in fact was not true; he did carry out raids to steal slaves, but not to give them their freedom but to sell them to other landowners. When asked why he fought for the South if he was against slavery, he replied it was due to an act of treachery. He and three other Confederates had planned to make a midnight raid on Morgan L. Walker, a rich farmer in Jackson County, Missouri, not far from Sarah's family's farm. Quantrill and the three with him were going to steal slaves and other property. In order to make sure the way was clear Quantrill rode ahead of the others.

On entering the Walkers' house he was pleasantly surprised at the family's kindly reaction to him when they welcomed him and gave him dinner. Their hospitality caused him to reconsider his actions, so instead of returning to his comrades and carrying out the raid, Quantrill revealed the whole plot to Walker and his sons, even to the point of telling them where the men were hiding out. Heavily armed, Walker and his sons crept up on the raiders. On catching them unawares the Walkers opened fire, and one of the raiders was killed. The other two escaped, but were eventually hunted down and killed. This was a perfect example of the devious and untrustworthy character of William Clarke Quantrill.

Not long afterwards William Quantrill persuaded Morgan Walker and his sons to join forces with him and his Raiders. By the end of 1860, Quantrill had convinced Sarah that he was at the head of a powerful guerrilla band on the side of the South. He bragged that when the war broke out his name was already a terror in the free state of Kansas.

Sarah was besotted with Quantrill and made plans to leave the family home and make a new life with him. Things came to a head when a neighbour saw her and Quantrill riding together and told her parents. Her father, furious that he been disobeyed, took her horse away from her. After a couple of days she walked to the Raiders' camp and told Quantrill what had happened. A couple of months later, in the spring of 1851 she and Quantrill decided to marry. He took her to the home of a country preacher where they exchanged vows, spending their wedding night in an abandoned cabin close by. Because he knew he was now a wanted man and had made many enemies, Quantrill insisted that Sarah changed her name to Kate Clarke (Clarke was Quantrill's middle name) to protect her identity to which she agreed.

The towns targeted by Quantrill and his Raiders were the pro-Union ones in Kansas and his wife Sarah accompanied him on a number of these and watched as they murdered innocent men, women and sometimes children. Just six months into the Civil War, William Quantrill and his raiders left the Confederate Army mainly because, in his opinion, they were not using his guerrilla tactics as they should. Over the next few months the guerrillas attacked Union mail coaches and soldiers in a series of hit-and-run raids. These skirmishes started to attract a certain kind of man, one that would kill without compunction and steal without thought. Sarah Quantrill shared a camp with these renegades seemingly untouched by the brutality of the guerrillas, but obviously enjoying a relatively luxurious lifestyle. On 7 September she accompanied her husband on an attack on the town of Olathe, Kansas.

One hundred and forty guerrillas entered the town after first blocking all the exits, and using their horses as shields, advanced towards the 125 Union soldiers who were supposedly guarding the town. All but one surrendered and he was subsequently shot. They then stood by whilst the guerrillas looted the town and then left. They headed for the town of Wellington in Lafayette County, Missouri.

Their stay was short lived as a large contingent of Union troops was discovered to be on their way. Sarah left with a large number of stolen horses whilst the remainder of the men split up to rendezvous later at a predetermined place. Once the coast was clear the renegades met up with Sarah who arrived with the fresh horses. She left once again, this time on her own and went to live in an area called Bone Hill close to the city of Missouri, Kansas.

Sarah moved to Fort Scott, Kansas in October 1862 just after her husband had attacked and sacked the town of Shawnee, Kansas, during which he burned the town to the ground and killed more than a dozen men and young boys by shooting them in the back of the head. The guerrillas then attacked the town of Lawrence, Kansas, where they murdered between 160 and 190 men and boys before burning over half of the town (154 buildings). Only one of the Raiders was killed, a man called Larkin Scaggs.

Drawing of Lawrence, Kansas, after the raid by Quantrill

13

Outside of the town, but watching the massacre, Sarah Quantrill (Clarke) waited for her husband. As the band of Raiders left, it was realised that the Union Army was going to descend on them and so it was decided to disband. Quantrill and his wife headed for Texas whilst the rest of his bloodthirsty renegades dispersed to various parts of the state. For the next few weeks, Quantrill and his wife moved about Missouri before settling for a while in Perche Hills in Howard County, Missouri. During their time there Quantrill showered Sarah with the jewellery that he had stolen during raids, the majority of which was from Lawrence.

The Raiders formed up two months later and attacked the town of Baxter Springs, Kansas, ransacking it. Once again they split up and for the next year the Quantrills kept a low profile, but William was planning and organizing his next band of guerrillas. He had kept in touch with some of his trusted men and arranged to meet up with them in Jackson County, Missouri and among these was Jesse James. In June 1864, as the band of renegades started to build, Quantrill sent his wife to St. Louis, Kentucky.

Then on 10 May 1865 Sarah Clarke heard that her husband had been badly wounded and taken prisoner. She found out that he was in the hospital of a military prison in Louisville, Kentucky. He had been given the barest of medical treatment and was dying of his wounds. Sarah managed to get into the prison and for the next two days stayed at his side in the appalling conditions of the prison 'hospital'. But she too was wanted by the Union Army and so was persuaded to leave. William Clarke Quantrill died on 6 June 1865. As one Confederate soldier put it, 'he was the bloodiest man in the annals of America'.

Sarah Catherine Clarke was later traced to a small town in Kansas where she had a boarding house. The authorities tried to take back some of the jewellery and monies that had been stolen during the raids by Quantrill, but were unsuccessful so abandoned the idea. Sarah Clarke died in the Jackson County Home for the Aged in February 1930, survived by a daughter, Bertha Ivins-Evans.

Chapter 3

The James Boys

Frank and Jesse James were born in Missouri, the sons of Baptist minister the Reverend Robert Sallee and Zerelda James. At the beginning of the Civil War, Frank James joined the Missouri State Guard and was wounded during a battle for Lexington, Missouri. He was left behind when the Confederate Army retreated and was hospitalised by the Union Army. He was paroled after swearing allegiance to the Union and allowed to go home. After recovering from his wounds, Frank James ignored his parole and joined up with a guerrilla band known as the 'Bushwackers', under the command of Fernando Scott. He later joined Quantrill's unit and was involved in the infamous Lawrence Massacre.

Whilst with the 'Bushwackers', Frank was joined by his brother Jesse, who had initially joined up with a local group known as Drew Lobb's Army who were involved in the Battle of Wilson's Creek. During the battle Jesse was seriously wounded, causing him to be hospitalised. Once he had recovered he joined up with his brother Frank, and together they fought throughout the remainder

Jesse and Frank James.

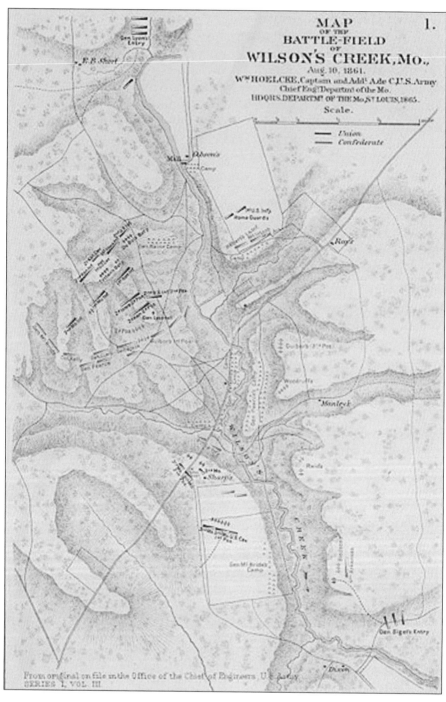

Map of the Battle of Wilson's Creek.

of the war with guerrilla units, initially with the 'Bushwackers' and later with 'Bloody' Bill Anderson and Quantrill. Towards the end of the war, when Quantrill's Raiders were being hunted by both the Union and the Confederacy, Jesse suffered a serious chest wound when they were ambushed by a Union patrol near Lexington, Missouri. He managed to get away and was able to recover at the home of his uncle in Harlem, Missouri, where he later met up with his brother Frank.

With the Civil War over the James Boys suddenly appeared again in 1866, when, together with the Younger Brothers, they robbed the bank at Liberty, Missouri, getting away with $15,000 in gold and $50,000 in non-negotiable securities. After bagging up the money, Jesse James locked the cashier and the rest of the staff in the vault, threatening to shoot them if they tried to escape. During the gun battle that followed, an innocent bystander, a young lad, was shot and killed. One year later they struck again,

Right: Jesse James aged 17 when with Quantrill's Raiders.

Below: Liberty Bank, Missouri.

this time in Savannah, Missouri and during the robbery killed the local judge, William McClain. Two months later they attacked the bank at Richmond, Missouri, which resulted in the deaths of the mayor, the sheriff and the sheriff's young son. Over the next few months the gang robbed the bank in Russellville, Kentucky where they stole $14,000 and then again at Gallatin, Missouri, where they killed a bank clerk who dared to try and stop them. With the whole state looking for them, the gang went into hiding and it was to be over a year before they went on the rampage again.

This time the gang headed into Iowa and held up the county treasurer's office in Corydon and then robbed the local bank of $10,000 immediately afterwards. They stole the Kansas City Fair takings in 1871 and the following year they moved to train robberies. Their first was the Rock Island & Pacific train which was attacked a few miles outside Adair, Iowa. The gang stole a tie hammer and a spike bar from a railroad shed, which they used to pry off the fishplate that connected two rails of the track. They then removed the spike securing the rail and tied a rope around the loose section of track and hid behind a bank and waited for the train. As the train approached they pulled the rail away from the track, expecting the engineer to halt the train before the

The former Davies Savings Bank at Gallatin, Missouri.

18

gap in the rail. With full brakes applied the train screeched to a halt, but too late to miss the gap. To the horror of the gang the engine and most of the carriages fell onto their sides in a sickening sound of metal crushing against metal. In the ensuing crash, the engineer was killed and the fireman injured when the engine overturned and crushed them. The gang entered the express car and stole just $2,000 from the safe and then went to the passengers and stole a further $1,000 in jewellery and cash all the time explaining to the terrified passengers that they had not intended to hurt anyone.

In the next couple of years the gang robbed stagecoaches and trains. They then split up and went their separate ways. Newspapers and writers back in the East picked up stories about the gang and the tales of their exploits were greatly embellished.

Overturned railroad engine and carriages.

An almost identical railroad engine of the Rock Island Line to the one that was held up by the James/Younger gang.

Wells Fargo stagecoach.

Magazines appeared telling stories of the James Boys' 'daring deeds' and that they were the 'Robin Hoods' of the time, stealing from the rich and giving to the poor. Nothing was further from the truth. They were a pair of murdering criminals, who kept their ill-gotten gains within their family and had little regard for human life.

Despite numerous attempts by sheriffs and US Marshals to catch them they always seemed to be one step ahead all the time. Then, on a cold night in January 1875, Pinkerton and railroad detectives were tipped off that the James Boys were hiding out at the family farm. Seeing movement in the kitchen they threw lighted turpentine balls in through the windows, followed by a 33lb bomb.

Some reports say that following the explosion, Frank and Jesse James burst out firing as they did so and managed to escape. Other reports say that they were not even there, and that was just an excuse to cover up the fact that a nine-year old boy was killed in the explosion and that the mother of Frank and Jesse James had her right arm blown off.

When news of this atrocity leaked out, the myth surrounding the gang took on more appeal and sympathy as their exploits grew. However, most local people feared and loathed the gang and this turned to hatred when, in September 1876, the gang, now reformed, rode into Northfield, Minnesota intending to rob the bank there. The James Boys and Younger Brothers

The home of Jesse James.

Northfield Bank, Minnesota.

and four other members of the gang entered the bank and shot one of the clerks dead when he said he couldn't open the safe. The robbers had failed to notice that the safe was already open so the killing was unnecessary.

The alarm was raised and as the gang ran out of the bank, the citizens were waiting for them and opened fire. Two of the gang, Clell Miller and Bill Chadwell, were shot dead in the street and all three of the Younger Brothers were seriously wounded, only the James brothers escaping uninjured. All three Younger Brothers were tried and convicted and sent to prison for life. Bob Younger died in prison, whilst his brothers Cole and Jim were paroled in 1901 after serving 25 years.

Jesse James's .45 Schofield revolver.

Above left: Postcard of the James/Younger Gang members after their capture whilst robbing the Northfield Bank, Minnesota, some showing signs of being roughly manhandled by their captors.

Above right: Postcard showing the photographs of the men who caught the Northfield bank robbers.

Right: Bodies of Clell Miller and Bill Chadwell on public display after the Northfield Bank raid.

Above left: Cole Younger.

Above right: Cole and Jim Younger.

Left: Bob Younger in the early years.

The hunt for the remainder of the gang intensified and two weeks later near Madelia, Minnesota, one of the gang, Samuel Wells aka Charlie Pitts, was shot dead by a posse after they had cornered him and the rest of the gang. Frank and Jesse James escaped and split up, Jesse heading for Mexico, whilst Frank went to Texas. They later joined up and for a while the two of them rustled cattle across the border, but then decided to make their way back to Missouri. Word of their returning reached the Governor of Missouri, T.T. Crittenden, and he was determined that one way or another he was going to put a stop to the James brothers once and for all. He offered a $10,000 reward and assigned Clay County Sheriff James Timberlake to take care of it. Timberlake immediately contacted two of the James brothers' distant cousins, and former gang members, Bob and Charley Ford, who he knew had been involved in the planning of a couple of bank raids. He promised them full pardons if they helped in the capture of the brothers and as a bonus, part of the reward money.

Above left: Charlie Pitts, a member of the James/Younger Gang that raided the Northfield Bank.

Above right: Portrait shot of Jesse James.

Governor Thomas T. Crittenden.

Above: Sheriff James Timberlake who arrested Bob Ford after he had killed Jesse James.

Left: Charley Ford.

There was no love lost between the two sets of brothers and when the James brothers returned to the family ranch, the Fords notified the sheriff that they were going to take care of them. Frank James, in the meantime, had moved on, leaving Jesse James at home with his wife and children. On 3 April 1882, Bob and Charley Ford went to Jesse James's home. Jesse's wife was in the kitchen and Jesse was standing on a chair to straighten a picture, when Bob Ford pulled out a nickel-plated revolver (that Jesse had given him), and shot him in the back three times.

Bob Ford was arrested for murder, tried and found guilty, but was immediately pardoned by Governor Crittenden and given the reward money. Bob Ford was killed on 3 June 1882 by a drunken gunman, when he opened a saloon in direct competition with another saloon, something to which the owner took exception.

Five months later Frank James walked in to Governor Crittenden's office, calmly unbuckled his gun belt, and placed it on the governor's desk. After a number of trials he was acquitted despite there being strong evidence that he was involved in a number of killings. It appears that his early war record, and the general feeling of disgust at the death of Jesse James and how he had died, was instrumental in acquitting him. Frank James never returned to crime and died in 1915 at the family home.

Bob Ford, cousin of Jesse James, who shot him in the back for the reward money.

The body of Jesse James lying in his coffin.

Chapter 4

Bill Doolin

One of the few outlaws who could be said to have continued the 'Robin Hood' legacy, was Bill Doolin. Doolin was the leader of the Doolin Gang that had raided many banks in Oklahoma. When on the run from the law, Doolin had no problem finding places to hide out, because in his early years he had used some of the proceeds of his robberies to support people when they moved into the territory and were struggling financially.

In August 1893, the gang consisted of Bill Doolin, 'Bitter Creek' Newcomb, Ole Yountis, Charlie Pierce, Dan Clifton aka 'Dynamite Dick', Bob Grounds, Alf Sohn, Tulsa Jack Blake, Little Dick West, Little Bill Raidler, Roy Dougherty aka Arkansas Tom Jones, and Red Buck Weightman. They first struck in Kansas, where they robbed trains at Cimarron and Spearville. The gang then split up and headed for Ingalls in Oklahoma, where they met up in a hotel/saloon/brothel run by a madam by the name of Mary Pierce. Their arrival had not gone unnoticed and word was sent out that the gang was holed up in the establishment.

Bill Doolin.

Above: Murray's Saloon, Ingalls, Oklahoma, scene of the shoot-out between the Doolin/Dalton Gang.

Below left: Dan Clifton aka 'Dynamite Dick'.

Below right: Richard 'Little Dick' West.

 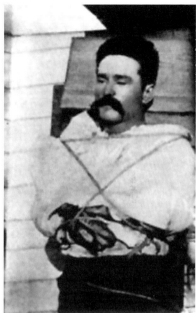

Above left: Roy Dougherty aka Arkansas Tom Jones.

Above right: Red Buck Weightman.

At the beginning of September, a covered wagon arrived containing fourteen deputy US marshals. As they got out, a young boy by the name of Dell Simmons pointed out 'Bitter Creek' Newcomb to the lawmen. However, Newcomb spotted the lawmen before they saw him and shouted a warning to the rest of the gang. Within minutes the silence of the street was shattered with the sound of gunfire and the whine of bullets. One of the first to be killed was young Dell Simmons, killed by Newcomb. In the ensuing gunfight three marshals were killed, Lafe Shadley, Dick Speed and Tom Houston. The gang made a run for the stables with the exception of Roy Dougherty, who was in an upstairs room when the firing started. Finding himself trapped, Dougherty started firing from the room. He gave himself up, when Marshal Jim Masterson, brother of the gunfighter Bat Masterson, threatened to blow the hotel up with dynamite if he didn't surrender.

A woman by the name of Rose Dunn, who had recently married Newcomb, aided the remaining members of the gang. She ran the gauntlet of bullets to take additional guns and ammunition to the outlaws, which enabled them to escape. Newcomb was badly wounded

Left: George 'Bitter Creek' Newcomb.

Below left: Deputy US Marshal Lafe Shadley.

Below right: Deputy US Marshal Richard 'Dick' Speed.

Right: Rose Dunn, George Newcomb's girlfriend.

Below: The three Guardsmen: 'Heck' Thomas, Chris Madsen and Bill Tilghman.

The Three Guardsmen

Heck Thomas   Chris Madsen   Bill Tilghman

during the shoot-out, but despite this he managed, aided by his bride, to get clean away. The gang headed for the lawless area of the Creek Nation, to hide up, but then were made aware that three of the toughest and most feared deputy US marshals, had been assigned to track them down – 'Heck' Thomas, Bill Tilghman and Chris Madsen.

To boost their rapidly dwindling funds, the gang carried out a raid on a bank at Woodward, Oklahoma where they netted $6,500. A number of other lawmen were also trailing the gang and amongst them was Deputy Sheriff Frank Canton who had served in Wyoming some years previously. He knew of Bill Doolin's practice of hiding out amongst friends who owed him favours, and so contacted the Dunn brothers, who were also suspected of having rustled cattle with Doolin. The offer of an amnesty and a reward for information leading to Doolin's capture, proved too tempting for the brothers. They told the lawmen that some of the gang were going to meet up at their place and some days later brought the bodies of Newcomb and Pierce into the town of Guthrie for identification. No questions were asked concerning how the two men met their death; such was the need to capture the gang.

One by one the gang was tracked down, the majority of them being shot dead when they refused to surrender. Among those captured were Bill Doolin and Bill Clifton who were held in the local jail at Guthrie. Somehow the two men managed to overpower the jailer and escape, along with a number of other prisoners. One of the Dunn brothers, Bill Dunn, told 'Heck' Thomas where Bill Doolin was hiding and even joined the posse that surrounded the house in which he was holed up. As he tried to make a break for it, Bill Dunn's shotgun cut him down, killing him. Concerned about his own safety, Bill Dunn later approached Frank

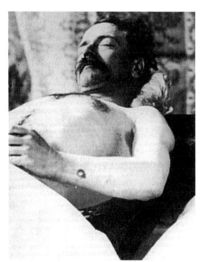 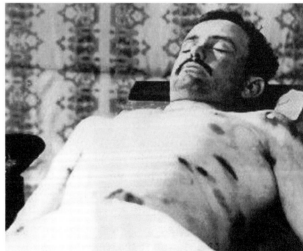

Above left: The body of George 'Bitter Creek' Newcomb after being gunned down by Rose Dunn's brothers for the reward.

Above right: Charlie Pierce's body after being gunned down by Rose Dunn's brothers for the reward money.

34

REWARD

$5,000.00

WANTED DEAD OR ALIVE!

BILL DOOLIN

NOTORIOUS ROBBER OF
TRAINS AND BANKS

ABOUT 6 FOOT 2 INCHES TALL, LT BROWN HAIR,
DANGEROUS AND ALWAYS HEAVILY ARMED

CONTACT THE GUTHRIE, OKLAHOMA TERR

U.S. MARSHAL'S OFFICE

Bill Doolin wanted poster.

Canton and threatened to shoot him if he told anyone about his double-dealings. He made the mistake of reaching for his gun as he did so, but Canton was faster and more accurate and killed him.

One of the other gang members, William 'Tulsa Jack' Blake continued to evade his pursuers, but whilst resting his horse, the posse, led by Deputy US Marshal William Bartling Murrill, caught up with him. Once again he managed to get away, but he was tracked to a hideout in Major County, Oklahoma. In a gun battle, that lasted almost an hour, Tulsa Jack made a break for it, but was shot and killed by Deputy US Marshal Murrill.

The break-up of the Doolin Gang didn't stop other outlaws from operating and one in particular, Henry Starr, was very active.

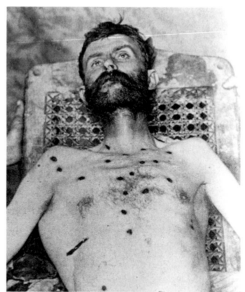

Above left: 'Heck' Thomas.

Above right: Bill Doolin's shotgun-peppered body lying on a slab.

Below left: William 'Tulsa Jack' Blake lying dead between the two lawmen who killed him.

Below right: 'Tulsa Jack' Blake lying in his coffin and 'dressed' for the occasion.

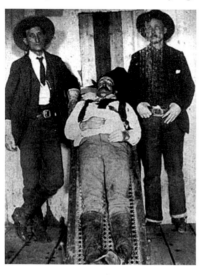

Chapter 5

Henry Starr

Henry Starr was born in the Indian Territory close to Fort Gibson, on 2 December 1873, the son of George Starr and Mary Scott Starr. His father was a half-breed Cherokee and his mother a quarter-breed Cherokee. His mother was a well-educated lady from a respectable family, whilst his father's family was rife with outlaws and criminals. His grandfather was the notorious outlaw Tom Starr, whilst his uncle was Sam Starr who was married to Belle Starr, also known as the notorious Outlaw Queen. She had been connected with the Younger Gang and had been involved in robberies and rustling throughout the Oklahoma Territory. Henry Starr disliked her intensely, saying that she was crude and unpleasant in every way and insisting that she was no relation to him, just his aunt by marriage.

Henry Starr, who was a distant relative of Belle Starr.

Henry Starr grew up in the north-east corner of the Indian Territory, which at the time was an area full of hideouts for a number of gangs that roamed the state. There was almost no law as only a handful of US marshals patrolled the vast area. The rugged terrain provided some natural hideouts that were almost inaccessible unless you were a member of these gangs.

Henry's father died in 1886, leaving his wife to care for their three children. Within a few months she married a man by the name of C.N. Walker, to who Henry took an instant dislike. Walker had no Indian blood in him and was a disciplinarian, which did not sit too well with Henry. After a couple of incidents between them Henry left and took a job as a cowboy on a ranch near Nowata, in the Indian Territory. It was while working on the ranch that he had his first contact with the law. He was driving a wagon into town when two deputy marshals stopped him and searched the wagon. They found some whiskey in the back and promptly arrested him and charged him with 'Introducing spirits into the territory'. Brought before the local judge, Henry Starr pleaded guilty on the basis that although it was found in the wagon he was driving, he maintained that he had no knowledge of it being there. He was convicted and fined.

Henry Starr resumed working at the ranch, and within a couple of months he was back in court, this time accused of the theft of a horse. He strenuously denied the charge but was remanded in custody at Fort Smith, Arkansas. One of his cousins put up bail money and Henry Starr was released. He immediately jumped bail and took to the road with an arrest warrant hanging over him. Henry Starr had decided that if he was going to be charged with offences that were not of his doing, he might as well commit offences

Deputy US Marshal Floyd Wilson.

38

and make money from them. The warrant for his arrest was given to two deputy US marshals, Henry Dickey and Floyd Wilson, both very experienced lawmen.

Henry Starr joined up with two friends, Ed Newcome and Jesse Jackson, and the trio started to rob stores and railroad depots. The first of their raids was in July 1892 when they attacked the Nowata railroad depot close to where they lived and stole $1,700. Four months later, after their money had run out, they robbed $300 from Shufeldt's store at Lenapah in the Indian Territory, quickly followed by robbing just $180 from the Carter's Store also in the Indian Territory. But the law was closing in on the three outlaws and in December the two deputy US marshals, Henry Dickey and Floyd Wilson, went to the XU Ranch, owned by a man named Arthur Dodge, after a tip-off that the three outlaws were going to meet there. Arthur Dodge denied knowing any members of the gang personally, but admitted having seen Henry Starr ride past occasionally. The two lawmen spent the rest of the day combing the surrounding area but without success, and then returned to the ranch. The following day they widened the search, but once again found nothing. Whilst having dinner at the ranch that evening one of the ranch hands told them that he had seen Henry Starr ride past an hour ago. Floyd Wilson immediately rushed to the barn where his already-saddled horse was waiting, and set off in the direction of where Starr was headed.

Floyd Wilson spotted Henry Starr close to an area called Wolf Creek. Starr saw Wilson at the same time and dismounted from his horse, whilst Floyd Wilson remained in the saddle watching Starr's every move. Wilson called out to Starr to surrender as he had a warrant for his arrest. Henry Starr appeared to just ignore him and was walking away when Floyd Wilson pulled his Winchester rifle from its scabbard and fired a warning shot over Starr's head. Starr immediately whirled around with a pistol in his hand and returned fire, hitting Floyd Wilson. In the ensuing gunfight Floyd Wilson fell to the ground wounded and attempted to jack another cartridge into the chamber of his rifle, but it jammed. Throwing the rifle aside he drew his pistol, but two more shots into his body forced him to drop it. Henry Starr then calmly walked over to the badly injured deputy US marshal lying on the ground and fired a single shot into his heart. A little while later Henry Dickey, who had had to saddle his horse, arrived to find his friend lying dead on the ground and Henry Starr gone.

Henry Starr was now wanted for the murder of a Federal officer, a deputy US marshal, and the efforts to find him were doubled. Starr teamed up with a man called Frank Chesney and together they started robbing railroad depots and stores. The first three of these took place in Choteau in the Indian Territory, where they robbed the MKT Railroad Depot of $189 and Haden's Store of $390. This was followed by robbing the railroad depot and general store in Inola of just $220.

Now having a total disregard for the law, Henry Starr and Frank Chesney went on a crime spree, only this time it was a bank. On 28 March 1893, the two men rode into the small town of Caney in Kansas and entered the Caney National Bank. Drawing their pistols as they walked in, the two outlaws forced the bank's employees and a couple of customers into a backroom and locked the door. They then entered the vault and stole $4,900 in cash, calmly walked out of the bank and rode away. By the time the alarm had been raised, the two outlaws were well away. One month later the pair robbed a passenger train at Pryor Creek in the Indian Territory, their first excursion into the world of train robberies and got away with $6,000.

Now considering himself untouchable, Henry Starr became arrogant and planned his next bank job. Three more outlaws had now joined him and Frank Chesney and they planned to rob the People's Bank of Bentonville in Arkansas late in the afternoon of 5 June just as they were closing. The five men rode brazenly into town and prepared to hit the bank. However, there was a problem because by now Henry Starr had become notorious and was instantly recognisable from the wanted posters springing up in the various states.

Two of the gang, Henry Starr, Kid Wilson and two others entered the bank just as it was closing, but they had been spotted and the alarm had been raised. The fifth member of the gang, tending the horses ready for a quick getaway, suddenly came under fire from members of the town. On hearing the gunfire Starr and Wilson ran from the bank, jumped on their horses and headed out of town. The remaining two outlaws in the bank grabbed what they could and they too jumped on their horses and headed out of town with a posse not far behind.

After riding hard for a number of hours they managed to give the posse the slip and met up in a prearranged spot share the proceeds of the robbery. After counting out the money they were bitterly disappointed to find that the total proceeds of the robbery was just $11,000, to be shared between five.

With the law closing in on the gang and a $5,000 reward now on the head of Henry Starr, the gang decided to part company and lie low for a while. At the beginning of July 1893, Henry Starr, Kid Wilson and a young woman caught the train to Emporia, Kansas. The three of them checked into the Spaulding House Hotel under assumed names, Henry Starr as Frank Johnson, Kid Wilson as John Wilson and the woman, who later turned out to be the wife of Henry Starr, as Mrs Jackson. Kid Wilson went to visit a friend in Colorado City whilst Starr and his wife went sightseeing and to buy some new clothes. It was whilst they were shopping in Emporia that Henry Starr was recognised and the law was informed. The following day Henry Starr was arrested in a restaurant and taken into custody. Officers then went to the hotel where they were all staying and, after waking Starr's wife, searched the room where they found $1,460 in cash and $500 in gold. She was arrested and taken into custody and after questioning told them where Kid Wilson was. The law in Colorado City was informed and Wilson was arrested and returned to Emporia. Deputy US marshals arrived from Fort Smith and took Starr and Wilson back to stand trial. There is no information of what happened to Starr's wife, but with the arrest of the two wanted men she probably became of no further interest to the authorities

Henry Starr was charged with thirteen counts of robbery and the murder of Federal officer Floyd Wilson. Appearing in front of Judge Isaac Parker, Henry Starr was found guilty and sentenced to hang. Starr's lawyers appealed the judgement successfully to the US Supreme Court and a retrial was ordered. A second trial produced the same verdict and sentence, but once again Starr's lawyers successfully appealed the judgement. At the third trial Starr pleaded guilty to manslaughter and was sentenced to three years for manslaughter, seven years for the robberies and one year for train robbery making a total of fifteen years in all. It was while in prison at Fort Smith awaiting transportation to the Federal prison at Columbus, that he met an old acquaintance, Crawford Goldsby, also known as 'Cherokee Bill'. An incident occurred when a trustee managed to smuggle a handgun in for Goldsby and he attempted to carry out a jailbreak. After a shoot-out with the guards, in which one of them was killed, there was a stalemate. They were unable to disarm Goldsby because he had barricaded himself in his cell. Henry Starr, who knew 'Cherokee Bill' quite well, offered to mediate and try and persuade him to give up, on the one condition that they promised not to kill 'Cherokee Bill' if he succeeded. Henry Starr entered the barricaded cell and, after a lengthy discussion, persuaded him that his situation was hopeless and that he should give himself up. 'Cherokee Bill' handed his weapon over and the two men exited the cell. Henry Starr then handed over the gun to the guards and was taken back to his cell.

Henry Starr was taken to the Federal prison at Columbus to serve his sentence, whilst 'Cherokee Bill' stood trial for murder and after being convicted, was hanged shortly afterwards.

In 1901 Henry Starr's father, with help from the Cherokee Tribal Government, made an application to President Theodore Roosevelt that his son might be pardoned. After careful consideration, including the part played by Henry Starr in resolving the stand-off in Fort Smith Prison, his sentence was reduced and in 1903 he was released.

For the next five years, Henry Starr lived a quiet, honest life working in his mother's restaurant in Tulsa, in the Indian Territory. During this time he married for the second time and produced a son. Then out of the blue came a warrant for his arrest after an extradition order from officials in Arkansas had been granted concerning the Bentonville Bank robbery in 1893. Henry left immediately, heading for the Osage Hills where he knew he could hide out with some old friends, one of whom was Kid Wilson now free from prison.

It didn't take long before Henry and his gang had planned the next bank robbery and on 13 March 1908, they rode into Tyro, Kansas and hit the local bank. Despite being pursued by a posse of over twenty men the gang got clean away and two months later Starr and Wilson robbed the bank in Amity, Colorado, for just $1,100. With it becoming more and more difficult to carry out robberies, because he was becoming very well known, Henry Starr and Kid Wilson went their separate ways. Henry Starr spent the rest of the year hiding out in New Mexico and Arizona. At the beginning of May 1909 he wrote to a friend back in Tulsa, who, obviously with one eye on the reward money, informed the authorities. Henry Starr was arrested in Arizona on 13 May and extradited to Colorado to stand trial for bank robbery.

After pleading guilty he was sentenced to seven to twenty-five years in Canon City Prison in Colorado. During his time in prison he studied law and wrote his autobiography entitled *Thrilling Events, Life of Henry Starr*. Four years later he was paroled by the governor on the condition that he never left Colorado, to which Henry agreed. True to form Henry Starr left Colorado almost immediately, headed straight for Oklahoma and went back to robbing banks. Fourteen banks in Oklahoma were robbed between 8 September 1914 and 13 January 1915, all attributed to Henry Starr and his gang. State legislature passed a bill called the 'Bank Robber Bill' appropriating $15,000 to the capture of the bank robbers and placing a $1,000 bounty, dead or alive, on Henry Starr.

US deputy marshals were convinced that Starr was hiding out in the rugged Osage Hills and scoured the area, but the wily Henry Starr was living in the centre of Tulsa at 1534 East Second Street, just two blocks from the Tulsa County Sheriff's office. Soon becoming bored; Henry Starr got a gang together and planned an audacious raid on two banks in the town of Stroud, Oklahoma. On 27 March 1915, Henry Starr and six of his gang rode into Stroud and hit the Stroud National Bank and the First National Bank simultaneously. Within minutes word had spread that the banks were being robbed and armed citizens opened fire on the robbers as they emerged from the banks. Henry Starr and Lewis Estes were shot and wounded during the gunfight, whilst the remaining members of the gang escaped with $5,815. After recovering from his wounds, Henry Starr pleaded guilty to the robbery of the bank in Stroud and was sentenced to 25 years and taken to the Oklahoma State Penitentiary at McAlester.

During his time in prison Henry Starr gave a number of interviews to the press about his life, saying that young people should take heed of what he was saying and not waste their lives like he had done. There was a certain method to this display of remorse as just four years later he was paroled once again. He stayed out of trouble for the next two years, even starring in a film called *A Debtor to the Law*, which included a scene depicting the Stroud Bank robberies. The film was a huge success and offers to make more films flooded in, including one from Hollywood. Henry Starr declined the Hollywood offer because he thought he was still wanted for the Bentonville bank robbery and they may take steps to extradite him. He did, however, make another three films and it was on the set of one of these that he met and married his third wife Hulda, who was from Salisaw, Oklahoma.

But the life of crime proved to be too irresistible to Henry Starr and on 18 February 1921, he and three others drove to Harrison, Arkansas, and entered the People's State Bank, robbing it of $6,000. But the citizens and the bank fought back and Henry was shot in the back and seriously wounded as he was leaving. The remaining members of the gang fled, leaving Henry lying on the floor of the bank. He was taken to the town jail where the local doctor removed the bullet from his back, but the following morning he died, with his wife, mother and son by his side.

Over his 32-year crime spree, Henry Starr robbed twenty-one banks, more than James/Younger Gang and the Doolin Gang managed together. He also claimed not to have shot anyone in the commission of a crime nor betrayed any of his accomplices.

Chapter 6

Belle Starr

The Starr family continued to make headlines throughout the West during this period and among them was the notorious Belle Starr. Born Myra Belle Shirley in Carthage, Missouri, on 5 February 1848, she was the youngest of three children. The family moved to Sceyene, Texas, in an effort to start a new life just after her elder brother was killed. At the age of 16, Belle met and became involved with Cole Younger, a member of the James Gang, who was in hiding after being involved in a number of bank robberies. Just months after meeting

Younger, Belle moved in with him in a remote cabin, where the couple stayed until the coast was clear.

Five months after Cole Younger had departed, Belle gave birth to a girl, who she named Pearl Younger, after the father. It was around this time that she met up with another outlaw by the name of Jim Reed, and when he was invited to join up with a gang of outlaws, Myra Belle, as she now called herself, went with him. After a couple of successful robberies, the gang split up, and Myra and her

A young Belle Starr.

Above left: Jim Reed.

Above right: Jim Reed and Belle Starr.

baby Pearl, and Jim Reed bought a small farm with their share of the proceeds. The law however was hot on Jim Reed's trail and so they sold up and headed for California.

The couple met up with the James/Younger Gang and settled down in the area. Over the next few years, the gang carried out a number of robberies and Myra had a second child, a boy, calling him Edward Reed after the father. Jim Reed became wanted by several law enforcement agencies forcing him to keep on the move, he eventually ended up hiding on Tom Starr's ranch. The Starr clan, headed by Tom Starr, had been given a large section of land by the Cherokee elders, as long as Tom Starr behaved himself after he had caused a great deal of trouble during the Civil War as a strong advocate for the Southern cause. The land was in a remote corner of Muskogee County, Oklahoma, and because of its remoteness became a haven for outlaws and the remnants of Quantrill's Raiders after the war.

Then in 1869, Jim Reed and Myra Belle, together with two other members of the gang, left to work on their own. They robbed a wealthy Creek Indian by the name of Watt Grayson of $30,000 in gold, torturing him and his wife for several days to find out where it was hidden, after

45

Tom Starr – head of the Starr family.

which they killed them both. The law was now hot on their trail and so the gang split up. Myra Belle and Jim Reed headed back to Texas to stay with relatives. Whilst there Jim Reed continued with his criminal activities and during an attempted robbery in August 1874, he was shot dead by Deputy Sheriff John Morris of Colin County, Texas.

With her partner dead, Myra Belle left her children with her relatives and went back to the Starr ranch, where she became involved with several men before joining up with Tom Starr's son Sam and married him. She renamed the ranch 'Younger's Bend', it is thought after her first lover Cole Younger. Myra took the name Belle Starr and organized a number of horse and cattle rustling offences, whiskey peddling and robberies over the next year or so. Sam Starr and Belle Starr set up one

Above left: A well-armed Belle Starr on her horse.

Above right: An older Belle Starr displaying her weapons.

of the most notorious rustling gangs of the time. Their luck ran out when they were caught stealing horses from a nearby ranch and taken to Fort Smith to appear in front of Judge Isaac Parker, a man not known for his leniency. Surprisingly they both received just a year in the state penitentiary and were released after having served just nine months. Within months of being released they were back to their old ways and were arrested for a second time. They were brought before Judge Isaac Parker once again, only this time they were released because of lack of evidence.

Moving away from the area, the pair continued with their activities and joined up with another outlaw, John Middleton, a cousin of Sam Starr. It soon became obvious that Belle Starr was attracted to Middleton. When Sam Starr found himself the centre of attention as far as the law was concerned, he headed for Arkansas to hide out, arranging to meet up with Belle Starr and John Middleton there. Middleton was also wanted by the law for the murder of Sheriff John Black of Lamar County and arson, so Belle Starr decided to take this opportunity to leave Sam Starr and run away with his cousin.

The two decided to travel separately so as not to attract attention, but somewhere along the way, someone caught up with John Middleton and killed him. It is though that Sam Starr might have had had something to with the murder, or had someone do it for him. Sam never saw Belle Starr again, as in December 1886; he was killed in a barroom during a shoot-out with a gunman by the name of Frank West. Frank West had been part of a posse that had in the past wounded and arrested Sam Starr. Starr was later rescued by his gang. The fatal chance meeting between Frank West and Sam Starr happened at a party given by one of the nearby ranchers. On seeing Frank West, Sam Starr accused him of shooting his horse and pulled out his pistol, shooting West in the neck. As he fell, Frank West pulled his pistol, and shot Sam Starr through the heart, killing him instantly. West died minutes later from his wound.

Belle Starr, now alone, was never short of admirers and even during her time with Sam Starr he realised that she was sharing her time with the other outlaws that were taking refuge on the ranch. One of these was a young outlaw by the name of Blue Duck, but this relationship didn't last long, as he was arrested after a robbery and sent to prison. Belle hired the best lawyers for his defence, but that was unsuccessful and she was soon romantically involved again, this time with a Creek Indian outlaw by the name of Jim July. All this time, Belle Starr's daughter Pearl had been growing up with relatives and in 1887, presented Belle

Belle Starr with Blue Duck.

with a granddaughter. Pearl refused to name the father, which angered Belle, and she refused to have anything to do with her granddaughter.

On the morning of 3 February 1889, Belle Starr and Jim July were riding toward Fort Smith, when Belle for some unknown reason suddenly decided to turn back, leaving July to go on alone. The next day Pearl Starr found Belle's horse in the yard still saddled and untethered. A search party was sent out and the body of Belle Starr was found face down in the mud, with shotgun wounds to her face and back. No one was ever charged with her murder; Jim July always suspected a neighbour, Edgar Watson, but no proof was ever presented. It transpired later that Jim July may have offered one of the outlaws at Younger's Bend, $200 to kill Belle after she had discovered that he had been seeing a young Cherokee girl and that Belle was refusing to help fund his defence in an upcoming trial. But once again there was no firm evidence to support this.

Whilst Belle Starr had been engaging in her outlaw ways, her daughter Rose Pearl Starr had been having thoughts about setting up her own business as an owner of a bordello. Whilst she was growing up, Pearl was well aware of her parents' lives of crime, mainly because they were always on the move trying to keep one step ahead of the law. Pearl's father was killed in a gunfight when she was six and so she was left with relatives.

Pearl Starr, who was Belle
Starr's daughter.

After her mother was murdered, Pearl left the Indian Territories where she had been living and set herself up as a prostitute in Van Buren, Arkansas. When people discovered that she was the daughter of the infamous Belle Starr her business increased as men, and occasionally women, flocked to see her.

Having made a considerable amount of money, Pearl moved across the river to Fort Smith, Arkansas, and established her own bordello. It was located on Fort Smith's water front street of gambling halls, saloons and bordellos, and was clearly lit up with a bright red star surrounded by lighted pearls. She set the bordello up with one of the best piano players around, making sure that her customers got only the best whiskey and the 'most beautiful girls west of the Mississippi'. Business boomed and so Pearl acquired some of the other bordellos and made a number of investments in saloons and other property.

As Fort Smith grew bigger and more people moved into the area, the city fathers decided it was time to clean the place up and in 1916, new ordinances made prostitution illegal. Pearl Starr was allowed to continue in business for a few years however, mainly because she kept strict, orderly houses but she was eventually arrested. The charges were dropped on the understanding that she left Fort Smith. She died in Arizona in 1925.

Chapter 7

The Wild Bunch

Amongst all the outlaws of the West, one group stands out alone, the Wild Bunch. Like a number of outlaws and outlaw gangs, they were glamorised by the newspapers and became the topic of a number of 'dime novels'. In later years the outlaws and the gangs became the

The Butch Cassidy gang aka The Wild Bunch. Seated L–R:
Harry Longbaugh (Sundance), Ben Kilpatrick, Robert Parker (Butch Cassidy).
Standing: William Carver, Harvey Logan (Kid Curry).

subject matter for numerous films as in the case of *The Wild Bunch* and *Butch Cassidy and the Sundance Kid*. The latter, starring Paul Newman and Robert Redford, became a huge cinematic success in 1969.

The Wild Bunch was the biggest and the last of the Western outlaw gangs. Originally known as the Hole-in-the-Wall Gang, their members became household names in later years.

Harry Longbaugh had acquired his nickname the Sundance Kid after having spent time in jail in the town of Sundance, Wyoming. How the gang got together is not known, but it was probably through meeting in the Hole-in-the-Wall hideout. This was a desolate natural basin

The Sundance Kid and Etta Place.

The Wild Bunch Hole-in-the-Wall hideout.

surrounded by steep, rugged buttes and bluffs. Within the walls of the basin were caverns and passages, which became a natural place to hide cattle and horses. The entrance to the valley was through a narrow gorge, which was impossible to enter without being seen by the men who were placed on guard there. The rustlers and robbers built cabins and corrals to accommodate themselves and the proceeds of their raids. The hideout became almost a small town and the occupants had to abide by the rules and regulations the men created to enable them to exist together.

Butch Cassidy had started life on a ranch in Utah, where his father Max Parker allowed rustlers to use his place as a way-station to water their stolen cattle or horses as they passed through. The young Butch helped drive the rustled cattle to a place called Robbers' Roost, where the rustling gangs kept their stolen cattle or horses. Inevitably he got drawn into this world and joined up with the Tom McCarty gang in Colorado.

He had taken the name Cassidy after an outlaw Mike Cassidy, who had helped him in his early years and who had now retired to Mexico. In November 1887 Butch and the McCarty gang attempted to hold up a Denver & Rio Grande train by piling wooden ties on

A young Butch Cassidy.

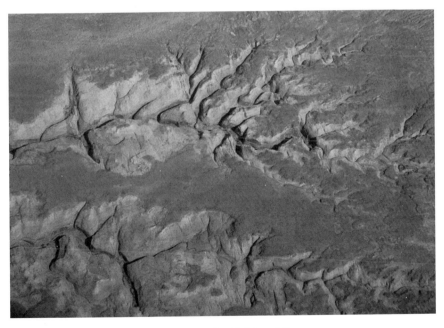

Aerial view of the canyon leading to the Robbers' Roost.

Stone cabin at the Robbers' Roost where Butch Cassidy and the Sundance Kid would hide out.

the track. The train stopped and the gang demanded that the express-car messenger open the safe, but he refused. The gang took a vote and decided that they wouldn't rob the passengers and removed the obstruction from the tracks. The train moved off to waves from the gang. This was typical of the sardonic sense of humour that was Butch Cassidy style and because of his prowess with a gun almost all were reluctant to challenge it.

It was this image as a lawbreaking prankster that was to keep him in the public eye for the next few years. Then in March 1889 the gang robbed the First National Bank of Denver. Tom McCarty walked into the bank holding a small bottle of colourless liquid claiming that it was nitro-glycerine, and that he was so desperate for money, that he would kill himself and destroy the whole building if they didn't hand it over. He walked out with $21,000, which he immediately passed to another member of the gang, before hightailing it out of town. He threw the small bottle, containing harmless water, on to the sidewalk as he left. It appears that Butch Cassidy's warped sense of humour was spreading amongst his fellow gang members.

A couple of months later the gang hit the San Miguel Valley Bank and liberated $10,500 from its safe. The gang split up and went their separate ways as the law closed in on them. Butch Cassidy went to Rock Springs, Wyoming, where for a short time he worked as a butcher and that is where he got his nickname Butch. It was whilst there that he ran afoul of the law, when he was accused of robbing a drunk. He pleaded his innocence and the case was found not proved, but Butch Cassidy was incensed: a rustler, train robber and bank robber he may have been, but stooping so low as to rob a drunk – never! He found the claim against him insulting and left Rock Springs.

He met up with some old friends who were herding cattle – not necessarily all theirs – and when he had acquired sufficient funds, went into partnership with a man named Al Rainer and bought a small horse ranch. It all went wrong when his partner brought thirty stolen horses to the ranch, followed closely by Sheriff John Ward of Uintah County, where the horses had originated. Before he could react, Cassidy received a graze to the head by a bullet from the sheriff's gun and was quickly disarmed. He and Rainer were taken into custody and hauled before the courts. Both Rainer and Butch Cassidy were sentenced to two years in the state penitentiary at Laramie.

After 18 months, the governor pardoned Butch Cassidy, who immediately promised not to commit any more robberies in Wyoming. In fact he kept his word and never took part in any of his gang's robberies in that state. He may have planned them and hid out in the state, but he never took part.

Immediately on his release, Butch Cassidy headed for an area called Brown's Hole in the Uintah Mountains. This was on the borders of the states of Colorado, Utah and Wyoming. Together with two other outlaws he built a log cabin on one of the highest points, which enabled him to keep a lookout over the three territories.

Matt Warner, a former member of Tom McCarty's gang, joined him briefly before moving on, but then was arrested a month later for the murder of two prospectors. Butch Cassidy persuaded two of his gang to engage the services of one of the top lawyers in the state, Douglas V. Preston. He demanded a retainer from them before agreeing to defend Warner, which they provided after 'borrowing' the money from a bank in Montpelier, Idaho. Unfortunately for the outlaws the bank belonged to the American Bankers Association, who were the main clients of the Pinkerton Detective Agency. From that moment on Butch Cassidy and the members of his gang were top of their wanted list. The gang suffered a setback when one of the gang, Bob Meeks, who was involved in the bank robbery in Montpelier, was captured and sentenced to 32 years in the state penitentiary for his part in the raid.

By now the Brown's Hole hideout was becoming known throughout the outlaw grapevine and a number of former members of the Hole-in-the-Wall Gang had now arrived. Known as the Wild Bunch, the gang enjoyed certain notoriety in nearby towns, Vernal and Rock Springs, where they spent most weekends and the proceeds from their criminal exploits. Cassidy and Elzy Lay carried out an $8,000 payroll robbery of a mine in Utah in 1897. Whilst the two outlaws were carrying out this raid, the Hole-in-the-Wall hideout was under siege from lawmen. In a desperate attempt to escape, George Curry and the Logan Brothers led over 100 men out from the hideout with the intention of joining Butch Cassidy in his new hideout.

Within days of joining up with Butch at Brown's Hole, trouble flared up in the now enormous outlaw camp, and a number of killings took place. The trouble was caused predominantly by one of the Logan Brothers, who shot dead the father of a former girlfriend during an argument. It was quickly realised that the Logans, who were part-Cherokee renegades, were just vicious killers, and the remainder of the outlaws soon made it clear that they were not wanted, and that it would be in their own interests if they left. The three brothers left and went back to the Hole-in the-Wall and joined up with George Curry, who had returned to the old hideout earlier.

The gang then carried out a series of raids on banks, post offices, trains and general stores. But Harvey Logan wanted revenge on a farmer, Jim Winters, who tipped off the law as the whereabouts of the Hole-in-the-Wall. Harvey Logan and his brothers went to visit him, but Winters was waiting for them, having been tipped off by another outlaw who despised the brothers. As they approached the farm, Winters opened fire with a shotgun, blasting Johnny Logan out of his saddle and killing him. The other two brothers fled, but some months later Harvey Logan returned and killed Winters in revenge.

The remaining two brothers joined up with George Curry and with three other outlaws rode into Belle Fourche, Dakota and held up the Butte County Bank. The hold-up turned into a farce. Grabbing what money they could they raced out of the bank and to their horses. One of the gang, Tom 'Peep' O'Day, got himself tangled up in his stirrups and was promptly captured, whilst the remaining five left. A posse was quickly organised and they were tracked to a deserted shack just 12 miles away.

Tom O'Day, a member of the Wild Bunch.

After a brief but violent gun battle, the gang ran out of ammunition and was captured. They were taken to Deadwood Jail and locked up. The following morning it was discovered that Curry and the Logans had escaped. The three men headed for Brown's Hole where they joined up again with Butch Cassidy. By this time a code of conduct had been drawn up for those who wanted to remain in the hideout. This was spelt out in no uncertain manner to the Logan Brothers, who had to agree to it or leave.

Butch Cassidy decided to organise the outlaws, who had now come to accept him as leader, into a regulated outfit. He created a hierarchy who planned raids and ensured that the code of conduct was upheld. They consisted of Butch Cassidy, the Sundance Kid, Bill Carver, Ben Kilpatrick, Harry Tracey, the Logan Brothers, Bob Lee, George Curry and Camilla Hanks, aka 'Deaf Charlie'.

Scouts were sent out to find out information regarding train times, what shipments they might be carrying, what mines and banks were in the area and when deliveries of cash or gold were arriving. Bribes to employees were handed out and the information relayed back to Brown's Hole. But there was a fly in the ointment, a Pinkerton detective by the name of Charles A. Siringo.

Looking like a tired man on the run, Siringo went to Brown's Hole and after convincing the guards that he just wanted somewhere to hide, they let him in. The hierarchy questioned him closely, as he was not known to any of them. He gave his name as Charles Carter and said that he was wanted for murder and was on the run from the law. He was so convincing, especially when he showed his admiration when introduced to the infamous outlaws that were there, that they accepted him without further checking. Siringo spent a number of weeks in the hideout collecting information on who were taking bribes, what shipments had been targeted and where to intercept messages from the gang. Then he left and passed the information on to his bosses, resulting in a number of arrests being made. The gang suddenly realised that they had been infiltrated and put all their plans on hold. Charles Siringo and another Pinkerton detective, Bill Sayles, trailed the gang for the next few years, gradually whittling down the members and preventing them from committing some robberies.

Despite knowing the location of Brown's Hole and everything about it, the authorities never moved to arrest the occupants. Some newspapers that got hold of the story maintained that the law was too afraid to go in. Things came to a head when one of the outlaws called Swede Johnson attended a steer-wrestling contest on one of the neighbouring ranches

Pinkerton detective
Charles Siringo.

and got drunk. During an argument he pulled out his gun and shot
dead a 16-year-old bystander. Realising what he had done he jumped
on his horse and rode off towards Brown's Hole. On the way he met,
and joined up with, three more outlaws on their way to the stronghold.
However, a large posse made up of ranchers and their cowboys were
hot on Johnson's trail and cornered the four outlaws in a gorge.

One of the posse, Valentine Hoy, was killed in the ensuing gunfight
but one of the outlaws was captured. The remaining outlaws slipped
away under the cover of darkness, and in retaliation and a degree of
frustration in not catching Johnson, the ranchers lynched their captive.
The three who escaped, including Johnson, were later captured after a
gunfight that lasted more than seven hours.

A series of violent incidents concerning neighbouring ranches, in
which two more of the ranchers were killed, resulted in stockmen's

associations demanding that the military be sent in to clear out the outlaws. But the brother of one of the murdered ranchers, Jacob Hoy, put forward another suggestion, and that was to offer a $1,000 reward for every member of the Wild Bunch captured – dead or alive.

Incensed but also frightened by this, the outlaws carried out a series of attacks on Hoy's ranch, killing his steers and horses. But the seed of greed had been sown, and the members of the Wild Bunch realised that their days were numbered. The $1,000 price on their heads would soon bring bounty hunters looking for them, and some of their so-called 'friends' would take the opportunity to cash in on the offer. After a meeting the Wild Bunch decided to split up and go their separate ways.

It was around this time that the Spanish-American War started and a number of cowboys were enlisting in Theodore Roosevelt's Rough Riders. Butch Cassidy saw an opportunity to move out of the state and

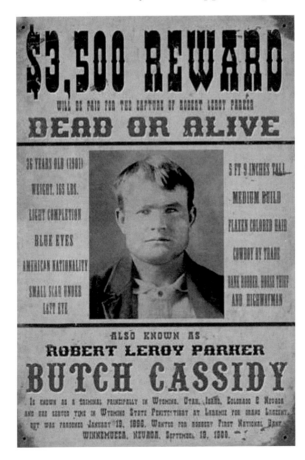

Butch Cassidy wanted poster.

proposed forming an outfit called the Wild Bunch Riders, but it was quickly pointed out that they were all wanted by the law and there were wanted posters out on all of them. The moment anyone of them attempted to join up at a recruitment centre, they would be arrested.

So the gang took advantage of the distraction of the war and its enlistments and decided to rob the Union Pacific's Overland Flyer. Butch Cassidy would be not there, as he had promised the Governor of Wyoming that he would never commit a robbery in the state.

Shortly after 2 a.m. on 2 June 1899, engineer William Jones opened the throttle on the Overland Flyer and began moving his train out of the Wilcox station. A second train containing 300 passengers remained behind to finish off its servicing and would not be ready to move for another 20 minutes. It was raining heavily as the train slowly made its way west toward Urora, the next stop on the line.

Less than a mile from Wilcox, engineer Jones saw a red and white signal light being waved by someone in the distance where he knew a small bridge spanned a gulch. Knowing there had been heavy rains, he became concerned that they may have caused a flash flood that could have damaged the bridge. Jones closed the throttle, slowing the engine down. The man holding the lamp was the Sundance Kid who was accompanied by an older man and both smiled as they saw the train slowing down. They blessed their good fortune for the raging storm that had arrived just in time. The two men had placed ten sticks of dynamite on the bridge just in case the driver of the train had ignored their signal. The idea of the dynamite was to blow the bridge, giving the engineer time to stop the train without sending it into the gulch and killing all the passengers and crew.

As the train drew near, Sundance kept waving the lamp until it pulled to a stop near the bridge and the engineer leaned out to see what was the matter. At the rear of the train, the rear brakeman immediately picked up his own signal lamp and started to run back down the line to stop the second train. In the meantime the Sundance Kid had approached the train with his pistol in his hand and climbed up into the cab. He quietly announced to the driver and the fireman that the train was about to be robbed and ordered them off the train. As the two men climbed down, they were met by the old man pointing a nickel-plated revolver at them.

In the mail car the three clerks were just finishing sorting out the mail. One of the clerks, curious as why the train had stopped so soon after leaving Wilcox, slid back the heavy door and peered out into the darkness. On seeing nothing untoward he shut the door again and resumed working.

By this time Sundance had been joined by the remainder of his gang, all wearing long masks. Glancing down the train they took in the position of the various carriages. Behind the tender was the Ogden mail car, then the express car (their target), then the Portland mail car, a baggage car, a sleeper coach and a private passenger car.

The two men had joined with the other members of the gang and after securing the engineer and fireman made their way back to the mail coach. They called for the clerks inside to open up and the heavy sliding door opened just a fraction and the outlaws could see just the eyes of someone peering out. The clerk could see riders with hoods over their heads and quickly shouted back 'Go to hell' and slammed the door closed.

One of the gang, Harvey Logan, fired a shot through the door just missing the clerk. In the express car, the clerk hearing the shot, realised that that there was trouble and grabbed a shotgun and a pistol, then extinguished the light and waited. Then a voice from outside called out, 'Come out or we will blow you out'.

On receiving no reply, one of the outlaws reached into a sack and produced a stick of dynamite and placed it on the door hinge. He then lit the fuse and everyone took cover. A loud explosion followed seconds later shaking the whole train and leaving the large sliding door hanging off. In the confusion that followed, the conductor took advantage and

The Dynamited Express Car after the Curry "Hold Up" between Malta and Wagner, Mont. July 3, 1901. "Kid" Curry's gang got away with $80,000.

The dynamited express carriage of the Great Northern Railroad after the Wild Bunch gang hold-up on 3 July 1901.

headed back down the tracks to warn the other train that was following. An enraged Harvey Logan then threatened to shoot all the clerks, but one of the other outlaws persuaded him against it.

The sudden appearance of a train light in the distance changed the situation and increased the urgency of the outlaws. Everyone was ordered back on the train and the engineer told to get the train across the bridge. With the train over the bridge and the knowledge that they had explosives tied to it, the outlaws concentrated on opening up the express car. With time of the essence Bill Carver placed a stick of dynamite against the hinge of the sliding door and lit the fuse. The explosion ripped off the door, and, after the smoke had cleared, a terrified clerk stumbled out of the wrecked carriage. Bill Carver climbed in and placed more dynamite on the two safes inside and blew them open. The outlaws immediately emptied the safes of their contents, a total of $50,000. In the meantime the conductor had met up with the second train to warn them with the result that it reversed back to Wilcox.

With all thoughts of robbing the second train now gone, the Wild Bunch gathered up all the proceeds of the robbery and headed away. Within hours the gang was being hunted by a large posse and a number of shoot-outs occurred in which several lawmen were either killed or wounded. Butch Cassidy had planned well, and had arranged for fresh horses to be waiting all along a pre-planned escape route. The gang easily outran the pursuers and headed for the Hole-in-the-Wall, but stayed only long enough to divide the spoils and then make their separate escapes. Elzy Lay headed for Mexico where he joined up with 'Black Jack' Ketchum, whilst Kid Curry and Butch Cassidy headed for New Mexico where they joined up with the Sundance Kid.

Elzy Lay was later involved with 'Black Jack' Ketchum in a series of robberies in which a

'Black Jack' Ketchum.

number of killings took place and both were arrested. Lay was never charged with the actual murders but as an accomplice and for robbery, for which he was sentenced to life imprisonment. Ketchum was hanged in New Mexico.

The Pinkerton detectives were closing in slowly but surely, and when one of the Logan brothers, Johnny, tried to cash one of the stolen Adams Express banknotes, Pinkerton detective Bill Sayles was immediately informed. Together with four other detectives, and travelling through heavy snowdrifts, he traced him to the home of Bob Lee, another outlaw. After a brief gun battle Johnny Logan lay dead in the snow.

Within a couple of months Bob Lee was arrested and sentenced to 10 years for his part in the train robbery and George Curry was killed by a posse. In an effort to spare any more blood being spilt, the Pinkertons offered Butch Cassidy an amnesty, thinking that if he accepted the offer, the remainder of the Wild Bunch would fall in with him. But Butch's sense of humour intervened, and he decided, after hearing that $100,000 was being transported by Union Pacific, that this was a temptation he could not turn down. His thinking behind the robbery was that he and the other members of the gang would be able to retire to South America if they succeeded in the job.

Somehow railroad detectives got wind of the intended robbery and sent the money by another route. As Union Pacific Train No. 3 passed

Photograph showing a posse alighting from a train when in pursuit of train robbers.

Pinkerton detective posse with their specially-converted railroad carriage.

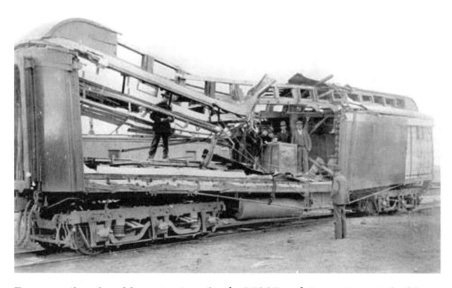

Express railroad car blown to pieces by the Wild Bunch in an attempted robbery.

through Tipton, Wyoming, Butch Cassidy and Kid Curry scrambled aboard and as the train struggled up a long uphill gradient, the two men jumped into the engineers cab and forced him to stop the train. The remainder of the gang who were waiting at a pre-arranged spot opened the express car and blew the safe. Unfortunately they overestimated the amount of dynamite required, and not only blew the safe, but demolished the express car. The explosion destroyed almost all the contents of the safe and the gang collected what was left – $50.40c!

To try and bolster their funds, the gang decided to relieve the passengers of their valuables, which they duly did. Two weeks later the gang struck again. This time it was the First National Bank of Winnemucca, Nevada and this time they got away with over $32,000. The gang immediately split up and headed towards Fort Worth using various routes, and on arrival enjoyed the nightlife there. It was whilst at Fort Worth that certain members of the gang bought some city clothes and posed for a group photograph which appears at the beginning of this chapter.

Ben Kilpatrick's girlfriend, Laura Bullion, had met up with the gang in Fort Worth and then left with Kilpatrick to visit his folks in Sonora, Texas. Some weeks later, Bill Carver went to visit them and it was whilst he was in town with George Kilpatrick, Ben's brother, that the local sheriff spotted them, recognising Bill Carver from the wanted posters that were around.

The same coach but from a different angle.

Above: Remnants of the express coach after the Wild Bunch had used too much dynamite.

Right: Laura Bullion, girlfriend of Ben Kilpatrick.

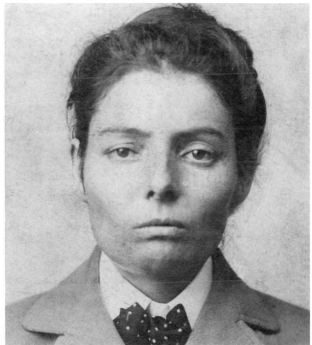

Carver, realising that he was about to be arrested, went for his gun and in the resulting gunfight, both Carver and George Kilpatrick were killed.

With things getting decidedly uncomfortable for the Wild Bunch, the Sundance Kid took his girlfriend Etta Place to New York, accompanied by Butch Cassidy. From there the Sundance Kid and Etta Place boarded the SS *Soldier Prince* which was bound for Buenos Aires. Butch Cassidy had agreed to go with them, but he was persuaded to carry out just one more train robbery by Kid Curry.

The robbery took place on 3 July 1901, when the Great Northern Express No. 3 pulled away from the station at Malta, Montana. Kid Curry climbed on top of the baggage car and made his way towards the engine. As the train approached a town called Wagner, Curry pointed his gun at the engineer and fireman and ordered them to stop the train near a bridge. Waiting there was Ben Kilpatrick, his girlfriend Laura Bullion and 'Deaf Charlie' Hanks. As the train ground to a halt, Laura Bullion and Kilpatrick held guns on the passengers and crew, whilst Kid Curry and Butch Cassidy blew the safe in the express car.

The gang netted $40,000 in unsigned banknotes that became negotiable currency once the forged signatures of the bank president and chief cashier had been added. With the Pinkertons now on their trail and rewards offered for their capture, the gang shared out the spoils and went their separate ways.

Above left: Will Carver, friend of Ann Bassett.

Above right: Ben Kilpatrick.

Butch Cassidy boarded a train for New York and once there took the ship to Buenos Aires to join up with his friend the Sundance Kid. In the meantime Ben Kilpatrick and his girlfriend Laura Bullion had been arrested trying to pass one of the forged banknotes. They were tried and convicted. Kilpatrick got 20 years, whilst Bullion received five years. Kilpatrick was released in 1911, and charged with an old murder but was acquitted. Almost immediately he went back to his old ways and attempted to rob the Southern Pacific Sunset Flyer No. 5.

Once inside the express car, Kilpatrick ordered the messenger to open the safe, but the messenger, a man called David Trousdale, grabbed a mallet and hit Kilpatrick on the side of the head, killing him instantly. He then grabbed Kilpatrick's gun and shot a surprised Howard Benson, Kilpatrick's accomplice, dead. Kid Curry by this time was also dead, killed during another attempted train robbery.

The bodies of Ben Kilpatrick and Ole Hobeck being held up for the camera after being shot by lawmen after an attempted robbery.

Butch Cassidy and the Sundance Kid were now domiciled in Argentina and had a homestead of four acres on which they had herds of sheep, cattle and horses. Their peaceful life was suddenly shattered by the arrival of a Pinkerton detective by the name of Frank Dimaio who approached the authorities with bundles of wanted posters, all with substantial rewards, for both Butch Cassidy and the Sundance Kid, alias Harry Longbaugh.

It was time to move on, but first they needed to be financially solvent, so in the spring of 1906, helped by Etta Place, they robbed the bank at Villa Mercedes in San Luis of $20,000. Then Etta Place was taken ill, and the Sundance Kid shipped her off to New York for specialist treatment – she was never heard of again.

After hitting another bank at Bahia Blanca, the pair decided that things were getting a bit too warm and headed for Bolivia where huge mining operations were building up. Over the next months, the pair robbed a number of mines and banks in Chile, Peru, Argentina and Bolivia. All the time they were doing this, they were working for the Concordia Tin Mines at La Paz, as wrangler and mule drivers, using assumed names.

Becoming arrogant at the ease at which they were able to pull off these robberies, they became complacent. They attacked a mule train in

Butch Cassidy, Etta Pace and the Sundance Kid in Argentina, relaxing away from the hassle of lawmen.

Bolivia, after learning that there was a suitcase full of money on one of the mules. They took the mule and the money and headed to the village of San Vicente to hide out, but the mule was a distinctive, large silver-grey beast and was immediately recognised by one of the villagers. He contacted the local militia, who immediately dispatched a detachment of cavalry to the village.

On arriving they saw Butch Cassidy and the Sundance Kid enjoying a drink in the afternoon sun outside one of the bars and immediately surrounded the building. An officer shouted for them to surrender, at which point gunfire started. It is not clear who fired the first shot, but a number of the militia were killed and the stand-off lasted well into the evening. The following morning the soldiers rushed the bullet-ridden bar only to find the two outlaws slumped against the bar – dead. It is not clear whether the soldiers had shot them or they had committed suicide after realising that there was no way out. So ended the last of the Wild Bunch, glamorised by the newspapers and later by the film industry, but in reality they were just thieves and murderers, who cared little for human life.

Chapter 8

Thomas 'Black Jack' Ketchum

Looking more like a bank manager or a preacher than a hardened criminal, Thomas 'Black Jack' Ketchum was nothing more than an uneducated, hard-drinking drifter, who had difficulty in keeping any job he took on. However, he cultivated a handlebar moustache and created an image of sartorial elegance, which belied his true characteristics.

Born in San Saba County, Texas, in October 1860 Ketchum was one of eight children. He and one of his brothers, Samuel, went to work as cowboys at the age of 15 and it was during the following few years

that his long-time sweetheart left him for another cowboy. Disillusioned and devastated, Ketchum left New Mexico and headed into Wyoming. Not much is known about him during this period, but he came to the fore when he joined up with the Hole-in-the-Wall Gang led by Butch Cassidy. Some people thought he was one of the leaders of the gang, but this was not true. His appearance may have given the impression of authority, but nothing was farther from the truth. He had a number of weird

'Black Jack' Ketchum.

eccentricities, probably brought about by mental illness, one of which was to self-harm. He would beat himself with either his gun butt or a rope end whenever he was depressed.

When 'Black Jack' Ketchum decided to go on a raid in New Mexico, only one of the Wild Bunch of outlaws agreed to go with him – William Ellsworth Lay, who also used the name of his childhood friend Bill McGinnis, but was known to the gang as Elzy Lay. Black Jack's brother Sam Ketchum joined his brother, together with another outlaw by the name of G.W. Franks, and the four of them rode to a town called Twin Mountains near Folsom, New Mexico. There they held up a Colorado & Southern Railroad train and robbed it of a mere $200 before making their escape. Some months later they held up the same train again, and again left with just a few hundred dollars. The gang were obviously not doing their research and finding out what trains were carrying large sums of money. Either they were satisfied with the small amounts of money they were stealing or they were totally inept. The gang carried out a number of other minor robberies over the next few months, but none that brought them substantial funds.

One other explanation put forward was that 'Black Jack' Ketchum was more interested in frightening and shooting than becoming rich and was hoping for a confrontation and a gun battle. He had been directly involved with two murders during July, the circumstances showing that he was not afraid to get involved in bloody gunfights.

At the end of July, Ketchum and his gang once again stopped and robbed the Colorado & Southern train at Twin Mountains, but two days later a posse trapped the gang in a canyon, near Cimarron. The gun battle that followed saw Sheriffs Edward Farr of Huerfano County and William Love of Cimarron County shot dead. Sam Ketchum and G.W. Franks escaped, as did 'Black Jack' Ketchum,

William Ellsworth 'Elza' Lay.

but he had a bullet through his shoulder. Elzy Lay was captured and later sentenced to 20 years in prison.

Ketchum was captured two days later and taken to Santa Fe, where US Marshal C.M. Foraker collected him, and after treatment had been administered, took him to Clayton to stand trial for the murders of Sheriffs Farr and Love. When word of his arrest got out and the impending move to Clayton for trial, rumours started to circulate regarding outlaw friends might be trying to spring 'Black Jack'. Judge Mills cabled Foraker, telling him to leave Santa Fe with the prisoner and take him to Clayton via the town of Trinidad and that a special deputy would be waiting there for them. Foraker, the special deputy marshal and their prisoner, arrived at Clayton a day later than expected. At no time was there any indication that there might be an attempt to rescue 'Black Jack' Ketchum.

At the beginning of September 1900, Ketchum was tried for the murder of Sheriff Farr and convicted. He was sentenced to be hanged and on 25 April 1901, the sentence was carried out. Arrogant to the last,

Above left: 'Black Jack' Ketchum about to be hanged.

Above right: 'Black Jack' Ketchum about to be dropped.

it is said that he bounded up the steps of the scaffold and as the black hood was placed over his head, he is purported to have said, 'I'll be in hell before you start breakfast, boys. Let 'er go!'

The hanging was a rather brutal affair, as the hangman, who was not at all experienced, misjudged the weight and the drop, and consequently Ketchum dropped through the trapdoor with such force that the jerk at the end of the rope ripped his head from his shoulders. As can be seen from the photographs, it was not a pretty sight.

Above: The decapitated body of 'Black Jack' Ketchum lying beneath the scaffold after his botched hanging.

Right: Close-up view of the decapitated body of 'Black Jack' Ketchum.

Chapter 9

John King Fisher

Born in 1854 in Collin County, Texas, John King Fisher (known as King) was the youngest son of Jobe and Lucinda Fisher, the other brother being Jasper. When Lucinda Fisher died two years after King was born, Jobe Fisher moved the family to Denton County where they lived throughout the Civil War. With the war over, the family moved to Williamson County, where Jobe's brother James, lived. Jobe became a successful rancher and married again to Minerva, but because she suffered from bad health the family decided to move to Goliad County,

which was near the coast. James also ran a freight wagon business, and when he moved his large herd and freight business to Goliad County, his eldest son Jasper drove one of the wagons.

After a few years, Jobe became concerned about the company his younger son was keeping whilst at school and sent him back to live with his brother James in Williamson County. King was an above-average student, good-looking and not afraid to get involved in a fight. A combination that was to lead him into all sorts of scrapes in the future.

John King Fisher, lawman and outlaw.

Whilst still at school he began buying wild horses, breaking them in and selling them for a good profit. It was then that his troubles with the law began. He was accused of stealing a horse, but claimed he only borrowed it to search for his own horse, which he said had strayed during the night. The courts did not believe him and on 5 October 1870 he was sentenced to two years in the state penitentiary. He was released four months later because of his age – he was only 16 years old.

He then started to work for various ranches in south Texas as a wrangler and it was during this period that he learned to handle a gun. It was also around this time that he killed his first man, a Mexican bandit who he caught trying to steal one of his horses. He was also running around with known rustlers and outlaws.

Realising that there was more to life than wrangling horses and that there were easier ways of making money, King joined up with a band of Mexican rustlers. The alliance didn't last long when, after a particularly successful raid, there was a dispute over the way the money was shared out. This was probably because King was the only 'gringo' in the outfit. They, however, had not reckoned on his prowess with a gun, and in less than a minute, three of the gang were dead, including the leader. King became the new leader and, using his intelligence, quickly gained control over three other gangs.

John King Fisher became increasingly flamboyant in his character. He wore a sombrero with gold braid attached, silk shirt and heavily embroidered waistcoats and chaps made from the skin of a Bengal tiger. His gun belt was embossed in silver, with silver-mounted holsters, in which there were a pair of ivory-handled, silver-plated .44 pistols.

Using the money from his crimes, King Fisher bought a ranch near Eagle Pass, Maverick County, Texas, which was across the Rio Grande River from Mexico. It was no accident that King bought the ranch so close to the border of Mexico, because a great deal of his business was dealing with stolen cattle from Mexico in exchange for stolen Texan cattle. It is said that he had a business arrangement on these lines with Porfirio Diaz, who was later to become President of Mexico.

With the wealth he was accumulating, John King Fisher became almost a law unto himself and ran his territory with an iron hand. On a number of occasions he used his skill as a gunfighter to make this point clear to anyone who questioned his word. In one incident with four Mexican rustlers at his ranch, he shot and killed three of them and clubbed the other to death with a branding iron, after a dispute over money.

John King Fisher
with an unknown
outlaw.

He loved to gamble and would frequent the saloons in Eagle Pass, causing many of the inhabitants of the town to be extremely wary of him. After several incidents with the law, after which he had threatened to kill a number of townsfolk, he was arrested. The prosecution dropped the case after no witnesses could be found who were prepared to testify against him.

In another incident, almost a thousand stolen cattle were found on his ranch and a troop of Texas Rangers was sent to arrest him and his men. The case was dropped after the cattle inspector refused to examine the stolen cattle, and the local sheriff refused to serve warrants on the men, even though it was known that they all had committed a number of murders.

The failure of the law to act created more problems for the local inhabitants, as it now meant that there was only one law in the territory and that was John King Fisher's. His men could take what they wanted, when they wanted, without fear of any retribution.

On one occasion he killed three Mexicans, who he said he caught trying to steal some of his cattle, claiming that acted in self-defence. He was arrested in one of the Eagle Pass saloons and put on trial. He of course could hire the best lawyers available and was acquitted, much to the anger of the Texas Rangers.

On a number of different occasions after that, King Fisher was involved in killings and rustling incidents, but then in 1876, he met and married Sarah Vivian and his violent lifestyle seemed to change. She bore him four daughters, but no sons. He expanded his business empire – legitimately – and started to become a pillar of society.

In 1881 he was invited to become deputy sheriff of Ulvdale County and three years later announced that he was applying to become sheriff. He took his role of peace officer seriously and would stand no nonsense from anyone. After a stagecoach was robbed by two brothers, Jim and Tom Hannehan, King Fisher trailed them back to their ranch. After a shoot-out, in which Tom Hannehan was killed, the other brother surrendered both himself and the proceeds of the robbery.

Then in March 1884 John King Fisher was in Austin, Texas on business, when he met his old friend Ben Thompson. Thompson was a notorious gunfighter, but well past his prime. The pair of them went from saloon to saloon talking about old times and past friends.

Ben Thompson was on his way to San Antonio and persuaded Fisher to go with him. What Fisher didn't know was that Ben Thompson had a long-standing feud with two theatre owners in San Antonio, Jack Harris and Joe Foster, over a gambling debt. Ben Thompson had gunned down Jack Harris in 1882, but Joe Foster, now with a new partner Billy Simms, still kept the feud going.

As Fisher and Thompson boarded the train to San Antonio, someone sent Foster a telegram saying that Ben Thompson was on his way there. On arriving in San Antonio, the two men went to the Vaudeville Variety Theatre, where Billy Simms met them. Thompson, still fuelled by drink, demanded to see Joe Foster and end the feud by having a drink with him. With Foster was one of his 'bouncers', Jacob Coy, and when Foster refused to shake Thompson's hand, Thompson went for his gun, but before he could get it out a hail of gunfire hit him. As he fell to the ground, Coy stepped up and fired three more bullets into his head.

When Thompson had gone for his gun, King realised that this had been a set-up to get Thompson, but before he could react, he too

Frank Wess's Vaudeville Theatre in San Antonio.

was caught in a hail of gunfire and was hit thirteen times. During the gunfight, Foster, whilst attempting to draw his own gun quickly, had shot himself in the leg, shattering the bone. Despite the leg being amputated, Foster died a short while later.

Although there was uproar over the killings and a grand jury investigation demanded, both the San Antonio police and the prosecutor showed no interest in investigating the shootings. Such were the reputations of Fisher and Thompson, that the consensus of opinion was that the world was better off without them, and they had got their just deserts.

Chapter 10

Henry Plummer

One of the most controversial outlaws of the west was Henry Plummer. Some say he was the leader of one of the most notorious gang of murderers, thieves, road agents and rustlers called the 'Innocents'. Others say that he was made the scapegoat, because he was the only member of the gang who was brought to justice.

Henry Plummer was born in Washington County, Maine, in 1832, the youngest of six children. The family all had strong connections with the sea and it was hoped that Henry would follow the family tradition. But Henry was not robust. He suffered from ill health and was not suited to a life at sea. The family was a prosperous one and gave Henry a good education and upbringing. When, in his late teens, Henry heard how gold fever had struck California he decided to head for the goldfields and hopefully make his fortune.

Within a year of arriving in California, Henry Plummer owned a ranch and a mine just outside Nevada City. So impressed were the local people that such a young man could have such a shrewd business brain, that they persuaded him to run

Henry Plummer – lawman turned outlaw.

for city marshal. Plummer realised that this could be just a stepping-stone to state recognition and promptly put his name forward. He soon persuaded the electorate that this young, well-mannered and smartly dressed candidate was just what the city wanted. He also realised that being the only law for hundreds of miles in any direction gave him a free hand to almost anything that he wanted to do – and get away with it.

In 1857 Henry Plummer was elected as City Marshal of Nevada City and quickly acquired a reputation for having impeccable manners, being an immaculate dresser and a man who took his office duties very seriously indeed. He was extremely fast and accurate with a gun, as a number of wrongdoers were to find out to their cost. Less than six months into his new role, Henry Plummer found himself on the other side of the law when he shot dead a miner, who had found Plummer in bed with his wife. He was convicted of second-degree murder and sentenced to ten years in San Quentin prison.

A number of friends petitioned the Governor, claiming that Plummer had acted in self-defence and that he was suffering from tuberculosis. For reasons best known only to himself, the Governor accepted all this and released Plummer after he had served less than six months.

Realising that his days of luxurious living were over unless he found a lucrative way of earning money, Plummer joined up with a gang of road agents, but their first job went painfully wrong and the Wells Fargo stage got away. He was arrested, then released for lack of evidence, but the mould had been set.

Henry Plummer returned to Nevada City and took up residence in one of the local brothels. Some months later he got into a fight with another man and shot him dead. He was arrested and put in jail, but realising that he was unlikely to get another pardon, he bribed the jailer, walked away and headed for Oregon. On the way he met up with another killer by the name of Jim Mayfield and headed toward Lewiston, Idaho.

It was here that Henry Plummer came into his own. Obtaining a job in a gambling house during the day, he organised a gang that specialised in stealing gold shipments, using information that he had gleaned from gamblers. He became a very respected citizen on the face of it, even funding the hiring of additional lawmen to help maintain law and order in the town. Things came to a head when one of his gang, a man called Charlie Forbes, was arrested. A lynch mob took Forbes and headed for the nearest tree, but Plummer stood in front of them and persuaded them to hand the man over to the sheriff. The mob dispersed and Forbes was handed over to the law. That night Henry Plummer helped Forbes escape. The activities of the vigilante committee, however, became a worrying sign for Henry Plummer, and he headed for the goldfields of Montana.

In Montana he joined up with a former partner-in-crime, Jack Cleveland. The two had never been friends, in fact at times they almost came to blows. It was in a saloon in Bannack that things came to a head. Cleveland, who was drunk, starting shouting about ex-City Marshal Plummer's illegal dealings, to which Plummer took exception. After warning him to be quiet, Plummer fired a warning shot into the ceiling. Cleveland went for his gun, determined to finish Plummer once and for all, but he underestimated his adversary's speed with a gun. Plummer's first shot hit him in the stomach, his second went in just below the eye and a third hit him in the chest. Cleveland collapsed, and died a little while later. Plummer was arrested and tried for murder, but was acquitted after witnesses testified that it was in self-defence.

Then the town was turned on its head when gold was struck in Alder Gulch, an area some ten miles out of town. Within six months over 10,000 miners were working along 17 miles of the creek and with them came the outlaws. These consisted of deserters from the Union and Confederate armies, gunfighters, thieves and professional gamblers. Gambling halls and brothels sprang up all over the place. The situation in Bannack quickly descended into lawlessness and the citizens realised that they needed a strong sheriff to try and regain control of the streets.

Plummer ran for sheriff but was beaten by the local butcher. After a confrontation with the man, Plummer 'persuaded' him that he would be a much better man for the job. With the job of sheriff now his, Henry Plummer set to work taking control of the town. Unknown to the townsfolk, he set about using many of his criminal friends to form an organised gang, as well as using them to enforce law and order. He placed a member of his gang in each of the mining camps, and with regular meetings between them, information was passed which enabled the gang to target the most lucrative of them. The main targets of his operations were the wagons that transported the gold from the creek to the major train stations. When the gang struck they killed everyone connected with the wagon train so no survivors could identify any of them. It is thought that during one four-month period in 1863, over 120 miners were killed and their bodies cut up for buzzard bait.

The gold was handed over to Plummer, who, it is said, buried it all over the hills. It soon became obvious that these robberies were not just random, but were well organised. It also became clear that the sheriff and his deputies were using their position unlawfully, when some killings by them went unpunished. There was always the excuse that it was in self-defence, and there always appeared to be 'witnesses' to support them.

Then one of Plummer's gang, called George Ives, shot and killed a prominent local businessman. When nothing was done about the murder, a mob of angry miners snatched Ives, and after a quick trial, hanged him from a ridgepole. By this time, the lawlessness and robberies had spread to Virginia City, and again it was Plummer who was suspected of being behind it. The citizens of Bannack, Nevada City and Virginia City had had enough and they organised a posse to hunt down the gang. The Vigilantes rode through the night visiting known criminals and warning them to desist or leave the area. They tacked up warning posters with the numbers '3-7-77' on them (it has never been discovered what the numbers meant or referred to). After `persuading' some of the known criminals to talk, they tracked down some of the outlaws and after a quick 'trial' hanged them.

One of the men seized was Erastus 'Red' Yeager who, after 'questioning', told them that Sheriff Henry Plummer was the brains

Gallows that Plummer had erected to hang a horse thief but which was used to hang him.

behind the gang. Armed with rifles and revolvers, the Vigilantes surrounded Plummer's house on the edge of town and demanded that he come out. On hearing that Plummer was in his sick bed, the Vigilantes went in and dragged the petrified man out to a makeshift scaffold. Along with Plummer were his two deputies, Ned Ray and Buck Stinson, who were both strung up first. Plummer pleaded for his life and even asked if he could pray, but this was denied him. The Vigilantes tied his hands behind his back, then placed a noose around his neck and slowly hoisted him up. The Vigilantes waited until the scourge of Bannack was dead, then rode off, leaving the body hanging for all to see. Over the next few weeks a number of other outlaws were hanged, while others left the territory, never to return.

What happened to all the gold that Plummer is said to have accumulated has never been discovered, but it is rumoured that it is still lies buried in the Montana hills.

For three years after the hanging of Plummer, the Vigilantes ruled with an iron fist. But the citizens began to tire of the night raids on suspected outlaws, and issued an ultimatum to the Vigilantes, saying that for every man lynched, five of the Vigilantes would die, unless it stopped – it did.

There is another version of the story regarding Henry Plummer, some say that he was not the head of a gang, but just a sheriff trying to do his job. It is also said that the Vigilantes, who hanged Plummer and his deputies, were in fact the real gang and that they disposed of Plummer and his deputies because they were close to identifying them. It is unlikely that the truth will ever be known.

Chapter 11

Sam Bass

Sam Bass was another of those outlaws whose reputation owed more to the pens of Eastern fiction writers than he actually deserved. He was born on a farm in Indiana on 21 July 1851, but within two years both his parents had died, so he and his brothers and sister were sent to live with their uncle and aunt and their nine children, on their farm. How many children lived there is not known, but they received no schooling. From a very early age all the children worked on the farm doing various jobs depending on their age.

Sam Bass.

At the age of 18, Sam Bass decided to break away from life on a farm and took a paddle steamer down the Mississippi to Rosedale where he took a job in a mill. It was in this environment that he learned how to handle a gun and acquired his card-playing skills. A chance meeting with a man by the name of Scott Mayes saw the pair heading for Texas, where they found jobs as farmhands on the farm of the local sheriff, Sheriff W.F. Eagan. In later years, it was Eagan who was to spend a great deal of time tracking down Sam Bass.

It was whilst working on the farm that Bass learned to become a teamster (multiple horse handler) and whilst learning this skill also learned about all the trails, backroads and normally inaccessible places that were going to become necessary to his later way of life. He also met a number of unsavoury characters that were also to become part of his life in later years.

Sam Bass was an extremely hard worker, and within a relatively short period of time had earned enough to purchase his own horse. This was not an ordinary horse, but a racehorse, and Sam Bass set about earning his living racing his horse and soon had earned enough to quit his job and rely solely on the profits of racing and gambling.

In San Antonio he met a man by the name of Joel Collins, who persuaded him that there was a great deal of money to be made running rustled cattle to the markets in the north. They took a herd to Nebraska and used the proceeds to finance their gold prospecting in the Black Hills of Dakota. This failed miserably, and finding themselves broke, they joined up with four other outlaws, James Berry, Jack Davis, Billy Hefferidge and Tom Nixon, and resorted to holding up stagecoaches. They soon realised that there was more money to be made holding up trains and on 18 September 1877, the gang forced the stationmaster at Big Springs, Nebraska, to signal the incoming express to stop at the station.

When the train pulled in, the gang forced their way into the express car and forced the messenger to open the 'way safe'. Finding only $450 inside, they beat the messenger almost unconscious in an attempt to make him open the 'through safe', which he was unable to do because it was fitted with a time lock. The messenger tried to explain by showing them written details about the time lock mechanism, but because all but one of the outlaws could neither read nor write, they didn't understand. It was Joel Collins who came to the rescue of the messenger by reading the notes, and explaining to the other gang members that the safe could not be opened by anyone at that time. Frustrated, the gang found some wooden boxes and, when they opened them, discovered $60,000 in freshly-minted $20 gold pieces from the San Francisco mint going to Eastern banks.

Dividing the money equally, the gang split up, Sam Bass and Jack Davis heading for Denton. The pair decided to take a buggy so as not to draw attention to themselves, and stowed their share of the gold under the seat. After travelling for about a day, they were joined by a troop of soldiers and Pinkerton detectives who were looking for the train robbers. Sam Bass told them that they too were looking for the train robbers, in the hope of getting a reward if they caught them. They were invited to go along with the posse and kept up the charade for four days. They then parted from the posse and continued to head for Denton.

On their arrival they explained their newfound wealth by a gold strike they had had in the Black Hills and then started to enjoy the high life. Word filtered back to them that two of the gang had been captured and the other two had been shot and killed. Amongst the outlaw fraternity word quickly spread that Sam Bass was looking for new members to join his gang. What remains a mystery is that Sam Bass and Jack Davis arrived in Denton around October 1877 with $10,000 each, yet in February 1878, less than four months later, the new Sam Bass Gang

Members of the Sam Bass Gang. L–R: Jim Murphy, Sam Bass, Sebe Barnes.

struck again when it held up the Texas Central train as it stood in Allen Station. The haul this time netted the gang a mere $1,300. Even knowing Sam Bass's reputation for wild living, it is hard to believe that he spent $10,000 in less than four months, which led to speculation that he had hidden most of it.

A second robbery on 18 March at Eagle Ford and a third on 4 April at Mesquite, netted the gang a further $2,000. Both times, however, the gang missed large sums of money because the express car messengers hid it under sacks when they realised they were about to be robbed. The only possible explanation as to why they missed these large amounts of money was because of the bungling of the Bass Gang.

A number of other bungled train robberies took place, but by this time the people of North Texas had had enough and complained angrily to the Governor to do something about the gang. There was a great deal of

Wanted poster for Sam Bass.

public concern around Texas at the time, reconstruction of the state had just finished and numbers of candidates for the top political posts were campaigning on a law and order ticket. The Governor ordered the Texas Rangers to take charge and to hunt down the outlaws still running loose (and in particular the Bass Gang) and bring them all to justice – one way or another!

The Texas Rangers saw this as an opportunity to consolidate their organisation, and to prove once and for all that they were a force to be reckoned with. The Rangers concentrated their efforts on the high-profile Bass Gang and started to hunt them down. However, Sam Bass used his knowledge of the trails and back roads he had studied when as a teamster, to his advantage. The Texas Rangers, whenever they seemed to pick up his trail, lost it almost as quickly. This gave the impression that they were inept, but it was Sam Bass's knowledge of the terrain, that kept him one step ahead all the time.

In an effort to flush him out, the Rangers performed a sweep of the area of those suspected of aiding and abetting the gang. Henderson Murphy, who was known to a friend of the outlaws, owned one of the farms they raided. Jim Murphy had been charged with robbing the US Mail, which was a Federal offence and carried a very heavy prison sentence if convicted. In an effort to get off the charge and get his hands on the reward, Murphy offered to inform on the Bass Gang and set it up for the Texas Rangers.

The gang was resting at Murphy's ranch when the Texas Rangers arrived, led by Captain Lee Hall. In the ensuing gunfight Sam Bass was hit twice: one bullet hit his gun belt, the other struck the stock of his rifle. The gang, despite being met with a hail of bullets, managed to shoot their way out without any serious injuries to either side. A very relieved Sam Bass appeared some weeks later in the northern part of the state, back to his old flamboyant ways of throwing his money around.

The Texas Rangers, however, were still on their trail, and in June they caught up with some of the gang. During a gunfight two of the gang were killed, whilst one of them, Henry Underwood, managed to escape and was never heard of again. In the meantime, Jim Murphy, who had escaped with the gang, contacted the Rangers informing them that the remainder of the gang was about to rob the bank at Round Rock.

Three Rangers were sent to Round Rock to see what they could find out and then informed the local sheriff of what they had been told about the robbery. Later Major Jones of the Texas Rangers arrived in Round Rock, together with Deputy Sheriff Morris Moore of Travis County. Two days later, on 14 July, Sam Bass, Frank Jackson, Jim Murphy and Seaborn

Sam Bass with other members of his gang. L–R: Sam Bass, John Collins, John Gardener, Joel Collins.

Seaborne Barnes.

Barnes arrived in town. Unaware that there were Texas Rangers in town, Bass and Seaborn suggested that they steal some fresh horses and hit the bank the following day, but Murphy warned against it, saying that stealing the horses might look suspicious and draw attention to the gang. The gang agreed to shelve their plans for a week and spend a little time in working out a plan for the robbery and their escape. Murphy, however, was hoping to make contact with Major Jones, unaware that the Rangers were already in town.

On Friday, 20 July, before the planned robbery of the bank, the remaining three members of the gang rode into town for a last look at the bank they were to rob. As they walked to the local store, Deputy Sheriff Grimes of Williamson County observed them. He had no idea who they were, but thought he saw one of them wearing a pistol, which was against the local ordinance.

Grimes confronted the men in the store, asking if they had a pistol. The three men replied by drawing their guns and shooting him dead. Deputy Sheriff Morris Moore, who had seen Grimes enter the store, heard the shots and ran over, only to be hit in the chest by a bullet from Sam Bass's gun. By this time the whole town was alerted to the gunfire, as were the Texas Rangers. The Rangers ran into the street drawing their pistols as they did so, and opened fire on the fleeing gang. Seaborn Barnes fell with a bullet in his head and Sam Bass was seen to stagger as he was hit. Frank Jackson managed to get to their horses and helped Sam Bass into the saddle and they rode out of town.

Because of his fearsome reputation, and the fact that there was a belief that there was a huge gang of outlaws waiting for their leader to return, there was no immediate call for a posse to be organised. The fear of retaliation was the main reason, but the fact was that Sam Bass's gang consisted of only four men, and one of them was dead and the others had deserted. Sam Bass himself was badly wounded and, unknown to the townspeople and the Rangers, was just outside the town unable to continue because of the pain.

Handing his guns, money, ammunition and his horse over to Frank Jackson, Sam told his friend to leave him. In the meantime the Texas Rangers also concerned for their own safety, decided to call off the search until the following day. Then, two of the searchers spotted a man propped up against a fence and went over to him. Sam Bass held up his hand and told them who he was. The remainder of the search team was called to the area, including Jim Murphy. One of the Rangers decided that it would not be wise for Murphy to be seen with the searchers, and told him to hide behind a nearby tree and carry out Bass's identification from there.

The Rangers put Sam Bass in the back of a cart and took him into Round Rock. It soon became obvious that Sam Bass was dying from his wounds and, despite being treated by the local doctor, all he could do was to make him comfortable. Bass refused to name any of his gang members and when questioned about the death of Deputy Sheriff Grimes, claimed, that if it was him who had killed the man, it was the first man he ever killed. Sam Bass died at 3.58 p.m. on 19 July 1878 just before his 27th birthday. He was buried in Round Rock cemetery.

Frank Jackson was seen to visit the grave some days later but was never seen again. Jim Murphy committed suicide by taking poison one year later on 7 June 1879, convinced that he was going to be killed by other members of the Sam Bass Gang in retribution for what he had done.

Chapter 12

Billy the Kid

Possibly the most romanticised outlaw of the Wild West, and without question the most talked and written about, was Billy the Kid. His real name is said to have been Henry McCarty and he was thought to have been born in New York in 1859, but recent research now thinks that his actual birthplace was Missouri. The young man who became known as Billy the Kid, moved with his mother, Catherine McCarty and her elder son Joe, to Indianapolis whilst Henry was still an infant. It was

there that she met William Antrim. Times were extremely hard at the time, the Civil War having taken its toll on the economy, and the search for work resulted in the four of them moving to Wichita when Henry was about 11 years old.

His mother contracted tuberculosis shortly afterwards, so William Antrim took her and the boys to Santa Fe, where it was hoped the dry, sunny climate would help her condition. Shortly afterwards Catherine McCarty and William Antrim were married and the family moved once again to Silver City,

Billy the Kid.

New Mexico, but sadly one year later Catherine died, leaving William Antrim to bring up the boys alone.

It was whilst in Silver City that Henry first got into trouble. He and another boy stole some laundry, but got caught by the local sheriff Harvey Whitehall, who locked him up just to scare him and hope that it would teach him a lesson. Terrified, the young Henry clawed his way up the jail's chimney and escaped. Frightened to go back home and face his stepfather, he fled to Graham County, Arizona. He called himself Billy Antrim, after his stepfather, who he liked, and started working as a teamster.

During this time he was called 'Kid Antrim' and then 'Billy the Kid' because of his youthful appearance and after a couple of years he got into his second scrape with the law. In the town of Fort Grant, which he used to visit on the odd occasion, the town bully, an Irishman by the name of Frank 'Windy' Cahill, took a dislike to the young Billy and would taunt him whenever he could. Then on 8 August 1877, the taunting turned into an assault and he punched Billy repeatedly. In desperation Billy grabbed the pistol from Cahill's holster and squeezed the trigger. Cahill fell to the ground mortally wounded. It was a clear case of self-defence, but Billy was arrested for murder and jailed pending a trial. In fear for his life, he escaped and headed for New Mexico and whilst on the trail, joined up with another man by the name of Tom O'Keefe. The two men rode together for some days before having a run-in with some Indians and losing their horses. Two days later Billy walked in to Seven Rivers, New Mexico, having travelled for two days without food or water. What happened to O'Keefe is not known.

When asked who he was he gave the name William H. Bonney, Bonney possibly being his mother's maiden name. He was offered a job as a hand on a ranch owned by an Englishman by the name of John Tunstall and an American by the name of Alexander A. McSween. A lot has been made of the association between Tunstall and Billy the Kid, some say Billy looked upon him as a father figure and was taught to read and write by Tunstall. The fact is, that Tunstall was only about 24 years old at the time, and Billy was more than able to read and write by this time, as is known by the letters he wrote and the fact that he was known to be an avid reader. He was also fluent in Spanish.

The arrival of Bonney coincided with the first rumblings of what was to later be known as the 'Lincoln County War'. The troubles stemmed from the accusations by a number of small ranchers and nesters (illegal homesteader) that one of the big ranchers, John S. Chisum, was beginning to acquire and monopolise vast areas of the cattle ranges.

The Tunstall-McSween faction and a number of the other small ranchers that bordered their land supported John S. Chisum.

Said to be representing the smaller independent cattlemen were two partners, Major L.G. Murphy and James J. Dolan, who also had interests in ranching, along with their other interests in storekeeping

and banking. This Dolan-Murphy consortium had strong contacts with a gang of rustlers known as the Jesse Evans Gang. US Attorney Thomas B. Carron backed the consortium along with the Santa Fe Cattleman's Association.

The law in Lincoln County at the time was Sheriff Bill Brady, who was in the pay of the Dolan-Murphy faction, whilst his deputy, Deputy Sheriff Billy

Left: John Tunstall.

Below: Jesse Evans with some members of his gang.

Mathews, was in fact a silent partner of the Dolan-Murphy faction. This of course meant that whatever the Dolan-Murphy faction did, they did with the full support of the 'law'.

Things came to a head when the Jesse Evans Gang was caught with a large number of Tunstall's horses and cattle, together with those of a number of other ranchers. The sheriff was forced to arrest them because of the overwhelming evidence, but almost immediately allowed them to escape, without bothering to form a posse to go after them.

In the meantime, the herd of cattle and horses that the Evans Gang had stolen was claimed to be owned by the Dolan-Murphy faction, who then laid claim in court for their return. The sheriff, who was in their pay, claimed he had been issued with a retaining order for the animals, until the issue of ownership had been resolved. John Tunstall and some of his men rode into Lincoln to contest the claim and whilst on the trail the group split up for various reasons, leaving Tunstall on his own. Suddenly a posse of men led by the sheriff and his deputy rode into view and, seeing Tunstall on his own, charged him and shot him dead.

They claimed later that Tunstall had resisted them when they had challenged him to give them lawful grounds to retain the disputed stock, and he had then drawn his pistol and fired upon them. The facts that Tunstall never carried a gun and that the stock was already in the sheriff's possession seem to have been ignored by everybody.

Billy the Kid and Dick Brewer, Tunstall's foreman, swore out affidavits on some members of the posse that they had seen riding away, but Sheriff Brady retaliated by trying to arrest members of Tunstall's party for theft and a number of trumped-up minor incidents.

Billy the Kid was known to be fiercely loyal to anyone who helped, respected and treated him with kindness, and Tunstall had done all these things. Dick Brewer formed a vigilante group intent on getting rid of the crooked sheriff and his deputy, and to stop the Evans gang from rustling any more cattle and horses. Things came to a head on the morning of 1 April 1878, when Sheriff Brady, his deputy and three gunmen in the pay of the Dolan-Murphy faction walked past Tunstall's store on their way to the courthouse. Waiting by a corral were Billy the Kid, Dick Brewer and four vigilantes. As the sheriff and his party appeared in view, the vigilantes opened fire and Brady and his deputy fell to the ground – dead. The three other gunmen fired back, hitting the Kid in the leg, but they too were cut down.

Wounded, Billy the Kid hobbled through the back streets looking for help, but despite leaving a trail of blood, the pursuers were unable to find him. Dr Taylor Ealy had found him and hid him whilst treating his gunshot wound.

Accused of Brady's murder, a warrant for Billy the Kid's arrest was issued by the new sheriff, Sheriff George Pepin. A posse was organised to search for the Kid, but to no avail. Three months later, Billy the Kid returned to Lincoln, together with a posse of fourteen armed men. Realising that they would be attacked, the posse immediately barricaded themselves into Alexander McSween's house, surrounded by a large number of gunmen belonging to the Dolan-Murphy outfit, and spearheaded by Sheriff Pepin and his deputies.

After three days of exchanging fire, troops from Fort Stanton arrived with a cannon and a Gatling gun. They had been summoned by the sheriff, who had contacted the commanding officer, Lieutenant Colonel Nathan Dudley, and requested his help in resolving the matter. Realising that Billy the Kid and his gang were heavily outnumbered, they responded to an order to ceasefire. In the meantime a group of Dolan-Murphy's men had set fire to the back of the house, with the full knowledge of Dudley. As the men ran out of the burning building, five of them were gunned down before they could reach their horses. The remaining gunmen mounted their horses and rode out. In the meantime Alexander McSween, unarmed and a pacifist, walked out with his hands in the air, but was shot dead by a man called Bob Beckwith. So incensed was Billy the Kid at this outrage, that although he was on his horse and heading away, he turned back and shot Beckwith dead before finally escaping.

Billy the Kid was now on the run, and wanted posters offering a $500 reward for the capture of 'William Bonney' sprang up everywhere in the state. With the deaths of Alexander McSween and John Tunstall, the Lincoln County War was in effect over, but so was the influence of the Dolan-Murphy organisation as they too had suffered serious losses in the 'war'.

In the meantime trouble followed Billy the Kid, and he was involved in a number of killings and robberies over the next few years. Then in 1880 a new sheriff was appointed in Lincoln County – Pat Garrett. One of the main reasons why he was elected was that he knew Billy the Kid well. The two of them had known each other for a number of years and had shared each other's company in gambling saloons.

Assembling a posse, Pat Garrett tracked Billy and four of his gang to a deserted hut at a place called Stinking Springs. After a brief gun battle, in which one of Billy's gang was killed, they surrendered. The journey to Lincoln was by train and took three days; Billy the Kid remained shackled with handcuffs and leg irons the whole time.

They were taken first to Las Vegas, and then transferred to Santa Fe. It was as they entered Las Vegas that Pat Garrett faced a screaming lynch mob wanting one of the prisoners, Dave Rudabaugh, who was wanted for the killing of a Las Vegas jailer. Garrett told the other passengers on the train to leave, as he knew things were about to turn violent. Garrett then told the mob that if they tried to take any of the prisoners, he would unchain them and give them weapons to defend themselves. The intervention of the deputy US marshal defused the situation when he clambered in to engine driver's place, pulled a few levers and took the train away from the station.

Finally, Billy was taken to Mesilla to be tried for murder. The trial was presided over by Judge Warren Bristol, who had been a close confidant

Pat Garrett.

of the Dolan-Murphy faction. He instructed the jury that there was no evidence shown to the court other than murder in the first degree. Unsurprisingly Billy was found guilty and sentenced to be hanged, he was then taken to Lincoln County for the sentence to be carried out.

On reaching Lincoln, Billy the Kid was housed in an old storeroom above the courthouse because the jail was crumbling and not fit to hold prisoners. In was during this time that Billy wrote a number of letters to Governor Lew Wallace (who wrote the book *Ben Hur*), asking to see him, but he never received a reply. The two guards assigned to watch Billy the Kid were Bob Olinger and J.W. Bell and Olinger detested the Kid. Olinger would allow no one to visit the Kid whilst he was on duty, whilst Bell would allow some visitors. One of these was a man called Corbett who worked in a local store and on one visit he slipped a note

Above: Pat Garrett with his shotgun.

Left: Deputy Sheriff Bob Olinger.

to the Kid saying that there was a gun wrapped in newspaper at the bottom of the latrine pit.

Billy the Kid chose the day that he knew Pat Garrett would be out of town carrying out his normal duties. Olinger was off duty and Bell was just lounging around, when the Kid asked to use the latrine. He asked for the leg irons to be taken off, but Bell told him that the only person with the keys for these was Pat Garrett. Despite the latrine having been searched every day, they never looked into the bottom of the latrine pit, and once inside the Kid found the gun almost immediately.

On opening the door, the Kid pointed the gun at Bell and ordered him upstairs, but Bell decided to make a run for it and ran downstairs. Billy fired and missed, but the ricochet hit the wall and hit Bell just below the armpit, killing him almost immediately. Billy hobbled back to the main room and picked up Bell's shotgun. Moving to the window he saw Bob Olinger, who had heard the shot, running across the street. Hearing his name called out caused Olinger to stop and look up, and for a fleeting second he had sight of a shotgun pointed at him. Billy the Kid pulled the trigger and Bob Olinger fell back dead.

Somehow Billy the Kid managed to get his shackles off, and grabbing a horse he rode away. Garrett never learned of the escape until the following day and set about tracing Billy. He followed a number of sources and then heard that Billy was still in the area and visiting a girl at a house owned by a Pete Maxwell. Maxwell ran a roadhouse that catered for passing ranch hands that were in need of female company and liquor.

With two of his deputies Pat Garrett headed out towards the house and arrived during the night. Garrett left his two deputies outside on the porch, whilst he made their presence aware to Pete Maxwell by sitting on his bed and waking him. Talking quietly to Maxwell so as not to wake anyone else in the house, Garrett warned him not to try and warn the Kid. Just then the door opened and Billy the Kid stood framed in the doorway, a pistol in his hand, but hanging down at his side.

'*Quien es* ?'('Who's there?') Billy muttered softly in Spanish. Garrett fired and two shots rang out. Seconds later Billy the Kid lay dead on the floor. The first bullet had struck him in the heart, killing him instantly. The second also hit him in the chest. A great deal of controversy surrounds the death of Billy the Kid: some say Garrett didn't kill him, but that he was killed by one of the deputies. A verdict later stated that Sheriff Pat Garrett had carried out a lawful killing. Billy the Kid was just 26 years old when he was killed. Pat Garrett was killed some years later when he tried to evict a young tenant farmer by the name of Wayne Brazil. Brazil claimed he shot Garrett in self-defence and was acquitted after a trial.

Chapter 13

Jefferson 'Soapy' Smith

Jefferson 'Soapy' Smith was born in Coweta County, Georgia, on 2 November 1860, the son of a wealthy plantation owner and lawyer. At the end of the Civil War, and the reconstruction of the Southern states that followed, the Smith family found themselves almost penniless and so moved to Round Rock, Texas, to start a new life. Jefferson Smith senior opened up a law practice whilst Jefferson Jnr. started work as a salesman, the first and only honest job he ever had.

Jefferson Smith was a tall, handsome young man who had been very well educated but he soon realised that there was more money to be made using his intelligence and sleight-of-hand skills than working.

He teamed up with two other unscrupulous characters, Texas Jack Vermillion and 'Big Ed' Burns, and together they carried out a series of scams designed to fleece unwary victims. One of these was the 'Thimble Rig' in which three thimbles, one with a pea underneath, would be moved around and the victim would select the one he thought the pea was underneath. The game would start with one of his associates playing the part of a player who would

Head and shoulders shot of Jefferson Randolph 'Soapy' Smith.

102

apparently win regularly. This inevitably would draw a crowd who would be encouraged to play, only to be fleeced by the sleight-of–hand of Jefferson Smith, who would delicately remove the pea from the chosen thimble. Together, with rigged poker games and other minor scams whilst moving from town to town, the trio made a very comfortable living.

Deciding to expand his dishonest career, Jefferson Smith moved to Denver, Colorado in 1879 with his two associates. It was here that he earned the name of 'Soapy' when he introduced his moneymaking scam of the selling of soap, with a chance of winning some money that was wrapped around the bars of soap. The soap was sold for a dollar a bar and was wrapped in plain paper, and then, when he had an audience, he would take a number of selected bars and wrap $20 or $50 bills around the bar and then wrap plain paper around them, which he then placed amongst the other bars of soap. Then one of his associates, or 'shills' as they were known, would buy a bar, unwrap it and exclaim loudly that he had just won some money. What the punters did not know was that

Above left: Texas Jack Vermillion who rode with 'Soapy' Smith.

Above right: Nathaniel 'Texas Jack' Reed.

was the only bar to have money wrapped around it, the other bars having had their money removed by a delicate piece of sleight-of-hand. Halfway through the sale of the bars, Jefferson would announce that there was still a $100 bill there somewhere, encouraging the punters to buy more bars of soap. On one occasion a policeman by the name of John Holland arrested Smith for running the scam. It is said that while he was writing Jefferson Smith's name in his notebook, he couldn't remember Smith's first name, so he wrote 'Soapy' and the name stuck.

Using his intelligence, 'Soapy' Smith began to expand his rackets until slowly but surely he drew into his net the vast majority of the criminal underworld in Denver. As his power grew he numbered amongst his contacts politicians and a number of police officers, including the chief of police, who were all on his payroll. Within three years of being in Denver, Jefferson 'Soapy' Smith controlled almost all of the underworld and gambling in the city. When in 1888 he opened the Tivoli Club, a gambling house, saloon and brothel, his younger brother, Bascomb Smith, joined his enterprise and operated a cigar store that was a front for illegal poker games that were played in the back room. The organisation ran fake lotteries, fraudulent stock exchanges and selling shares in non-existent businesses together with fake diamond auctions.

Although 'Soapy' Smith used his intelligence and wit to establish his enterprises, he was not averse to using violence himself, although he usually had his own enforcers take of any problems that required force. One such incident arose when the editor of the *Rocky Mountain News*, who was always hostile to Smith's dealings, ran an article about his family. 'Soapy' Smith had married a young lady by the name of Mary Noonan, with whom he had had two children, but they were kept well away from his business dealings. The article came as an unwelcome surprise to Smith because almost no one knew he was married. When the article appeared in the paper, all her neighbours much to the anger of 'Soapy' Smith shunned his wife.

He immediately put his wife and children on the first train to St. Louis, and then, arming himself with a heavy walking stick, he went to the offices of the *Rocky Mountain News*. As he approached the paper he saw the owner, Colonel John Atkins about to enter and challenged him. Without a moment's hesitation 'Soapy' Smith lashed out and beat the unfortunate man to the ground, fracturing his skull in the process. He was arrested and tried for attempted murder. His defence team argued that had 'Soapy' Smith wanted to murder Colonel Atkins he would have chosen a more suitable weapon to do it. He was acquitted.

In 1889, an electoral fraud trial highlighted the illegal ties between 'Soapy' Smith's empire and corrupt politicians. At the end of the trial the mayor and the chief of police lost their jobs, but Jefferson Smith somehow remained untouched. But he was not without enemies, there was a continuing power struggle within the underworld, mainly because certain factions did not like one person controlling everything, and taking a percentage of what others had made. There were several attempts on his life and a number of would-be-assassins paid the price, as did those who paid them.

In 1892, Jefferson Smith's influence over Denver's politicians waned, so he decided to sell the Tivoli and move his operation to the silver mining town of Creede. There had been a major silver strike and because of it the town was flourishing with miners desperately wanting to be parted from their money – and 'Soapy' Smith was ready to oblige. He imported prostitutes to incite property owners in the main street to sell their leases, which he in turn rented out to his associates. Within a matter of months he had control of almost the whole of the main street and the criminal section of the town. He opened a gambling hall and saloon called the Orleans Club where he exhibited a petrified body of a man known as McGinty. He would charge ten cents to see the exhibit and while the queue waited, he would encourage them to play the shell game amongst other games of 'chance'.

One of his main competitors in Creede was Bob Ford, the man who shot Jesse James in the back to claim the reward. The competition was short lived when on 8 June Ford was shot dead by a man called Ed O'Kelley, leaving 'Soapy' Smith in control of the thirty-nine out of forty saloons in Creede. Why O'Kelley shot Ford is not known: some say it was in retaliation for the killing of Jesse James, while others think that 'Soapy' Smith might have had a hand in it. The only saloon Smith did not control was the Denver Exchange owned by Bat Masterson, but Smith was not foolish enough to go up against a man with the reputation of being one of the most feared gunfighters in the West.

What is not so very well known about 'Soapy' Smith, is that he used some of his ill-gotten wealth to help poor families, build a church and bury destitute prostitutes, some of whom had been the initial core of his business. By the end of the year 'Soapy' Smith had become a very rich man, but he realised that the silver bonanza was starting to decline, and when word from some of the corrupt officials in Denver reached him that the reforms were coming to an end, 'Soapy' decided to return to Denver.

The petrified body of an unknown man that 'Soapy' Smith named 'McGinty' and used as an attraction in his saloon in Skagway.

On his return he quickly built up an organisation and within weeks was taking a percentage from almost all the illegal activities in the town, offering them 'protection' in return. He enlisted the aid of a number of people, including two disbarred lawyers who would tie up any court with their exceptional talent for quasi-legalese that would totally confuse any jury having to listen to it. They were very useful when any of 'Soapy' Smith's men were arrested for enforcing his organisation's rules. One particular case brought by two men, claimed that on a visit to 'Soapy' Smith's gambling saloon they had been swindled out of $1,500 in a rigged game. In his defence 'Soapy' Smith claimed that his

'Soapy' Smith at the bar of his saloon in Skagway.

gambling establishment was designed to cure gambling addicts much like other institutes treated alcoholics. Furthermore, he claimed that both the players had sworn never to gamble again, so endorsing his statement. He was acquitted.

In 1894 the state had a new governor, Davis Hanson Waite. His first act was to fire three Denver officials who he claimed were corrupt and the pay of 'Soapy' Smith. The three men refused to leave City Hall and barricaded themselves in, accompanied by a number of others who thought that jobs were being threatened. On hearing this, Smith and some of his men joined the protesters and the governor ordered the state militia to attend. Realising that the siege could end with considerable loss of life, Governor Waite withdrew and left it to the Colorado Supreme Court to decide. They ruled that although the governor was well within his rights to remove the officials, he was wrong to involve the state militia and reprimanded him for doing so.

With the approval of the law Governor Waite set about cleaning up Denver and ordered the closure of all gambling halls, saloons and brothels. The writing was on the wall for 'Soapy' Smith and his gang and when he and his brother Bascomb were arrested for the attempted murder of one of his saloon managers, things turned from bad to worse. Bascomb Smith was convicted and sentenced to prison, but 'Soapy' Smith escaped and went on the run. So much for brotherly loyalty.

Jefferson Smith surfaced again in Skagway, Alaska, in 1897, at the beginning of the Klondike Gold Rush. His first attempt at opening up in the town ended in failure when a committee of townspeople and miners persuaded him to leave after numerous complaints about his three-card 'monte' and pea and shell games were found to be rigged. One year later in 1898, he appeared again and this time managed to gain a foothold in the town. He based his new empire in the same way he had in Denver and Creede, firstly managing to get the deputy town marshal on his payroll and then 'persuading' business holders in the main street to transfer their leases to him. He then opened a fake telegraph office, with wires that only reached the other side of the room, and charged for sending messages. The telegraph didn't reach Skagway until 1901. His gambling saloon Smith's Parlour started to relieve miners of their money in the rigged poker games after they had been 'befriended' by some of 'Soapy's' associates. Within the year he had acquired a hotel, a couple more gambling dens, brothels and even a fake shipping company.

The local townspeople were becoming more and more concerned about the control 'Soapy' Smith was gaining over the town and formed

Skagway in 1897.

Above: Members of 'Soapy' Smith's gang outside the JS Parlour in Skagway.

Right: 'Soapy' Smith's saloon in Skagway.

Group of vigilantes outside of City Hall in Skagway discussing what to do about 'Soapy' Smith.

a vigilance committee called the 'Committee 101' and threatened to get rid of Smith and his men. Smith in retaliation formed his own 'Law and Order Society', which outnumbered the Committee 101, and so forced them to back down. However the threat caused many of the cardsharps and the like to leave town.

The Spanish-American War erupted in 1898 and Smith formed his own volunteer army with the approval of the United States department of War. They were known as the 'Skagway Military Company' commanded by Captain Jefferson 'Soapy' Smith. It is not known if any of the company actually fought in the war, but it is most unlikely that they did, because Smith used his position to strengthen his position in the town.

Things came to a head on 7 July 1898 when a Klondike miner by the name of John Douglas Stewart came to Skagway with a sack full of gold worth $2,700. He was persuaded by a couple of 'Soapy' Smith's men to play three-card 'monte' and lost a considerable amount of his gold. When he was asked to pay up he questioned the way the game had been played and accused them of cheating. The two men grabbed his sack of gold and ran off. Stewart complained to Committee 101 that

Decoration Day in Skagway, Alaska, with 'Soapy' Smith on the white horse leading the procession.

he had been cheated out of his money and that the two men had stolen what was left. On confronting 'Soapy' Smith, the committee demanded that he return the gold, but they were told that the game had been fair and that the miner had lost. That evening the vigilance committee had a meeting on the Juneau Wharf to decide what they were going to do about the theft and the numerous other complaints that were continually coming to their notice.

When 'Soapy' Smith heard of the meeting he and a couple of his thugs went down to the wharf to confront the committee. Armed with a Winchester rifle, Smith began to verbally berate one of the guards, Frank Reid, who was blocking his way to the wharf. Smith swung his gun in the direction of Reid, threatening him with it. Reid grabbed the end of the rifle and pushed it away at the same time as drawing his own pistol, and pulled the trigger. The first shot misfired, giving Smith the opportunity to point his rifle again at Reid. He pulled the trigger, shooting Reid in the groin just as Reid squeezed of another round, hitting 'Soapy' Smith in the heart. The crime lord of Skagway was dead and his control over the town gone. Frank Reid had been shot in the leg and in the groin and died twelve days later from his injuries.

111

Above: The dock at Skagway where 'Soapy' Smith was shot and killed.

Left: Frank Reid who killed 'Soapy' Smith.

Right: Drawing from a San Francisco newspaper depicting the killing of 'Soapy' Smith.

Below: The bullet that killed 'Soapy' Smith being removed from his body, watched by members of the town council. Interesting to note the cigar-smoking onlooker observing the hygiene regulations of the day.

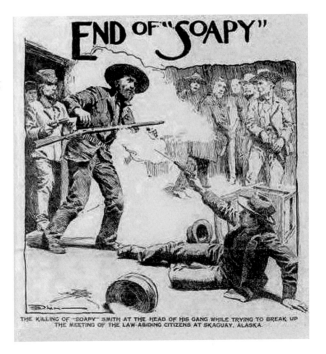

THE KILLING OF "SOAPY" SMITH AT THE HEAD OF HIS GANG WHILE TRYING TO BREAK UP THE MEETING OF THE LAW-ABIDING CITIZENS AT SKAGUAY, ALASKA.

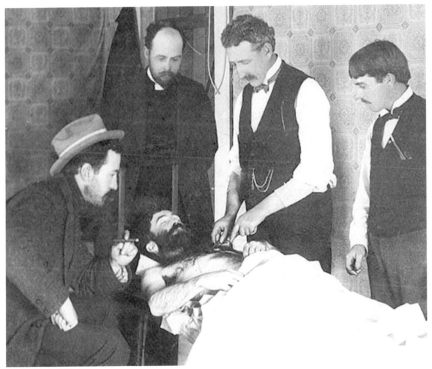

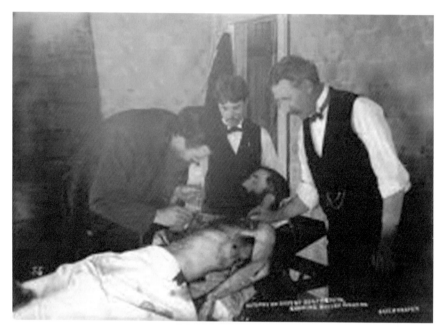

Post mortem of 'Soapy' Smith.

With 'Soapy' Smith dead and his control gone, the townspeople armed themselves and took to the streets. Within hours twenty-six of 'Soapy' Smith's gang were in custody, amongst rumours of lynchings coming from the ever-increasing crowd of townspeople and miners. Fortunately a detachment of troops had been summoned by Judge Sehlbrede, who was concerned that law and order was breaking down. Martial law was quickly introduced and the crowds dispersed as the troops patrolled the main street. Later the three members of 'Soapy' Smith's gang who robbed John Douglas Stewart were captured and sent to prison.

With the situation calmer and the town under strict control by the officials, the Army left. The leading figures of 'Soapy' Smith's gang were sentenced to lengthy terms of imprisonment, whilst the remaining members were placed aboard a steamer bound for Seattle, and told that if they were to set foot in Skagway or any of the other towns nearby again, they would suffer the consequences.

A rough board with a stark inscription marked the grave of the 'Crime Lord of Skagway': 'Jefferson R. Smith, Age 38, Died July 8, 1898.'

Chapter 14

Crawford 'Cherokee Bill' Goldsby

One of the least known of the outlaws who left his mark in the west, was Crawford Goldsby or as he became known – 'Cherokee Bill'. Goldsby's reign of terror was short, violent and bloody, and lasted just two years. A mixed-blood Cherokee Indian, Crawford Goldsby was born on 8 February 1876, at Fort Concho, Texas. He was the oldest son of Ellen Beck and George Goldsby, there were three other children, older sister Georgia Eller and brothers Clarence and Luther.

Their father, who was part mulatto, enlisted in the Confederate infantry during the Civil War and after Gettysburg, escaped to Harrisburg where he joined the 21st Pennsylvania Cavalry Regiment. After the Civil War he returned to Alabama, but he was told that he was not welcome because he had joined the Union Army after Gettysburg and fought against the South.

The family moved to the Indian Territory and George Goldsby joined the 10th Cavalry Regiment, known as the 'Buffalo Soldiers'. Within three years he had been promoted to sergeant major and on finishing his time rejoined and became the first sergeant of D Company, 10th Cavalry. It was around this time (1878) that serious

'Cherokee Bill'.

problems arose between the black soldiers and the local cowboys, residents and hunters of San Angelo. Things came to a head when one of soldiers who was having a quiet drink in the local saloon was attacked and had the chevrons ripped from his uniform and the yellow stripes ripped from his trousers. The battered soldier returned to Fort Concho, whereupon fellow soldiers armed themselves and returned to the saloon. In the ensuing gunfight, one of the hunters was killed and two others badly wounded, whilst one of the soldiers was killed and one wounded.

Although George Goldsby was not directly involved in the incident, it was claimed later by Texas Rangers that he had been responsible for issuing the rifles to the men. Realising that he was not going to get a fair trial, George Goldsby went on the run, leaving his wife and children at the fort.

Unable to cope with all the children, Ellen Beck left Crawford Goldsby with an elderly black lady known as Amanda Foster. When he was seven years old, Crawford was sent to the Indian School at Carlisle, Pennsylvania, where he stayed until the age of 12. In the meantime his mother had moved to Fort Gibson and remarried a man called William Lynch.

From the start, when he returned from Pennsylvania Crawford did not get on with his stepfather. He started to drink and mix with the local villains, getting into all sorts of minor scrapes. At the age of 15 and in desperation, his mother sent him to live with his elder sister Georgia and her husband Mose Brown in Nowata, in the Oklahoma Territory.

The visit lasted less than a month. Mose Brown and Crawford disliked each other right from the very moment they met, so Crawford returned to Fort Gibson. He lived with a distant relative, Bud Buffington, for a while and then found work on a local ranch doing odd jobs. He was described by the owner of the ranch as a hard-working, pleasant young man, who never caused any problems whilst he was there.

At the age of 18 his troubles began, when, at a local dance at Fort Gibson, he got into an argument with a 35-year-old man, by the name of Jake Lewis, who had picked on one of Crawford's younger brothers. Crawford received a beating from the man that left him humiliated and angry. Two days later he confronted Jake Lewis again, only this time he was carrying a pistol. He shot Lewis twice and, thinking he had killed him, got on his horse and fled, heading for the Cree and Seminole Nations. There he joined up with two locally-known outlaw brothers, Jim and Bill Cook who were already wanted by the law for numerous robberies and other offences.

Jake Lewis recovered from his wounds and named Crawford Goldsby as the person who had shot him. The sheriff in the Cherokee Nation went after him with a warrant for his arrest but was unable to find him.

During the summer of 1894, the government purchased land from the Cherokees called the Cherokee Strip. Anyone who could claim and prove title to some of the land and was one-eighth Cherokee blood was to be paid $265.70.

The Cook brothers, who were also part Cherokee, went with Crawford Goldsby to Tahlequah, to claim their share. On their way, they stopped at Fourteen-Mile

Bill Cook, leader of the Cook Gang.

Creek at a small hotel and restaurant owned by Effie Crittenden. The Cooks' brother-in-law worked as a cook at the restaurant, and together they put pressure of Effie Crittenden to go to Tahlequah to make the claim on their behalf. The reasoning behind this was that both the Cook brothers and Crawford Goldsby knew they were on the wanted list and if they turned up there was a chance that they would be arrested.

Effie Crittenden turned up on the last day for the claims to be made and collected the money. However, Sheriff Ellis Rattling Gourd had been made aware of the arrival of the outlaws at Effie's establishment and, together with seven of his deputies, including Dick and Zeke Crittenden, followed her home. Dick Crittenden was the estranged husband of Effie. Any hope they had of surprising the gang disappeared when the outlaws spotted the lawmen trailing her. A gunfight ensued and some thought that Dick had started the gunfight in the hope his wife would be killed.

The gunfight lasted all evening, during which one of the deputies, Sequoyah Houston, was killed and the outlaw Jim Cook was wounded. Under cover of darkness the two Crittenden brothers left and on discovering this the sheriff and his posse withdrew. The following morning the Cook brothers and Crawford Goldsby left. When Effie Crittenden was later questioned about the three men, she was asked to identify Crawford Goldsby as one of the gunmen, but she said that the man's name was 'Cherokee Bill', a name that stayed with Crawford Goldsby until he died.

Some weeks later the Cook Gang was formed and consisted of blacks and men of mixed Indian blood, the majority of the Indians being Cherokee freedmen. During the next couple of weeks a series of murders and robberies took place, all pointing to the work of the Cook Gang. Their first major raid was carried out on 14 July 1894 when they held up the Muskogee–Fort Gibson stage, followed two days later by the robbing of a prominent Cherokee tribal chief. Within days the gang had also held up a train at Red Fork and had robbed the passengers as well as the express car.

At the end of July the gang entered the town of Chandler in the Oklahoma Territory and robbed the Lincoln County Bank. A barber across the street from the bank raised the alarm and was shot dead for his trouble by one of the gang. Other citizens opened fire and wounded one of the gang resulting in his capture, but the remaining members of the gang escaped to the hills.

The reign of terror throughout the Indian Territory was brought to the attention of the Office of Indian Affairs in Washington. They in turn summoned Chief United States Marshal Crump to Washington to give an account of what was going on. The US Attorney and the Secretary of War both threatened to break off the treaties they had with the Indians, abolish all tribal relations and establish a territorial government if the gang were not caught. Reward posters appeared almost overnight for the capture of any or all of the gang members.

A breakthrough came after a man by the name of Burl Taylor, who lived in the Creek Nation, mentioned to the authorities that 'Cherokee Bill' had visited him several times. The last time he had visited him he was accompanied by members of the Cook Gang, who he named as Jim Cook, Texas Jack, Sam McWilliam, who was also known as the Verdigris Kid, Jim French and a man called Skeeter. Taylor had taken a real risk in talking to the authorities about his meetings with the gang, as they were known to have killed a number of others who had talked to the sheriffs and US Marshals.

Such was the fear that the gang instilled in the people of the Indian Nations, that a number of towns actually passed an ordinance that permitted them to pass through their town without hindrance. This was of great benefit to 'Cherokee Bill', as he was reputed to have had a girl in every town. It was his love of the ladies that was to be his final undoing.

His killings were not restricted to victims of robberies or anyone else who may have upset him, but also members of his own family fell beneath his guns. It appears that 'Cherokee Bill' wrote to his sister inviting her to visit him, but her husband, Mose Brown, refused to let her go alone and accompanied her. The relationship between 'Cherokee Bill' and his brother-in-law had always been one of hostility and just after the pair had reached the place where 'Cherokee Bill' was hiding out, an argument broke out between the two men. Minutes later Mose Brown lay dead on the floor – shot by 'Cherokee Bill'.

The killings and robberies continued unabated, but then on 8 November 1894 'Cherokee Bill' and the Verdigris Kid rode into the small town of Lenapah, which was situated between Coffeyville, Kansas and Nowata, Indian Territory. Their intended target was the store owned and operated by Schufeldt & Son. On entering the store, 'Cherokee Bill' held a gun on the owner and forced him to open the safe. After taking the money he decided to help himself to some new clothes and more ammunition. It was then that he noticed a group of men looking through the window and, without warning and for no reason, 'Cherokee Bill' fired at the window, killing an innocent bystander by the name of Ernest Melton.

The senseless killing enraged the people of the territory and a huge manhunt began. So intense was it, that it forced the gang to split up and almost all the members of the gang were either shot dead or captured. Those who stood trial were given either lengthy prison sentences or hanged. However, 'Cherokee Bill' remained as elusive as ever and, because most lawmen were reluctant to face him on account of his reputation with a gun, it was decided that the only way to catch him was by stealth.

Then came the breakthrough. A man by the name of Clint Scales told Deputy US Marshal W.C. Smith that 'Cherokee Bill' was seeing a girl by the name of Maggie Glass, a girl of African-Cherokee descent, at a friend's house. The friend was Ike Rogers, whose wife was the aunt of Maggie Glass. Deputy Smith persuaded Ike Rogers and Clint Scales to help him catch 'Cherokee Bill', and promised them a share in the substantial reward now being offered for the capture of the outlaw.

They were to use Maggie Glass as bait and invited 'Cherokee Bill' over for drinks with them and Maggie. In the meantime, Ike, his wife and Clint Scales, who had just joined them, tried to ply 'Cherokee Bill' with whiskey laced with morphine. Bill knew that something was not quite right and kept his rifle over his knees all through dinner and in the meantime refused to drink. The next day, after breakfast, Ike Rogers persuaded Maggie to go to a nearby neighbour and purchase some chickens for dinner that night. When she was gone, Bill was lighting a cigarette by the fire, when Ike struck him across the back of the head sending him crashing to the ground. Such was the force of the blow that Ike later said that had it been a normal man, it probably would have killed him. Ike's wife grabbed Bill's gun as it fell to the floor, whilst Ike and Clint fought with Bill and managed to get a pair of handcuffs on him after a long struggle.

Left: Crawford Goldsby ('Cherokee Bill') under arrest.

Below: 'Cherokee Bill' (above centre with left hand in his pocket), who killed for the pleasure of killing, and his captors, on his arrival in Fort Smith, Arkansas, to face the Hanging Judge. L–R: Zeke Crittenden and Dick Crittenden, deputy marshals; Bill; Clint Scales; Ike Rogers and deputy marshal Bill Smith.

The two men then manhandled Bill onto the back of a buckboard and took him into Nowata. He was handed over to Deputy US Marshals George Lawson and Bill Smith, who then transported him to the federal jail in Fort Smith. There he was brought before Judge Isaac Parker and charged with the murder of Ernest Melton.

'Cherokee Bill's' mother arranged for her son to be defended by the top lawyer in the territory – J. Warren Reed. At the trial the prosecution produced seven witnesses that identified 'Cherokee Bill' as the man who shot Ernest Melton down in cold blood. All J. Warren Reed could do was to produce a couple of shady characters, who said unconvincingly under oath that Bill was 50 miles away on the day of the murder.

The jury returned a unanimous verdict of guilty, at which both his sister and mother started to cry. 'Cherokee Bill' is said to have said, 'What's the matter with you two? I ain't dead yet.'

He was brought back to court on 13 April 1895 for sentence and an execution date was set for 25 June. He was returned to the Federal prison where he was reunited with his old friend Bill Cook who had been captured in New Mexico. The jail at the time housed over 200 prisoners, some awaiting trial, some waiting sentence and others waiting to be executed. All the time there was an underlying tension that prisoners were plotting escapes.

The arrival of 'Cherokee Bill' in his prison so concerned the head jailer J.D. Berry that he ordered a sudden search of the entire prison. A number of weapons were found secreted in various places, and in 'Cherokee Bill's' cell nine .45-calibre bullets were found. A fully-loaded .45 calibre revolver was then discovered in a bucket of lime in the communal bathroom. What they didn't find was the one secreted by Bill himself.

The following evening at 7.00 p.m., two guards, Campbell Eoff and Lawrence Keating, entered 'Murderers Row'. They were challenged by 'Cherokee Bill' from his cell and ordered to give up their weapons. The two guards refused, so Bill opened fire, killing Keating. The other guard ran down the corridor and sounded the alarm. Within minutes other guards appeared and shots were exchanged. There was stalemate until Henry Starr, the grandson of the Cherokee outlaw Tom Starr, a prisoner serving a sentence for robbery, volunteered to go and talk to 'Cherokee Bill'. The authorities agreed and promised to hold their fire whilst he talked and tried to persuade him to give up his gun.

After some time, Henry Starr emerged holding 'Cherokee Bill's' gun and the siege was over. Brought before Judge Parker again, this time for the murder of Lawrence Keating, Bill was sentenced to be hanged on 10 September 1895. Bill's lawyers managed to get a stay of execution and appealed to the Supreme Court on 2 December. The appeal was rejected and the execution date reset for 17 March 1896.

The time set for the execution to take place was 11.00 a.m. on the morning of the 17th, but it was delayed until 2.00 p.m. because Bill's sister Georgia wanted to see him before he died. At 2.0 p.m. 'Cherokee Bill' stepped on to the gallows, and when asked if he had anything to say, he replied, 'I came here to die, not make a speech'. Ten minutes later the trap was sprung, ending a short reign of terror that had haunted the territory for less than three years. For his part in helping to end the siege in the prison, Henry Starr's sentence was reduced.

Chapter 15

Charles E. Bolton/Boles, 'Black Bart'

One of the most unusual outlaws who haunted the West was Charles E. Bolton/Boles, or as he was to call himself – 'Black Bart'. The name Bolton, it is thought, was originally Boles as a bible found in his room in later years had the inscription: 'This precious bible is presented to Charles E. Boles, First Sergeant Company B 116th Illinois Volunteer Infantry, by his wife as a New Years gift.'

Born in 1829 in Norfolk, England, Charles Boles's family emigrated to America when he was just two years old. His parents, John and Maria Boles, farmed a homestead in Jefferson County, in upstate New York. Almost nothing is known of Charles Boles's early years, but when he was 20 years old, he and his cousin David set out for the goldfields in California. For the next three years the two men prospected along the Californian rivers and streams and finally headed back home. On the way back one of the places he stopped at was Decatur, Illinois, and it was here that he met and later married his wife Mary Elizabeth Johnson.

With the Civil War now affecting almost everyone, on 13 August 1862, Charles E. Boles joined the

Charles Bowles, also known as 'Black Bart'.

A smartly dressed Charles Bowles ('Black Bart').

116th Illinois Volunteer Infantry Regiment at Decatur. On 8 November the regiment went to Memphis, Tennessee to join up with General Grant's army and take part in his Mississippi campaign. For the next three years Charles E. Boles took part in several campaigns, fighting in numerous battles. In 1865 he was honourably discharged after having been severely wounded during a battle in Georgia. He set up home with his wife and two daughters near New Oregon, Iowa, and started farming, but the mundane life soon got to him and he decided to head for pastures new.

Charles wrote to his wife from Silver Bow, Montana, saying that he was heading for the goldfields of California once again. Surprisingly he preferred to walk rather than ride and would easily walk 20–30 miles in a day and he also enjoyed living in the open air. During the next four years nothing was heard of Charles Boles and he even stopped writing to his wife, which led her to believe that he was dead.

What happened during this period appears to have turned a hardworking, honest man into one of the most notorious stagecoach robbers of the time. The only clue was a comment he is said to have made whilst in Silver Bow, when he had some sort of altercation with Wells Fargo & Co. and swore to get back what was his!

The first stagecoach robbery attributed to Charles E. Boles, or Bolton as he was now known, was in July 1875, when he stopped the Sonora to Milton Wells Fargo stage in Calveras County, California. He carried a rifle, which he pointed at the driver, John Shine, and said him to 'Please throw down the box'. He presented an unusual sight as he wore a long white linen coat down to the ankles, and a hood made out of a flour sack, which had eyeholes cut out of it. This was what he wore for all subsequent hold-ups and his attire became his trademark.

He always picked his spot near a dense wood, so that he could quickly make his escape on foot, making it extremely difficult to follow him on horseback. He wore socks over his boots so as not to leave footprints and when the empty strongbox was found, there was a note inside which read:

I've laboured long and hard for bread
For honour and for riches
But on my corns too long you've tred
You fine haired sons of Bitches
'Black Bart', the Poet.

From that moment on, every time 'Black Bart' carried out a robbery, he left behind a poem. The second robbery, the Wells Fargo stage from North San Juan to Marysville in Yuba County was carried out in similar circumstances, the only difference being that this time the driver reported that whilst the robbery was taking place, four other members of the 'gang' were keeping the passengers and driver covered with rifles from hidden positions. After 'Black Bart' had left it was found that the 'rifles' were in fact just sticks, giving the robber ample time to make his escape.

Then followed the Quincy to Oroville stage, which netted 'Black Bart' $379, a diamond ring and a silver watch, all of which were in the strongbox. He left behind the following poem:

Here I lay me down to Sleep
To wait the coming Morrow
Perhaps Success perhaps defeat
And everlasting sorrow . . .
Let come what will, I'll try it on
My condition can't be worse
And if there's money in that Box
Tis munny in my purse.

It is interesting to note that when 'Black Bart' was finally brought to book, he insisted that he never once robbed a passenger and only took that which belonged to Wells Fargo. The robberies took place irregularly and he appeared to carry them out only when he needed the money.

The Wells Fargo detective put in charge of the case was James B. Hume, one of the company's most successful investigators. He distributed wanted posters with examples of the poems that 'Black Bart' left behind, in a hope that someone might recognise the handwriting. Over the next five years 'Black Bart' carried out twenty-nine hold-ups and it was the last one that was to be his undoing.

The first clue to the identity of the outlaw came with the hold-up of the Sonora to Milton stage on 3 November 1883. When the driver had thrown down the strongbox Charles Bolton had cut his hand opening it and had used a handkerchief to bandage it. He had dropped it when a rider approached and fired a shot at him. On examining the handkerchief it was discovered that there was a San Francisco laundry mark on it. James Hume went to San Francisco only to find that there were ninety-one laundries in the city, but he painstakingly visited them all until he reached the Ferguson & Biggs California Laundry, who identified the mark as theirs. Their records showed that the handkerchief belonged to Charles E. Bolton, a mining engineer.

Accompanied by the local police, Hume went to Bolton's hotel and arrested him. At first Bolton denied that he was 'Black Bart', but when confronted with the fact that he had registered with the hotel under a false name – T.Z. Spalding – he finally admitted that it was he who had carried out the stagecoach robberies. In his hotel room the police also found the bible his wife had given him, with its inscription to 'Charles E. Boles'.

After a trial he was sentenced to six years in San Quentin. The reasons given for his relatively light sentence were his age and the fact that he never fired a shot at anyone during the robberies, was always courteous and never robbed a passenger. Charles E. Bolton/'Black Bart' served four years of his six-year sentence and was released on 21 January 1888 and disappeared. A stagecoach robbery later that year had all the hallmarks of being carried out by 'Black Bart', but the poem left at the scene was examined by Hume and said to be a fake. Someone was copying 'Black Bart's' methods.

Chapter 16

'Big Nose' George Parrott

A short but violent reign of terror and ruthlessness began in January 1879, when a gang led by a man by the name of 'Big Nose' George Parrott robbed a merchant of $14,000. The merchant, Morris Cahn, was in a military wagon, being escorted by soldiers who were several hundred yards to the rear. At a point where the wagon was out of sight of the escorting soldiers, the gang struck and was away before the escort arrived.

The gang went on to rob stagecoaches and freight wagons in various states, among them Montana, Dakota and Wyoming. The appeared to make their headquarters in Miles City and if the law started to show an interest in their whereabouts, they would retreat into the Big Mountains of Wyoming, the Dakota Badlands or the prairies of Montana.

After one of their raids, the gang went to Miles City to live it up and spend their ill-gotten gains. The law, who was collecting evidence about the gang, was told that 'Big Nose' George Parrott was spending large amounts of cash in the city. Marshal Hank Wormwood and some of his deputies arrived in Miles City and arrested Parrott and some of his gang.

Put on trial, a number of witnesses came forward to swear on oath that Parrott and his men were in Canada at the time of the alleged robbery.

Big Nose George Parrott.

It was quite obvious that all the witnesses had lied, but nothing could be proved against them.

The robberies continued and when an attempt to derail a Union Pacific train in order to get to the express car failed, two lawmen who trailed the gang were murdered. Investigations and information from an informer showed that George Parrott had led the gang that attempted the robbery and had killed the two lawmen.

The authorities placed a reward of $1,000 for the capture of George Parrott and approached US Marshal John X. Biedler, who had a reputation for being one of the best manhunters in the West. After weeks of trailing the gang, Biedler traced them to a small town in Montana. In front of a saloon called John Chinnick's, Biedler recognised two of George Parrott's gang. There was a problem in that US Marshal Biedler had a pronounced limp and was well known to most of the criminals in the various states. If he were to be recognised then the gang would probably escape, so Biedler enlisted the help of a local farm hand by the name of Lem Wilson, who risked his life in helping the marshal. The two men outside the saloon were obviously keep watch and so would suspect anything out of the ordinary. Lem Wilson was wearing the normal bib-and-braces overalls worn by all farm hands and so was completely in place. Placing two handguns behind the overall bib, Wilson walked toward the saloon and was confronted by one of the outlaws who wanted to know where he was going. Wilson told him he was going into the saloon and walked past. The moment he was past them and behind them, he pulled out the guns and told them to raise their hands. Minutes later it was all over and 'Big Nose' George Parrott and most of his gang were in custody.

George Parrott was taken to Rawlins, Wyoming, where he was charged with the murders of the two lawmen and found guilty. Whilst in jail awaiting execution, he tried to escape by beating a guard, but was foiled by the wife of one of the other guards who raised the alarm. When the local citizens heard of this, they were so enraged that they dragged George Parrott from his cell and lynched him from a telegraph pole.

That would normally be the end of that episode in the life of an outlaw, but 'Big Nose' George Parrott's body was claimed by Doctors Thomas Maghee and Eugene Osborne. They made a death mask of him, and then carried out a series of experiments on the body. They took out the brain to see if it showed any abnormalities that might explain his criminal behaviour – which it didn't – then had the body skinned and the skin sent to a tannery in Denver, Colorado. Doctor Osborne then asked the tannery to make him a pair of shoes using the skin, which they duly did. The top of Parrott's skull that was crudely sawn off was presented to 15-year-old Lillian Heath, then a medical assistant to Maghee. She became the first female doctor in Wyoming and is said to have used the cap as an ashtray, a penholder and a doorstop.

Dr Osborne wore the shoes for many years and when elected state governor, is said to have worn the shoes to the inaugural ball. The shoes are now on display at the Carbon County Museum, Rawlins, Wyoming.

The remaining parts of George Parrott's body were crammed into a whiskey barrel and buried. It was found in 1950 when construction workers were digging new foundations for a building behind Doctor Maghee's old office. The bones were reburied, but the skull given to the museum in Wyoming.

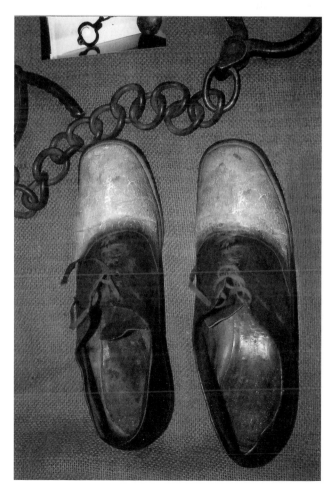

Pair of shoes made from the skin of George Parrott.

Chapter 17

The Evans Gang

John and George Sontag were the owners of a quartz mine in Visalia, California, for a number of years, but in 1892 when the quartz started to peter out, they decided to sell up and move on. They met up with Christopher Evans, a farmer who was struggling to make ends meet, and the two brothers moved in with Evans and his family in their tiny farmhouse. This proved to be the catalyst for the forming of a violent and vicious gang that came to be known as the Evans Gang.

Evans had started his farm when the railroad announced their intentions to run their tracks past the little town of Visalia, in the hope of using the railroad to his advantage. But it was not to be and the railroad ended up 10 miles away, turning the already quiet little town into almost a ghost town.

Train robber Chris Evans. This photograph was taken after his arrest and shows signs of him being manhandled.

It was around this time that the train robberies started, and almost all were credited to the Dalton Gang. When the train had been stopped, dynamite was used to blow open the express cars and on two occasions passengers were killed when they stuck their heads out of the windows of their carriages to see what was going on. The gang members were never identified, despite other passengers giving quite detailed descriptions of the robbers.

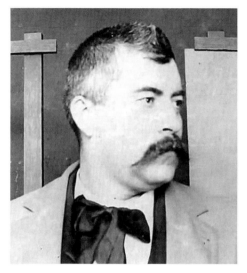 

Above left: George Sontag.

Above right: Poor-quality photograph of John Sontag.

Chris Evans' ranch outside Vistalia, California.

With financial desperation setting in, Christopher Evans and the Sontag brothers decided to turn their hands to robbing trains themselves. Evans himself had no qualms about robbing the railroad, thinking that they had let him and his family down badly by not bringing the railroad track close to his farm as they had originally planned.

The gang held up the Southern Pacific Railroad train as it neared Visalia and one of the 'passengers' interviewed by the sheriff after the robbery, was George Sontag. He gave the sheriff a vivid account of the robbery and a false description of some of the robbers, in an effort to throw them off the scent. However, the train's conductor knew George Sontag and had not seen him amongst the passengers during the trip but only after the hold-up.

Wells Fargo detectives were quickly on the scene of the hold-up and followed the tracks of a cart from the scene to the Evans' ranch. It was decided to lay a trap for the gang and so the sheriff's office, going along with George Sontag's account of the robbery, asked him to come to Visalia to identify a suspect. The moment he turned up, he was arrested and thrown into jail. A large posse then went to the Evans' place with the intention of arresting the remaining members of the gang. However, word had reached Evans, and before the posse could surround the house, the barn door flew open and Chris Evans and John Sontag opened fire with their shotguns. By the time the shooting had stopped and the posse had to time to reorganise themselves, the two gang members were long gone. They left behind one dead deputy sheriff and three badly wounded ones, whilst they themselves had escaped unharmed.

The two were now on the run with rewards on their heads for their capture dead or alive. Over the next year the two of them continued to rob stagecoaches and stores, and all the time the reward on them grew until it reached $10,000. Surprisingly, they were harboured by a number of people to whom $10,000 was a fortune, but who never attempted to collect the reward. Whether or not this was through some misguided loyalty or fear, it is not known. But it is suspected that on two occasions, when a posse arrived and questioned the owners of the homes where the two robbers had visited, they were actually asleep in the house at the time.

The posses came close to the outlaws a number of times and shots were exchanged, resulting in a number of lawmen being wounded, but never the pursued robbers. Then came a breakthrough. An informer said that the two men were heading for a hideout that they had been using at a place called Sampson Flats. There was a cabin at the foot of a hill in which the sheriff's men hid for three days. They were just about to give up when the two men appeared. With the trap about to be sprung, the two outlaws sensed something was wrong and as the deputies opened fire, the men dove behind a pile of manure. In the ensuing gunfight, which lasted most of the day, just one of the deputies was hit. At dusk, Chris Evans staggered away from the manure pile bleeding heavily from a number of gunshot wounds, whilst nothing was heard from John Sontag.

The posse decided to wait until morning before venturing out and then found John Sontag behind the manure pile, dying from his wounds. Evans in the meantime had been captured and taken to jail – he was later sent to prison for life. John Sontag died where he had made his last stand and when his brother heard of his death, he tried to escape from prison and was shot dead.

Above: George Sontag lying dead.

Right: Chris Evans.

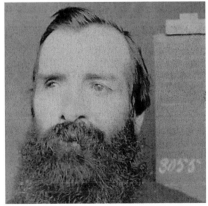

Chapter 18

The Rufus Buck Gang

One of the most ruthless and violent gangs in the Indian Territories was the Rufus Buck Gang. The gang consisted of five teenagers, Maoma July, Sam Sampson (both Creek Indians), brothers Lewis and Lucky Davis (both Creek Freedmen), and the leader Rufus Buck, a negro. During the space of one year, the gang carried out two murders, two rapes and a succession of robberies.

All five had been in trouble from an early age, but just for minor offences. But like some of the gangs of today, the five teenagers wanted to make a reputation for themselves as a gang to be feared, without really considering the consequences. Their troubles started on 28 July 1895, when Deputy US Marshal John Garrett stopped them near the town of Okmulgee. Rufus Buck immediately drew his pistol and shot him dead. This was a deliberate act as John Garrett had been following the gang for some time and Rufus Buck took the opportunity to get rid of him.

Rufus Buck.

Realising they had killed a Federal officer, the gang now threw caution to the winds and continued on their rampage. They intercepted two wagons that were moving a family from one farm to another, a mother and her son and another young man. The gang ordered the two boys to continue, but abducted the woman a Mrs Wilson, and took turns in raping her. When they had finished they let her go, firing at her feet to make her run.

Over the next couple of months they carried out a series of robberies, including taking all the clothes and money from a cowboy and firing after him as he ran away naked. Caught trying to steal some horses belonging to a man by the name of Gus Chambers, the gang just gunned him down when he tried to stop them. Two days later the gang carried out a robbery at a house belonging to Henry Hassen. They forced his wife to cook them a meal and after eating everything they could, they beat her husband, tied his wife, Rosetta, to the bed and took it in turns to rape her whilst keeping the her family at bay with their rifles. The whole family was witness to this outrage, but was helpless to do anything about it.

The gang's next target were two stores, Norbett's and Orcutt's, both close to the town of McDermott, where they stole ammunition, clothes, tobacco and food. By this time an intensive manhunt was underway by both the law and the Creek Indians, who were outraged at what members of their tribe had done. The posse, consisting of Deputy US Marshals Sam Hayne and Bill Irwin, the Creek Lighthorse (Indian Police) under the command of Captain Edmund Harry, who together with a large number of Creek Indians found the gang camped in a small valley sharing out their loot. So occupied were the gang that they failed to notice the posse until they found themselves surrounded. They were called upon to surrender but responded with gunfire and a seven-hour siege followed. Realising it was futile to continue and running short of ammunition, they gave up. Initially the Creek Indians wanted the law to hand them over to them, so that they could carry out summary

Choctaw Indian Lighthorsemen.

Creek Lighthorsemen.

justice in their traditional way, but they were told that the gang would have to stand trial in a court of law and if found guilty would be hanged, and they agreed to abide by that. The gang were taken under heavy guard to the town of McDermott where Town Marshal Morton Rutherford took control of them and placed them in the town jail. Such was the anger that developed when people found out what they had done and that they had been caught, that mobs started to gather in the town and the mutterings turned to shouts for a lynching. The situation

The execution of Choctaw Indian Sian Lewis by the Choctaw Indian method. This was the last execution they carried out: all future executions would take place in jails under the control of the local sheriff.

became very tense as the mobs grew larger and more vociferous and Rutherford knew that unless he could get his five prisoners away to Fort Smith, they would not be alive in the morning. The Creek Indians had set up a camp nearby and posted sentries to make sure that the prisoners were not moved by the marshal.

Marshal Rutherford talked with his deputies and then told the prisoners that they were going to get them out and move them to Fort Smith. Because they were all in chains and the marshal was reluctant to remove them, he told the prisoners that they were going to have to make sure the chains did not rattle when they moved or they would end up being lynched. Just after midnight Marshal Rutherford and his deputies together with the five prisoners, slipped away to the town of Muskogee and boarded a train to Fort Smith. A huge crowd was waiting to meet the train at the end of the journey, but with heavily-armed deputy US marshals and deputy sheriffs front and back, the entourage made its way up the main street to the Fort Smith jail.

The five were found guilty of murder and rape and sentenced to be hanged. They appealed to the Supreme Court, but the verdict of the court was upheld, and the death sentence was passed on all five young men.

In sentencing the gang, Judge Isaac Parker outlined the horrendous crimes the five had committed and then passed his sentence on Rufus Buck:

> Listen to the sentence of the law, which is that you, Rufus Buck, for the crime of rape, committed by you upon Rosetta Hassen, in the Indian country, and within the jurisdiction of this court, of which crime you stand convicted by the verdict of the jury in your case, be deemed, taken and adjudged guilty of rape; and that you therefore, for the said crime against the laws of the United States, hanged by the neck until you are dead; that the Marshal of the Western District of Arkansas, by himself or deputy, or deputies, cause execution to be done in the premises upon you, on Wednesday 1 July 1896, and that you be taken to the jail from whence you came, to be there closely and securely kept until the day of execution, and from thence on the day of execution, as aforesaid, you are to be taken to the place of execution, there to be hanged by the neck until you are dead.

A similar sentence was passed on the four other members of the gang. The hangings of the Rufus Buck Gang were the last multiple hangings to take place at Fort Smith. As the men were led into the execution yard where the gallows waited they showed not one flicker of emotion.

All five were dropped at the same time, Rufus Buck taking over three minutes to die.

After Buck's death, a photograph of his mother was found in his cell. On the back, Buck had written a poem:

Rufus Buck's Gang. L–R: Maoma July, Sam Sampson, Rufus Buck, Lucky Davis, Lewis Davis. Photograph taken the day before their execution.

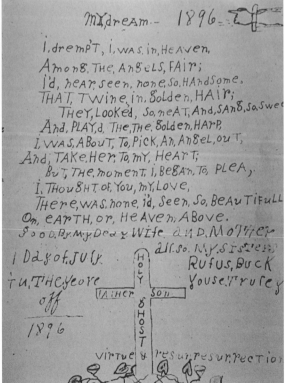

Poem written by Rufus Buck on the back of his mother's photograph whilst he was awaiting execution.

Chapter 19

Clay Allison

The Rufus Buck Gang were not the only young killers around at that time, however. Today Clay Allison would have been regarded as a schizophrenic psychopath. One of the most feared gunmen of the West, he was also one of the most unpredictable. Any level of emotional or physical excitement had an effect on him, creating one of the most unstable characters of the time.

Born in Wayne County, Tennessee in 1840, Robert Clay Allison had what can only be described as a normal childhood, but had a fascination for guns. In his teens he used to practise fast draw and on one occasion shot himself in the foot. This was often a hazard for wannabe gunfighters, as they had never learned from the experts about loading their guns with only five cartridges and dropping the hammer on the empty chamber.

A tall, well-built and handsome man, Clay Allison had very small hands and a limp; the result of the self-inflicted shooting injury, and it was these minor peculiarities that would often lead him into gunfights, or, during his time as a soldier, prove advantageous to him. During the Civil War he served with the Tennessee Light Infantry and on a number of occasions slipped over

A young Clay Allison.

Above left: Clay Allison after shooting himself in the foot.

Above right: An older Clay Allison.

the enemy lines to gain information. He was caught one time and tried as a spy, but fortunately, because of his small hands, he was able to slip out of the handcuffs and escape, killing a guard in the process.

After the war, like many of his contemporaries, he drifted between the states finding work as a cowboy or ranch hand. In 1860, at the age of just 20, he became a trail boss working for the legendary cattleman Charles Goodnight. It was during this period that his reputation as a gunman started to flourish, helped by an occasion when he became involved in a friendly 'fast draw' competition with a man called Mason Bowman. The two became friends and over the next few months Bowman taught Clay Allison how to improve his fast draw technique, something that helped later, when a renowned gunfighter by the name of 'Chunk' Colbert sought him out.

The story has it that the two men met in a bar in Red River Station, Texas, and for most of the day drank beer and 'enjoyed' each other's company. Then during dinner at a diner known as The Clifton House, Allison placed his pistol alongside his plate whilst he sat across the table from Colbert. Suddenly Colbert made a grab for Allison's gun whilst attempting to draw his own. Unfortunately for him, he was sitting too close to the table and as he drew his gun, with the hammer cocked, it hit the edge of the table. The gun fired harmlessly into the wooden floor, but Clay Allison had reached his gun, which was already cocked, and shot Colbert in the head. It is said that Allison finished his dinner before attempting to move the body away from the table.

With the death of Colbert, Allison's reputation became more and more fearsome and it also attracted the attention of would-be gunfighters who wanted to add Clay Allison's name to the list already notched up on their guns. One of these was a young cowboy by the name of Buck Bowman (no relation to Mason Bowman), who displayed twelve notches on his gun. He rode into Cimarron with the intention of facing up to Clay Allison and adding him to the list.

Going into the saloon, Bowman sought out Clay Allison and made pointed remarks about 'Rebels from the South' and when that didn't get a response, he then made comments about Allison's small hands. This did get a response and Bowman found himself face to face with Clay Allison. Minutes later Bowman lay dead on the floor of the saloon having found out to his cost that those small hands were deadly.

Although Clay Allison was a member of the Stockgrowers' Association, he actually supported the homesteaders, regarding them as the underdogs. It was this stance against the stockgrowers that prevented a lot of bloodshed, mainly because no one would go up against him. His support for the underdog was never more apparent than when a local preacher, Reverend F.J. Tolby, was murdered. The preacher had written numerous letters to newspapers about the political hierarchy, known locally as the Santa Fe Ring, that were attempting to influence the running of the territory. The preacher had just left a mining camp one Sunday morning after holding a service there, when his body was found lying beside the trail – shot in the back. This so incensed the local citizens that they started to make their own investigations into the killing. A vigilante group, headed by Clay Allison, found out that a man by the name of Cruz Vega was involved and, after 'questioning' him, lynched him from a telegraph pole. He had named a local criminal by the name of Manuel Cardenas, saying it had been Cardenas who had fired the shot.

By this time the local sheriff had got involved and it was when he was in the process of taking Cardenas to the jail, that the vigilantes rode up and gunned the prisoner down. It became common knowledge that Clay Allison had been primarily responsible for both the killings and two days later, a friend of the two men, Francisco Griego, rode into town intent on avenging their deaths.

He went straight to the St. James Hotel in Cimarron and demanded that Clay Allison meet him. The two men sat down at a table in the

A horse thief by the name of Johnson lynched from a telegraph pole after being caught.

saloon, then suddenly there were three shots and Griego lay dead on the floor. Whether the killing was in self-defence or not is unclear: suffice to say that nobody asked.

Three months later Allison was standing at the bar in the same hotel, when three black soldiers walked in. Allison looked up and within seconds the three soldiers lay dead on the floor. Clay Allison's excuse was he did not think it right that 'Negroes should be allowed to drink in a white man's establishment'.

The commanding officer of the troops, Captain Francis Dodge, demanded that the sheriff arrest Clay Allison for the murder of his three men. Allison by this time had returned to his ranch and when the sheriff arrived with a warrant for his arrest, he was accompanied by a troop of soldiers. For some unknown reason Clay Allison was never detained or arrested for the murder of the three soldiers, the whole episode was just swept under the carpet by the authorities. This was an indictment of the way black people were regarded by both the white population and the military at the time.

In December 1876, Clay Allison and his brother John went to Las Animas for an evening's entertainment. After doing the rounds of the local bars they went to the Olympic Dance Hall, but refused to hand over their guns as they entered the hall. After some minutes the two brothers, who were both drunk and obnoxious, were asked to leave by the law – they refused. The constable, Charles Faber, realised who they were and left to arm himself with a 10-gauge shotgun and then deputised two of the local citizens to assist him. As he entered the hall he opened fire on the two brothers without warning. The first blast hit John Allison sending him crashing to the floor. Clay Allison moved with the speed of a striking snake and shot back, killing Faber. As he fell, Faber's finger pulled the other trigger, sending another load of buckshot into John Allison.

Clay Allison rushed after the two deputies, who by this time were well on their way out of the hall, and fired a few shots after them. He returned to look after his brother and was with him when Sheriff John Spear appeared and arrested him. John Allison was taken to the local hospital where he was treated for his wounds. When he had recovered sufficiently he was arrested and charged with complicity in the death of Charles Faber, but was released for lack of evidence.

Clay Allison, on the other hand, was charged with the manslaughter of Charles Faber and released on $10,000 bail. He later appeared before a grand jury and managed to convince them that he had acted in self-defence. He was released.

Clay Allison sold his ranch to his brother in March 1877 and moved first to Sedailia, Missouri and then to Hays City, Kansas, setting himself up as a cattle broker. On his first trip to Dodge City on business he discovered that his reputation as a gunman had preceded him. The deputy town marshal at the time was Wyatt Earp and he was well aware of Clay Allison's reputation. A local ordinance forbad the wearing or carrying of guns within the town and Clay Allison and some of his men, according to Wyatt Earp's account, had entered the Long Branch Saloon and refused to hand over their weapons. Wyatt Earp and Bat Masterson had apparently confronted Clay Allison and forced him and his men to back down and hand over their weapons, such was their reputation. However, one of the cowboys in the saloon at the time was Charlie Siringo who later became a well-known Pinkerton detective, who said he had witnessed the whole incident. His version was that a rancher by the name of Dick McHulty and the owner of the Long Branch Saloon, Chalk Beeson, had persuaded Clay Allison and his men to hand over their weapons. He also added that Wyatt Earp was never present and that Bat Masterson was not even in town at the time. It is interesting to note that Wyatt Earp never mentioned the incident in his biography until after Clay Allison's death.

His reputation as a gunfighter was established, but his death on 3 July 1887 was as far removed from gunfighting as it could be. Clay Allison had gone to the town of Pecos to pick up supplies for his ranch. It is said that one of the sacks of grain he had placed on the back of the wagon started to slide off as he was making his way out of town. He reached back to stop it and lost his balance and fell under the wheels of the wagon. One of the wheels went over his neck, breaking it.

This ignominious end to one of the most feared gunfighters of the West was, to some people, nothing more than he deserved. As one citizen put it, 'It was a pity that it wasn't a rope that broke his neck.'

Chapter 20

The 'Cowboys'

One group of outlaws, known as the 'Cowboys', was one of the largest and best-organised criminal gangs in the West and was led by a man by the name of Robert Martin. The name 'cowboy' is normally associated with the hardworking drovers who look after cattle, but in 1878 the name took on another meaning – outlaw gang.

They came to the attention of the law when the Mexican government complained about a large gang of American outlaws who raided ranches over the border in Mexico, stole cattle and sold them in Arizona. The Governor of Arizona, John C. Fremont, carried out an investigation into the allegations. He accused the Mexican government of allowing outlaws, both Mexican and American, to use the lawless town of Sonora as a refuge, from which they carried out raids in Arizona, stealing horses and taking them into Mexico. Fremont contended that these outlaws probably stole Mexican cattle on their way back to Arizona.

It was estimated that there were over 100 members in the gang. The original leader was killed during one raid and Newman H. Clanton took his place. Together with his sons Billy, Ike and Phin and the brothers Tom and Frank McLaury and Johnny Ringo as dominant members, the gang continued to flourish. The gang had sections that carried out stagecoach robberies, especially around the Tombstone area of Pima County. It wasn't long before the residents of the county became seriously concerned about the lack of law and order, and demanded that something be done about it.

So concerned were the residents of Tombstone and the surrounding area that they put forward a bill in the assembly that a new county, Cochise, be created. This bill was passed and the new county appointed Sheriff John Behan to take care of law and order. Behan came with a

The Clantons in 1877: Top clockwise: Newman Haynes, William Billy, Phineas Fin and Joseph Ike.

reputation as a top lawman, having served with some distinction as sheriff of Yavapai County for some years.

One of the other persons considered for the post was Wyatt Earp, who had a somewhat tarnished reputation, having once been arrested for horse theft in the Indian Territories. He had hoped to get the post, so that he could appoint his brothers as deputies, thus controlling the town and everything in it. Virgil Earp, however, was offered the post of deputy sheriff, which he took, and carried out the duties diligently.

When in October 1880, 'Curly Bill' Brocius, one of the 'Cowboys' leaders, was arrested for the murder of US Marshal Fred White, Virgil Earp appointed Wyatt and Morgan, his two brothers as special deputies and took Brocius to Tucson to prevent him from being lynched by the angry citizens of Tombstone.

In November 1880 Virgil Earp stood for election as City Marshal, but lost by just fifty votes. By this time there was open hostility between Wyatt Earp and Sheriff John Behan, after Wyatt Earp had failed in his election attempt for the position of sheriff. This hatred between the two

Above left: Deputy US Marshal Fred White, shot by 'Curly Bill' Brocius.

Above right: A young Virgil Earp.

Virgil Earp in later years.

men was also reflected in the way Virgil Earp, who was still a deputy US marshal, performed his duties. More time was spent bickering than was spent searching out criminals, and a number of robberies and stagecoach hold-ups took place, all of which were attributed to the 'Cowboys'. The Attorney General contacted US Marshal Dake ordering him to take action against the 'Cowboys' using all means possible. He also placed him on notice regarding Deputy US Marshal Virgil Earp, stating that 'He was more inclined to quarrel than co-operate with the local authority'.

Things came to a head when after one hold-up, when $9,000 was taken, Wells Fargo temporarily closed the service between Benson and

Tombstone. Virgil Earp deputised his two brothers, Morgan and Wyatt, and set off after the robbers. After a chase, which was said to have covered over 100 miles, the Earps made just one arrest.

The 'Cowboys' continued their reign of terror by carrying out raids into Mexico, and in one incident they attacked and murdered four Mexicans and stole $4,000. Incensed by these attacks, Governor Pesqueira of Sonora sent one of his men to Tombstone to complain about the lack of law and order, but he was murdered en route. The people of Sonora had had enough, and during one incident in the town, four of the 'Cowboys' were killed in a gun battle with enraged citizens. Two weeks later Mexican soldiers killed Newman Clanton, the leader of the 'Cowboys', along with two of his henchmen when they were caught in the act of rustling cattle. Things had reached the stage where the governments of each country were getting involved, and in the United States, a law was repealed to allow the army to be used to track down and apprehend the 'Cowboy' gang.

In Tombstone, Wyatt Earp accused Sheriff Behan of being in league with the 'Cowboys' when he and his brothers arrested one of Behan's deputies, Frank Stilwell, for stagecoach robbery. The open hostility between the Earps and Behan was beginning to affect the townspeople's concern about law and order and the law's ability to capture the 'Cowboy' gang.

Wyatt Earp contacted Ike Clanton, who had taken over as leader of the 'Cowboys', with a suggestion that if he gave up the outlaws who had carried out the stagecoach robberies, and aided in their arrest, Wyatt and his brothers would either kill or arrest them, and give the reward money to Ike.

Word somehow leaked out about the suggested conspiracy and Ike Clanton accused Wyatt Earp of trying to set him up and threatened to kill him. Then word came out that Ike Clanton was looking for the Earps and was carrying a Winchester rifle and a pistol. Virgil, Morgan and Wyatt Earp met up and then decided to split up and try and locate Ike Clanton. Virgil and Morgan spotted Ike walking down the main street and quietly came up behind him

A young Ike Clanton.

147

and 'buffaloed' him, knocking him to the ground. After disarming him, the Earps took him to the courthouse and charged him with carrying a concealed weapon. In the court building there was a violent verbal confrontation between Ike Clanton and Wyatt Earp. Wyatt Earp called Clanton a 'cattle thieving son of a bitch', and told him he'd threatened his life enough. 'You've got to fight!' Clanton replied, 'Fight is my racket and all I want is four feet of ground'. Witnessing this was R.J. Campbell, clerk of the Cochise County board of supervisors.

Ike Clanton was brought before Judge Wallace and fined $25 for carrying a concealed weapon. On his release Ike Clanton went to a gun shop where he was joined by Billy Claiborne and Frank McLaury, who had just ridden into town. In the meantime Wyatt Earp had been involved in a confrontation with Tom McLaury after accusing the latter of having a concealed weapon. Angry words were spoken with the result that Wyatt Earp drew his pistol and clubbed Tom McLaury to the ground. According to some witnesses, Ike Clanton sensed trouble and had wanted to get the rest of his men out of Tombstone, whilst others said he was spoiling for a showdown with the Earps.

Virgil Earp approached Sheriff John Behan and called upon him to help disarm Ike Clanton and his men. Behan was reluctant to get involved at this time because he knew that the Clantons would not give up their weapons to the Earps. Other witnesses testified that they had sensed something was going to happen and approached the sheriff

about their concerns and that the Clantons and their men should be disarmed. Witnesses watched as Ike Clanton, Frank and Tom McLaury and Billy Claiborne made their way towards an empty plot between Papago's Cash Store and Bayer's Meat Market that had an alleyway leading to the OK Corral. Sheriff John Behan approached the Clanton gang and asked them to give up their weapons, to which the reply was, 'only if the Earps do'.

At that moment John Behan saw Virgil, Morgan and Wyatt Earp, together with Doc Holliday, walking

Doc Holliday at the time of the purposefully side by side down the gunfight at the OK Corral. main street in the direction of the

148

OK Corral. All four men were armed with revolvers, but Virgil was also cradling a short-barrelled shotgun in his arms. Sheriff John Behan confronted them and asked them to disarm, but there was no response, and the four men just brushed past him. As the Earps and Doc Holliday turned the corner into the vacant plot they came face to face with the Clanton gang. Billy Claiborne and Frank McLaury were carrying single-action Colt revolvers and there is some dispute about what weapons Ike Clanton and Tom McLaury were carrying. Some say that Ike Clanton had no weapon, as he had had them taken away from him when he was arrested earlier, but Tom McLaury was said to have been holding a Winchester rifle.

What happened next at 3:00 p.m. on 26 October 1881 has been the subject of discussions, arguments, debates, books and films so the truth will always be open to controversy. The only people who knew what really happened were the participants and they are all now dead, and even when alive, they had differing accounts.

The two parties were only 10–12ft apart when they faced each other. Virgil Earp is said to have told the Clanton gang to throw down their guns. Tom McLaury is then said to have opened his coat saying that he was not armed. Billy Clanton was heard to say 'I do not want to fight' and had his hands in the air. Ike Clanton later said that one of the Earps said, 'You sons of bitches, you ought to make a fight'. Seconds later gunfire erupted and bullets were flying everywhere.

The Earps of course had a totally different story saying that when asked to throw down their guns, the Clanton gang immediately grasped their weapons in a threatening way. Virgil Earp then said that Billy Clanton and Frank McLaury started to draw their guns from their holsters and he heard the click of the hammers

Billy Clanton.

as they were pulled back. Tom McLaury was then seen to raise his Winchester rifle. Almost immediately gunfire erupted. Who fired first is not known, but Wyatt Earp claimed that he had seen Frank McLaury draw his weapon and that he had immediately drawn his own and shot McLaury in the stomach. Witnesses said that it was in fact Doc Holliday and Morgan Earp who had initiated the gunfight. Nevertheless it was all over in 30 seconds. Tom and Frank McLaury and Billy Clanton were dead, whilst Virgil and Morgan Earp were wounded. Later word got out that the Earps, along with Doc Holliday, had been arrested by Sheriff John Behan on a charge of murder, but were later released awaiting trial.

US Marshal Dake requested additional funding to carry out his investigations, but also defended the Earps, saying that they had removed three of the leaders of the 'Cowboys' and by doing so possibly brought an end to their reign of terror. Virgil Earp, after recovering from his leg wound, was to head up a special posse to go after the outlaws, but then on the night of 28 December he was shot and seriously wounded. Wyatt Earp sent a cable to Governor Gosper requesting that he be appointed a deputy US marshal with the power to appoint other deputies, as he felt fit.

This was approved and Wyatt Earp appointed Morgan Earp and three of their friends, two of whom were suspected of having carried out stagecoach robberies in the past, the other one being a professional gambler/gunman. On hearing of these appointments, the remaining gang leaders did not relish a violent confrontation with what can only be described as five professional gunmen. In an effort to trim the odds, they attempted to assassinate Wyatt and Morgan Earp as they played billiards together. Morgan Earp caught the full blast of a shotgun and died, whilst Wyatt escaped unharmed.

Bent on revenge, Wyatt Earp and his 'deputies' went after the men whom they felt were responsible and one by one caught up with them. They meted out their own justice without bothering with the law. Sheriff Robert Paul of Pima County was given arrest warrants for Wyatt Earp and his 'deputies', but they had already returned to Tombstone.

The charges of murder brought against the Earps and Doc Holliday were later dropped but no reason was ever given. Maybe it was the killing of the leaders of the 'Cowboy' gang that persuaded the authorities that they had done the country a service, albeit in an unorthodox way. The gang's reign was in effect over as they went their separate ways. Robberies continued to be committed, but not in the same violent way.

Chapter 21

The Dalton Brothers

The Dalton Brothers came from a very respectable family and lived on a homestead in the Oklahoma Territory. There were five brothers, Frank, Grattan (Grat), Bob, Bill and Emmett, and all were hardworking young men. Frank Dalton became a deputy US marshal serving under Judge Isaac Parker, but was killed in 1887 whilst attempting to arrest three whiskey runners in Fort Smith. Although two of the criminals were killed during the incident and the third hanged, the brothers became disillusioned with the law and grew less law abiding as time went on. Grat Dalton was appointed a deputy US marshal in Frank's place and later his two brothers Bob and Emmett joined him.

Bob Dalton was the first to step outside the law, when he shot dead a man by the name of Charlie Montgomery, who had been seeing Bob's girlfriend. He and his brother Emmett took the body to Coffeyville claiming that they had caught the man stealing from a stable and that he had been shot resisting arrest.

Then Grat and Bob were involved in the theft of horses from a ranch near Baxter Springs, Kansas, and had their badges taken away. A little while later their brother Emmett was dismissed. Deciding that there was more money to be made on the other side of the law, the brothers formed a gang by recruiting a number of known outlaws, including Bill Powers, Dick Broadwell and George 'Bitter Creek' Newcomb.

The gang's first robbery took place at a gambling saloon in Silver City, New Mexico. Chased by a posse, the gang split up in an effort to confuse them, Emmett and Newcomb went to the Indian Territories, whilst Bob Dalton and some of the others headed for their brother Bill Dalton's ranch in California. The arrival of the members of the Dalton Gang could not have come at a worse moment for Bill Dalton, as he was in the process for running as an assemblyman on a ticket against the

Bill Dalton with his wife.

Southern Pacific Railroad and their land-grabbing methods. The problem was that just prior to the gang arriving, the Southern Pacific Express had been held up and robbed as it passed through Tulare County. Suspicion fell upon the Younger Brothers who were related to Bill Dalton and his own brothers who were wanted for a robbery in New Mexico.

The railroad detectives dealing with the robbery saw a chance to get Bill Dalton off their backs and indicted Bill and Grat Dalton for the robbery. A second charge of train robbery was laid against the two men, as 'witnesses' placed both men at the scene. Grat Dalton, fearful that his record would go against him, broke out of jail and hid out for some time in a cave. In the meantime his brother Bill, who had not tried to escape, was tried and found not guilty. This, of course, acquitted his brother in absentia, because the evidence was that both men had been seen together committing the robberies.

The incident ruined Bill Dalton both financially and politically and so he returned to the Indian Territories in an effort to rebuild his life. Finding it impossible to live within the law, Bill Dalton joined with his brothers, including Grat who had found his way back, and the gang set about concentrating on the robbing of trains. Between May 1891 and July 1892, four trains were robbed in the Indian Territories and it was all done with military precision.

In October 1891 the gang robbed a train at Lillietta, Indian Territory, and relieved it of $10,000. The following year they struck again, this time at Red Rock, where they robbed not only the express car, but also the passengers. Supremely confident, almost to the point of arrogance, the gang struck again, this time at Adair, Oklahoma, near the Arkansas border. Instead of stopping the train, they went to the station, robbed the express and baggage rooms and then sat on a bench on the platform and waited for the train to arrive.

As the train drew to a halt, some of the gang backed a wagon up to the doors of the express car and ordered the guard to open the doors.

They then unloaded the contents of the car onto the wagon and made off. In the meantime other members of the gang engaged the guards in a gunfight in which three of the guards were wounded and a stray bullet killed the local doctor. None of the gang was injured and they escaped, realising that this time they had been lucky.

The Dalton Gang decided that the robbing of trains was becoming decidedly risky, as the railroad companies were putting more and more armed guards on board. It was decided to switch to robbing banks and in a typical arrogant gesture, Bob Dalton decided that they would rob C.M. Condon & Company's Bank and the First National Bank in Coffeyville, Kansas, in broad

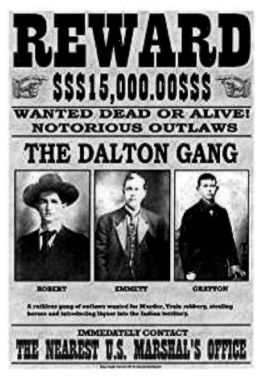

Reward poster for the Dalton Gang.

daylight. One of the problems they faced was that the local people knew them, so it was decided to carry out the robberies in disguise.

On 5 October 1892 at 9:30 a.m., five members of the Dalton Gang rode into town. Three of the gang, Grat Dalton, Bill Powers and Dick Broadwell, went into Condon's Bank, the other two, Bob and Emmett Dalton, entered the First National Bank. The first indications that the banks were being held up came from one of the tellers in the Condon bank, when he saw a Winchester rifle being pointed at him. His shout that the bank was being robbed alerted people outside, who then saw two other suspicious-looking men entering the First National Bank.

The townspeople rallied and a number armed themselves with rifles and started shooting at the robbers. In Condon's Bank, the employees attempted to stall the robbers by saying that the safe was on a time lock and could not be opened for another 10 minutes. Grabbing what money he could, Grat Dalton asked if there was a back door, but was told there was none.

Deciding to make a dash for their horses, the three men ran out of the bank firing across the road as they did so. Grat Dalton and Bill

The C.M. Condon Bank showing signs of the attempted bank robbery by the Dalton Gang.

The bodies of Bob and 'Grat' Dalton being help up for photographs after the failed bank robbery.

Powers fell under hail of bullets, whilst Dick Broadwell made a dash for his horse, but collapsed when a bullet smashed into his back. For a moment there was a lull in the firing and Broadwell managed to pull himself onto his horse and started to ride out of town. He was shot again, this time by a shotgun, but despite both bleeding profusely, his horse managed to get him clear. His body was later found half a mile outside of the town crumpled up on the side of the road. It was discovered later that Grat Dalton, whilst exiting from the bank firing his gun, had shot Marshal Connelly in the back as he did so.

In the First National Bank Bob and Emmett Dalton had escaped down an alleyway alongside the bank. They came under fire from a store across the road from the bank, and one of the first volley of shots hit Bob Dalton, sending him crashing to the ground. He pulled himself up and sat on a pile of rocks and returned fire with his Winchester rifle. He got

The bodies of the Dalton Gang thrown into a cell just after the bank raid in Coffeeville, Kansas.

The bodies of Bill Power, Bob Dalton, Grat Dalton and Dick Broadwell laid out for public display. Note that all their boots are missing.

Bill Dalton.

to his feet and attempted to move down the alleyway, but a second volley of shots sent him sprawling in the dust.

His brother Emmett had managed to get to his horse and still had hold of the money. Instead of heading out of town, he turned his horse and went back to try and drag his dying brother on to his horse. As he did so, one of the townspeople, Carey Seamen, emptied both barrels of his shotgun into him and he fell beside his brother.

Emmett Dalton survived the shooting, suffering twenty-three wounds. He was later sentenced to life imprisonment in the Kansas State Penitentiary at Lansing. He was released after having served 14 years of his sentence and died in California in 1937.

After the train robbery Bill Dalton decided to form his own gang, and on 23 May 1894, Bill Dalton and his new gang robbed the First National Bank at Longview, Texas. This was their one and only job. Over the next few weeks various posses hunting the robbers killed three of the gang and captured the other who, after a short trial, was sent to prison for life. Bill Dalton was still on the run, but then on 8 June 1894 a posse, led by Deputy US Marshal Buck Garrett (no relation to Sheriff Pat Garrett) from Ardmore in the Indian Territory, tracked Bill Dalton to his home in Pooleville, Oklahoma. Garrett, together with deputy James H. Mathers and six other deputies, surrounded the house and called for Bill Dalton to give himself up. He replied with a volley of shots and the two parties exchanged gunfire for over two hours, in which the posse reported over 100 rounds being exchanged between them and Dalton. Suddenly the firing stopped, and after getting no response from Dalton, deputies entered the cabin and found him dead with a gunshot wound to the head. The violent days of the Daltons were finally over.

Chapter 22

The Female Outlaws

Belle Starr was not the only female outlaw around at the time. There were a number of others, such as 'Cattle Annie' McDougal, Jennie Metcalf Stevens (aka 'Little Britches') and Fat Ella Watson (aka 'Cattle Kate') to name but a few. Amongst these Florence Quick, a former schoolteacher and mistress of Bob Dalton, was probably one of the most notorious and operated under a number of aliases. Whilst out with the Dalton Gang, she was known as 'Tom King', 'Lucy Johnson' or 'Daisy Briant' and dressed and rode like a man. When in town or in their ranch, she was the epitome of femininity and often seen dressed in an elaborate buckskin outfit.

She would go out at night looking for horses for the gang to rustle, or searching for hideouts in the Indian Territory. When she found them she would make sure they were well stocked with food and water. She was

Lucy Johnson (R) with her sister Julia in 1930s. Lucy was also known as: Eugenia Moore, Florence Quick, Flora Quick, Flo Quick, Daisy Briant, Lucy Howard, Lucy Alderman (Alterman), Minnie Johnson and Tom King, among other names.

also the go-between when information was required regarding the train schedules and whether or not the trains were carrying anything worth stealing. Florence would even go to the extent of sleeping with a railroad worker or express agent, if they could supply information to the gang.

During her time with the Dalton Gang, Florence Quick was arrested and jailed a number of times, but somehow managed to escape every time. She became renowned as a 'jailbreaker' and was sought after by sheriffs and deputy US marshals all over the territory.

Then after the infamous raid on Coffeyville in 1892, when her lover Bob Dalton was killed and the remainder of the gang decimated, Florence Quick organised her own gang and carried out a number of train robberies. Deputy US Marshal Chris Madsen described Florence Quick as one of the 'most hard-bitten bitches' he had ever come across.

Just over a year after setting out on her own life of crime, it was rumoured that she had been killed during an attempted robbery, but it was never substantiated. Nevertheless she was never heard from again. Recent research discovered that she moved to Canada for a number of years before returning to America. She lived in Tulsa, Oklahoma, with her sister Julia until she died in the 1940s.

A young Florence Quick when working with the outlaws.

Two young women who believed the tales about the Dalton Gang were Annie McDougal and Jennie Metcalf – aka Jennie Stevens. The girls, both 17 and 16 respectively, were farm girls who read the so-called 'dime novels' avidly and believed every word that was printed in them. Then one day at a local dance, Bill Doolin and some of his gang arrived for a night out. The girls, enraptured by the sight of these outlaws come to life and right off the pages of their novels, left with them and joined the gang. Known as 'Cattle Annie' McDougal and Jennie 'Little Britches' Stevens, the two girls soon found themselves doing all the washing and cooking for the gang. They soon tired of this and went to work for themselves rustling cattle and horses, together with some whiskey peddling, and soon came to the notice of the law.

Anna Emmaline McDoulet ('Cattle Annie') and Jennie Stevens ('Little Britches').

Over the next couple of years, the Doolin Gang was gradually being reduced as one after another they were either caught or killed. Then in 1884, two deputy US marshals, Bill Tilghman and Steve Burke, tracked the remainder of the gang to a farmhouse near Pawnee. By the time the two marshals arrived only the two girls were there, but the authorities wanted them, so they decided to arrest them.

'Little Britches' Stevens had spotted the two lawmen arrive and dived out of a window and on to her horse. Bill Tilghman set off in hot pursuit and at one time Stevens fired a shot at him over her shoulder. The shot missed, and had she been a man, there is no question that Bill Tilghman would have fired back with the intention of killing the fleeing criminal, but because she was a young girl, he decided to shoot her horse instead, bringing her tumbling to the ground. After spanking her, Bill Tilghman placed her on his horse with him and returned to the farmhouse.

In the meantime Marshal Burke had had a fight with 'Cattle' Annie McDougal after she had levelled her rifle at him, before finally subduing her.

Ella Watson ('Cattle Kate').

The pair were arrested and later sentenced to two years in the state Federal reformatory. Annie McDougal married soon after her release and settled down on a ranch near Pawnee, never to get into trouble again. 'Little Britches' Stevens went to New York to work in the settlements there, but died of consumption just two years later.

Another potential outlaw was Ella Watson or 'Cattle Kate' as she was to become known. Born on a farm in Kansas in 1862, she quickly established a reputation in her teens as being a brawler, when she started working in the brothels of Cheyenne and Denver as a 'bouncer'. A rather large girl, she weighed close to 200lbs and knew how to use every pound. When she was 26 years old a cattleman, by the name of Jim Averill, hired her to 'look after' the cowboys who stopped at one of his saloons after corralling their cattle in his stockyard. Later she was married to Jim Averill and the two went into business developing their expanding herd.

Over the next few years she acquired a reputation as being a fearsome woman, who could handle a six-shooter, a rifle and a branding iron as well as any man. The majority of this information came from the pen of a reporter for the *Cheyenne Mail Leader*, who was out to make a name for himself and sell papers.

Other cattlemen quickly became suspicious when a number of their cattle appeared in Averill's other stockyards, bearing their brand. They also discovered that 'Cattle Kate' was also using her 'charms and favours' to acquire cattle from the cowboys who visited her. It was during the severe blizzards of 1888, when a large number of the herds were lost, that it was noticed that 'Cattle Kate's' herd seemed to be increasing. When challenged by another ranch owner about some of the cattle in her herd that bore the brand of his ranch, she levelled a rifle at him and said that she had purchased them legitimately from a cowboy

Above left: Drawing of 'Cattle Kate' and Jim Averell being lynched.

Above right: Ella Watson, 'Cattle Kate'.

as maverick cattle (after Samuel Maverick, a rancher who refused to brand his own cattle). When, some months later, another disgruntled rancher traced some of his missing cattle to her herd and received the same response, the ranchers in the area decided to take action.

One hot morning in July 1989, a posse of vigilantes appeared outside her cabin. Inside were 'Cattle Kate' and Jim Averill and within minutes, the pair had been bundled into a wagon and driven to some cottonwood trees, one of which they were hanged from.

The lynching of 'Cattle Kate' and Jim Averill caused three of the men involved to be brought before the grand jury, but although there had been a witness to the lynchings (a young boy who happened to be killed just before he was to give evidence), no one was convicted of the murders. All the perpetrators of the crime were cattle barons and members of the Wyoming Stockgrowers Association, some of the most powerful people in the state, so it came as no surprise when they walked free.

Another female outlaw was Susie Raper, a beautiful young lady whose life had been tragically shattered in 1866, by a renegade band

James Averell.

'Calamity Jane' holding her rifle and showing her gun belt with its pistol in cross-draw position.

of Indians, who attacked and killed her family. Susie Raper charmed the owner of a freight company to give her a ride from Nevada to California and by the time she arrived, she owned the company. How she achieved this is open to speculation.

On arriving in California she sold the outfit for cash and returned to Nevada, where she joined up with a former officer from the Nevada Volunteers. Together they set about carving themselves a career in cattle rustling and brazenly stole herds from ranches, changing the brands and selling them on. Their luck ran out and although her companion escaped, Susie Raper was arrested and put on trial. She turned her considerable charm on the twelve male jurors and was acquitted. After her release she once again joined up with her former accomplice and started rustling again. Once again she was arrested, and realising that a jury would not fall for her charms a second time, somehow persuaded the two deputy sheriffs that were taking her in to let her go. She was last seen galloping across the desert towards Colorado. The next time she was heard of was when she was on trial for murder in New Mexico, after killing the man she was living with had signed over the deeds to his ranch to her. She was found guilty and hanged.

It doesn't seem right not to mention possibly one of the most famous women of the West, and that is Martha Jane Canary, better known as 'Calamity Jane'. She was never an outlaw but was very friendly with a large number of them. Born on a farm in Missouri in 1848, she was brought up more as a boy than a girl, working on the farm as a labourer. At the age of 15 she left home and started drifting around the territory. She wore men's clothes most of the time as it didn't seem appropriate for a young girl to be seen wandering from town to town. There are many, many stories attributed to her early years: some say she joined the army and fought against the Indians and acquired the name of 'Calamity Jane' because of the number of escapades she apparently got involved in. The truth is thought to be that she acquired the name after getting drunk in barrooms on numerous occasions, throwing glasses and breaking mirrors. It is thought she may have turned to prostitution to support herself, but, dressed as a man, she did join General

'Calamity Jane' when a scout for the army.

Cook's Sioux Peace Talks Expedition as a muleskinner. It was whispered around the camp that she was in fact a woman, probably because she had been recognised by some of her many 'clients'. Later she joined a government wagon train as a teamster, but after being caught swimming in the nude with some of the other drivers, she was dismissed.

By now, she had achieved a certain notoriety, mainly because of the company she kept and that she was often seen drunk in barrooms brawling or causing mayhem. She was mentioned in a number of the stories being written about the Wild West by eastern newspaper correspondents. She dressed almost always like a man, carrying sixguns at her hip and would try and show off her expertise with a pistol by shooting bottles and streetlights when she was drunk.

She befriended Wild Bill Hickok and is said to have tagged along with him and his colourful Wild West Show for a while. But he soon tired of her drunken escapades, although by this time her fame had been firmly established because of her connection with him. She worked for a time in brothels in Dead Tree Gulch, and then in Miles City, one of the most lawless towns in the state.

The only time that 'Calamity Jane' ever seriously broke the law was in 1895, when she was arrested for drunken brawling in a barroom and

Above: Martha Jane Burke, popularly known as 'Calamity Jane', on horseback, wearing an elaborate Western costume, in front of tepees and tents at the Pan-American Exposition in Buffalo, New York.

Left: Martha Jane Canary ('Calamity Jane') leaning on her rifle.

'Calamity Jane' drinking with friends outside a saloon.

jumped bail rather than pay the $100 fine. She appeared some months later in Kansas City with a little girl. 'Calamity Jane' claimed that her daughter's father was Wild Bill Hickok, but this was untrue. The father of the little girl was a Lieutenant Summers, who was known to have been co-habiting with her, on and off, for a number of years. What eventually happened to the little girl is not known, but she probably ended up with relatives, because of the lifestyle of 'Calamity Jane'.

In 1900, 'Calamity Jane' was discovered in a brothel, drunk and in poor health. Such was her reputation, however, that she was taken out of there and nursed back to health, so that she could be hired by the Pan American Exposition of 1901 to represent the West, and she was well paid for it. Unfortunately with all the extra money in her pocket, she reverted back to her old ways and got roaring drunk most evenings, shooting up the barrooms and even shooting at the feet of the local policemen in an effort to make them dance. She was dismissed!

"CALAMITY JANE" IN 1885 (*Above*)

I FOUND "CALAMITY" SMOKING A CIGAR AND COOKING BREAKFAST (*Below*)

Two views of 'Calamity Jane'. Top: With her horse. Bottom: In her house.

'Calamity Jane' at Wild Bill Hickok's gravesite.

Very little was heard of her again, but it is known that she married a Texan called Clinton Burke, who left her soon after the marriage. In 1903, 'Calamity Jane' Canary died of alcoholism and pneumonia, and in poverty, living in a dilapidated, crumbling cabin just outside Deadwood. After her death she was buried alongside the grave of Wild Bill Hickok, as was her wish (although when he was alive Hickok said that he had no time for her).

What is rarely mentioned about 'Calamity Jane' is the time that she was in Deadwood, when a major smallpox outbreak occurred. The only doctor in the territory, Doctor Babcock, said that she worked tirelessly throughout the epidemic, nursing women and children and asking for nothing in return. Certainly she cursed and drank a little, but rarely slept and, although she bragged about her exploits with the army as a scout, she never ever mentioned the tireless work she carried out in Deadwood during the epidemic. It is said, that the man, who closed the lid on her coffin was one of the boys she tirelessly nursed back to health during the smallpox epidemic.

Chapter 23

Ned Christie

Ned Christie was born in Wauhillau in the Going Snake District of the Cherokee Nation on 14 December 1852, the son of Watt and Lydia Christie, members of the Keetowah tribe. There was nothing unusual about his early years and he was a popular fiddle player and excellent stickball player.

In his early teens he trained as a blacksmith and gunsmith in his father's blacksmith's shop. Both professions suited him, as he was a large young man 6ft 4in (1.93m) tall. In the blacksmith's shop, Ned and his brothers heard stories about the forced removal of the Cherokees from the East to the Indian Territory in 1838. They were told that thousands had died upon the Trail of Tears, as it was called, including Christie's grandmother, an Irish woman who had given the Christie family its last name.

During the Civil War, Christie's father and his uncles joined the Union Army. Young Ned Christie remained behind to help defend the rest of the family. After the war, several of Ned's brothers and his father served in the Cherokee legislature from the Going Snake District. Ned Christie married Nannie Dick at the age of 19. Four years later, after divorcing her, he

The outlaw Ned Christie.

married Peggy Drake, and two years later he married for a third time to Jennie Scraper. This marriage lasted 11 years before he divorced her and married his fourth wife Nancy Greene in 1888. In 1885, Ned Christie, followed in the footsteps of his father and brothers and was elected to his first term in the National Council. He

Ned Christie with his brother Jim Christie.

became known for his hot-tempered speeches on the legislative floor in defence of Cherokee sovereignty, as movement was underway to open to white settlement a two-million-acre tract, known as the Unassigned Lands, in the heart of Indian Territory. The Indians were being pressured to take their lands in individual allotments, thus eliminating the tribes as separate nations. Christie knew that once this happened, the white man would soon be in charge of those allotments, legally or otherwise. In the meantime, intruders and illegal whiskey were plaguing the Cherokee Nation.

Like many of his peers Ned liked to go downtown after supper to find a drink of whiskey and on the odd occasion he drank too much and became violent and belligerent. On 24 December 1884, after a period of heavy drinking, he got involved in a drunken brawl with a young Cherokee Indian by the name of William Palone, resulting in the young man's death. Christie was brought to trial at the Tribal Court but was found not guilty.

On the night of 5 May 1887, in downtown Tahlequah, Christie met John Parris. This was to be the night that would change Ned Christie's life forever. A half-breed, Parris had been in trouble with the court in Fort Smith for years for introducing and peddling whiskey and he always knew where to find a drink. He and Ned Christie walked toward Dog Town on the northern edge of Tahlequah. There they crossed the bridge over Spring Branch and passed Big Spring, where a team and wagon, belonging to two deputy US marshals, was camped. The past three days had been cold and rainy, but this evening was clear and pleasant.

Christie and Parris went to the home of Nancy Old Lady Shell, where they found Thomas 'Bub' Trainor, Jr., eating supper, all dressed up and ready to attend the local dance. Trainor was known as one of Tahlequah's

Saturday Night Outlaws. His family was well known and respected, but 'Bub' was wild and reckless. Christie and Parris bought a bottle of whiskey from Nancy. Not having a cork for the bottle, she tore a strip from her apron to use as a stopper. Christie and Parris left Nancy and 'Bub' behind and made their way back to Spring Branch Creek where the wagon was camped. They came across three other acquaintances close to the wagon camp, and soon all five men were drinking.

Back in Big Spring, US Deputy Marshal Dan Maples and posseman George Jefferson were at work, after John C. Carroll, the Western District of Arkansas US Marshal at Fort Smith, had sent them there to investigate the growing illegal whiskey operations in the Tahlequah area. Maples had inquired quietly about the matter and discovered that his main suspects were 'Bub' Trainor and John Parris, and so he had warrants issued for each of them.

The major supplier of illegal whiskey in Dog Town and a frequent visitor to Old Lady Shell, amongst others, was 'Bub' Trainor. Content with what he had learned, Maples used storekeeper James S. Stapler's phone to notify US Marshal John Carroll of what he had discovered. But one of Trainor's friends was standing outside unnoticed by an open window and heard everything.

After making the call, the two marshals walked back toward their wagon camp. The moon shone brightly as they approached a footbridge across Spring Branch Creek. Then George Jefferson suddenly saw the muzzle of a revolver resting against the side of a tree on the opposite side of the creek. 'Don't shoot! he shouted, but too late: the assassin fired. The bullet struck Dan Maples in the chest, knocking him to the ground. As he fell he managed to draw his revolver and fire in the direction of where the shot came from. George Jefferson pulled his gun and fired, too, but none of their shots found their mark. A few hours later, shortly after midnight, Maples died of internal bleeding.

The following morning Ned Christie awoke, slumped against a tree where he had spent the night after passing out after his drinking session. He was shocked to hear of the shooting the previous night and shocked even more when he learned that he was the main suspect for the murder of Deputy US Marshal Dan Maples. Talking with his father and a senator from the National Council, they advised him to leave the area as killing a white man was serious, more so when he was a deputy US marshal. If he were to be convicted of this it would carry the death sentence, especially when in Judge Isaac Parker's court. Ned Christie pleaded his innocence saying that he didn't even have a gun that night, and anyway he had been too drunk to even fire a gun, and refused to leave.

Later that day Christie heard that a warrant for his arrest had been issued and a number of deputy US marshals were on their way to arrest him. Ned Christie immediately headed out of town and went to ground in Rabbit Trap, an area in the Cherokee Nation. In a letter to Judge Parker in Fort Smith, he offered to give himself up if Judge Parker would grant him bail so he could prove his innocence. The reply from Parker was an unequivocal no! Ned Christie felt he would not receive justice in a white man's court especially where the death of a Federal officer was concerned. He stated that he would rather die at home fighting than go to Parker's court to be hanged. After consulting with the tribe's medicine man and going through a number of rituals, Christie returned home feeling protected by the spells cast and confident the deputy marshals could not catch him now. His family and friends in the Keetoowah Society set up a system of signals in the hills and warned him when one of the deputies was near. If a deputy did get close, Christie would utter his defiant Cherokee gobble and fire a warning shot to scare him off. One too-persistent deputy was shot in the heel, another in the neck.

Meanwhile, in Fort Smith, two of Ned Christie's drinking partners on that fateful May night, John Parris and Charley Bobtail, were in jail beneath the Federal Court. Along with Christie and 'Bub' Trainor, they too had been charged with the murder of Dan Maples. Trainor said he could prove he had been at Nancy Shell's eating supper at the time of the killing, and he was released on bail. Even on bail he continued to commit offences, and during 1888 he appeared in court on a number of occasions for a variety of drink related charges. Judge Parker said that whilst Ned Christie was still at large, the Maples case could not go ahead, but Christie remained elusive. It seemed almost every crime in the Indian Territory was now being blamed on him.

On 18 May 1889, in Fort Smith, Jacob Yoes replaced John Carroll as US marshal. A man of strong determination, Yoes set about clearing up the backlog of unsolved cases. Of particular concern to him was the long-pending case of the murder of Marshal Dan Maples. It was unthinkable to Jacob Yoes that such a crime could go unpunished. He called in his most able lawman, US Deputy Marshal 'Heck' Thomas, and handed him a writ for Christie, reminding him there was a $500 reward for the outlaw's capture.

'Heck' Thomas, had joined the US marshal's force in Fort Smith in late 1885, and had quickly become one of the most active officers of the court. He consistently brought in more prisoners than anyone else. On 21 November 1887, he had set a record for a single trip by bringing in forty-one prisoners.

Christie was now being reported as one of the most vicious men to ever raise a gun in the Indian Territory. He was reputed to be a born killer, cold-blooded and ruthless. Dime novels of the time said he walked the isolated paths of the Cherokee Nation, relentless in his maniacal hatred of the white man. He was said to have murdered eleven or more people, though officially he was charged with only one, Marshal Maples. For five years Christie, who maintained his innocence, had evaded the lawmen attempting to bring him in to stand trial for that murder. Ned Christie became increasingly bitter and began drinking heavily. It was said that he started bootlegging whiskey to support his family.

With 'Heck' Thomas was Deputy US Marshal L.P. Isbell of Vinita, a skilled tracker. The two of them set off on 'Heck' Thomas's usual circuit through Indian Territory, handing out subpoenas and making arrests. At Muskogee, they left thirteen prisoners under guard and met 'Bub' Trainor. Trainor, still on bail, knew Ned Christie and his habits well and wanted him captured or, better still, killed in an effort to clear his own name for the murder of Maples.

At the end of September 1889, 'Heck' Thomas and his posse located Christie at his home in Rabbit Trap. As dawn broke on the 26th, the deputy marshals crept quietly toward Christie's home. The dogs in the yard barked, warning Christie. Thomas ordered the deputies to rush the cabin and as they did so they could hear Christie crawling into the loft. 'Heck' Thomas shouted, 'United States Marshals' and ordered Christie to surrender. Instead, Christie knocked a plank off the gabled end of his cabin, and opened fire with his Winchester. Thomas shouted to him to send out his women and children. Christie ignored the call from 'Heck' Thomas and kept firing. The deputies decided to set fire to a small outbuilding, hoping to smoke Christie out. With that Nancy Christie ran out of the house, and the lawmen held their fire. However, young James, Christie's son, remained inside, scrambling into the loft to load his father's weapons.

As smoke swirled around the cabin, Nancy disappeared into the woods. The firing continued and Deputy Marshal Isbell, trying to use a tree for cover, took a bullet in the left shoulder. Flames from the outbuilding now took hold of the log cabin, and the deputies waited for Christie to run out. But unknown to them, during an exchange of gunfire, a bullet had smashed Christie's nose, struck his left eye, ran around the side of his head, and lodged in the back just beneath the skin. Blinded, he fell on his back, unable to move or speak. James grabbed his father's Winchester and kept firing at the deputies to make them believe Ned Christie was still alive and dangerous. The fire crackled below. James could not move his father, so he decided to leave the house alone. Slipping through a window he tried to climb the fence, but he was spotted by one of the deputies who shot him in the back. Despite being in great pain James Christie managed to get over the fence and stumble off into the woods.

With the cabin burning fiercely, the deputies decided Ned Christie was probably dead and left. Deputy US Marshal Isbell was bleeding badly, and they knew that Nancy Christie, who had fled the house, was certain to bring help. Shortly after they had gone, Nancy returned and ran inside the burning cabin. In the loft, Christie's eyesight had partially returned, but he still could not move or speak. He heard his name being called in Cherokee, '*Nede Wade!*' Ned saw his wife's frightened eyes peering at him from the opening at the top of the ladder.

Friends and relatives came running to see what the shooting was about and discovered a wounded Ned Christie in the loft. They managed to get Christie out of the burning house and hid him in the woods, where they also found the badly wounded James. They sent for Dr Bitting, a white man who was sympathetic to the Indians and owned a gristmill nearby.

Deputy US Marshal Isbell was taken back to Tahlequah for treatment. 'Heck' Thomas telegraphed Yoes telling him what happened and that they believed Ned Christie to be dead. However, Yoes was not satisfied and sent 'Heck' Thomas back to get confirmation. It was then he learned that Ned Christie had been rescued from the burning cabin, but badly wounded. The attack on Ned Christie's home and the wounding of his son now increased Christie's hatred for the white man. The bullet that had hit Ned Christie had broken his nose and blinded his left eye, leaving him badly scarred. He was now being hunted for what he still claimed a crime he did not commit.

Ned Christie made it clear that he would never surrender or be taken alive. He said he bore no law enforcement officer any ill will, but would shoot at them whenever they came within range of his gun. Christie said there was only one man whom he would like to shoot and that was 'Bub' Trainor, who, he claimed, was responsible for the death of the US Marshal and was now doing all he could to assist the officers. But Trainor kept well out of the range of Christie's Winchester.

Christie's friends and relatives built him a rock fort on a hilltop less than a mile west of his burned cabin. They stocked the fort with food, water and ammunition and also cleared the trees from the top of the hill, making Ned's Mountain virtually impregnable. Feeling secure in the rock fort with his guards, Christie sent word to 'Heck' Thomas where he could be found, telling the marshal to come on up if he thought he could capture him, and they would shoot it out.

'Heck' Thomas, on hearing the challenge, returned to Rabbit Trap with a posse that included 'Bub' Trainor. It became obvious, after seeing the rock fort, that Ned Christie was in an impregnable position and it would take a regiment of soldiers and some heavy artillery to move him. Thomas did not want to expose his men needlessly to danger, so he called off the assault.

It was decided to leave Ned Christie alone for a while, whilst another plan to capture him was devised. The main problem being that his friends and relatives had built him a new two-storey, double-walled house, that had sand poured between the walls. There was just the one door and there were no windows as such, but loopholes through which Ned could fire if attacked. The house was also well stocked with food and ammunition.

As time passed Ned Christie's reputation as an outlaw grew, as the number of robberies increased in the state, but most of them were unfairly attributed to him. He was also losing the support of many of his friends, who started to believe the stories of violence carried out during these robberies and they felt that they could not support or condone these acts. Despite his denials, support for him dropped away and this did not pass unnoticed by Marshal Yoes in Fort Smith.

Jacob Yoes increased the reward on Ned Christie to $1,000 confident now that sooner or later someone would bring Ned Christie in to claim the reward. The warrant for his arrest was still outstanding and lawmen and bounty hunters roamed the woods in Going Snake District in the hope of catching Ned Christie. There were reports that he had exchanged fire with some of his pursuers and his reputation was rapidly turning into becoming the legend that he was invincible amongst the Cherokee Indians.

In Fort Smith Marshal Jacob Yoes and Judge Isaac Parker decided that enough was enough, it had been five and half years since the death of Deputy US Marshal Dan Maples and Ned Christie was still at liberty. He summoned Deputy Marshal Dave Rusk, who had been with 'Heck' Thomas in the failed 1889 attempt to capture Christie, and told him to get Christie at any cost.

At dawn on 12 October 1892, Dave Rusk and five other deputies approached Ned Christie's house. Once the again the Christies' dogs alerted the occupants of the house and a gunfight started, resulting in two of the deputies being wounded. Rusk set fire to one of the outbuildings, but it wasn't close enough to the main house. Even the use of dynamite didn't work against this impregnable fortified house. Rusk sent a message back to Fort Smith requesting more help. Yoes replied that help was on its way, but Rusk was to keep Christie pinned down inside the fortified house.

The arrival of a twenty-strong posse with Deputy US Marshal 'Cap' White in charge increased the firepower and throughout the day the assault on the fortified house continued. It soon became obvious that bullets were having no effect and what was needed was a cannon to smash through the walls.

Some of the deputies were dispatched to a nearby fort and returned with a cannon that fired a 3lb projectile. Under the cover of darkness, the men surrounded the outlaw's home and concealed themselves in the underbrush. White knew that Christie kept a pack of dogs to warn him when intruders were near, and earlier the deputies had heard dogs barking down in the hollow, but now the dogs were strangely silent.

Since the last raid, Christie had stayed close to his fortified house. With him that morning were his wife Nancy, daughter Mary, granddaughter Charlotte, Little Arch, Charles Hare, a young full-blood Cherokee who had recently joined the gang, and Charles Grease, a seven-year-old nephew of Nancy's. James Christie was not at home.

Just before dawn on 3 November a posse of twenty-five men lay in wait outside Ned Christie's fortified house in Rabbit Trap. Deputy US Marshals Gus York and Gideon S. 'Cap' White, the posse leaders, issued their final orders. Under no circumstances can Ned Christie be allowed to escape and Christie's supporters must be prevented from coming to his aid.

At sunrise, the door slowly opened and Arch Wolf, Christie's nephew, stepped out. Wolf started for the nearby spring and Cap White shouted for him to surrender. Wolf pulled his pistol from his belt and replied with gunfire. The deputies opened fire struck Wolf in the leg and arm. As he staggered back towards the cabin, another bullet grazed his head just he made it inside. Christie whooped as he always did when a fight began. Within minutes a hail of bullets blazed from the portholes that had been cut into the upper portion of his home. The final battle to capture Ned Christie was on.

A little while later, during a lull in the fighting, Nancy and Mary came out of the house briefly and then went back inside. Little Arch came out soon after, and when he refused to surrender he exchanged fire with the deputies and was wounded.

Following Little Arch's wounding, Gus York once again called for Ned Christie to surrender. With York was Sheriff Ben Knight, a full-blood Cherokee, so York had the order repeated in Cherokee to make sure Christie understood. A hail of bullets was the only response from the fortified house. Once again Cap White told him to send out the women and children. This time Ned Christie called Nancy and the others up from the cellar and told them to leave which they did except, for some unknown reason, young Charley Grease.

The arrival of the cannon gave hope that the siege would soon be over, but after firing thirty-eight cannon balls at the fortified house, all of which just bounced off the walls, the posse gave up that tactic. The deputy marshals kept firing at long range whilst a dozen sticks of dynamite with long fuses were placed at the side of the house.

The explosion wrecked the side of the house and knocked out one corner and the house began to burn. Christie and the others inside were once again called upon to surrender but once again they refused and kept up the fight. Then the roof fell in and Arch Wolf's hair caught fire, and burning timbers struck Charles Hare. Young Charley Grease was probably already dead.

Thick smoke bellowed from the burning house and enveloped the clearing. While the blaze was at its fiercest, the deputies saw Christie emerge from the cellar, firing at the nearest deputies. In the smoke and confusion Ned Christie tried to slip away and almost did. But then young Deputy Marshal Wesley Bowman heard a yell and saw Christie running towards him and two other deputies, firing his rifle as he came. The deputies returned the fire, riddling Christie's body with bullets. Then there was silence as the deputies gathered around the dead body of Christie, and then suddenly Sam Maples, son of Dan Maples, ran up, and, in a frenzy of revenge, emptied his revolver into the lifeless body of Christie. The Indian women supporters, waiting on the knoll above the fort, trilled in mourning. The sun rose, and a light wind scattered the drifting smoke. The officers found a badly-burned Charles Hare trying to escape and arrested him.

Ned Christie's body was strapped to the charred door of his cabin and carried to their camp. A photographer, who was in the crowd that had gathered, took pictures. The deputies then took Christie's corpse to Fort Smith to collect their reward. The body was placed in the front entrance of the jail and the public were allowed to see the disfigured remains of a once-notorious outlaw.

Judge Parker personally congratulated each man who had accompanied Christie's corpse to Fort Smith. The body remained on public display until it was placed on the 4 p.m. train to Fort Gibson. Ned's father claimed the body at the fort and brought his son to Rabbit Trap for burial in the family cemetery. Gus York received the $1,000 reward at the end of December, but after paying expenses and dividing the rest among posse members, he and the others each received just $74.

Right: The body of the notorious Ned Christie propped up against the wall of a shack on public display.

Below: The posse that killed Ned Christie posing with his body.

1.Paden Talbot. 2. Captain G. White, 3. Coon Rataree, 4. Enoch Mills, 5. Ned Christie's body, 6. Thomas Johnson, 7. Charles Copal, 8. 'Heck' Bruner.

There were mixed emotions regarding Ned Christie's death. Many in the Indian Territory felt safer now that Ned Christie was dead. Others considered his death a tragedy, believing he was a peaceable man who had been the victim of a miscarriage of justice and had desired nothing more than to be left alone to enjoy family life.

Charles Hare and Arch Wolf, who survived the fire, were brought to trial and convicted of resisting arrest and intent to kill. They were both sent to prison. Arch Wolf became mentally ill whilst in prison and was later admitted to a hospital for the insane. He didn't get out until 1907. James Christie was shot and killed by an assassin near his home in July 1893, eight months after the death of his father.

With Ned Christie dead, the Deputy Marshal Dan Maples murder case never came to trial. It was not until 1918 that what is said to be the truth in the matter became public knowledge. In a story in the *Daily Oklahoman* it was revealed that Tahlequah blacksmith Richard A. (Dick) Humphrey, a former slave who has been adopted into the Cherokee Nation, had witnessed the murder. He told his story 31 years later. He stated his reason for waiting so long was that he was in fear of reprisals from 'Bub' Trainor's friends and family if he told what happened. In his statement Humphrey said:

> Trainor was wild and reckless and carried a big revolver in his belt. I saw Trainor cross the creek where Ned Christie was slumped against a tree sleeping of an alcohol-induced stupor. I saw Trainor take off Ned Christie's coat and put it on. He then took a position behind a tree and waited for Dan Maples. When Maples appeared he opened fire with his pistol, mortally wounding him. There was an exchange of gunfire and Trainor slipped away. He then took off the coat and shook Ned Christie telling him to get up, but Christie just staggered a few steps and collapsed again.

How much is truth and how much was made up we will never know, but the likelihood is that Ned Christie was innocent of the murder of Marshal Dan Maples and became a victim of treachery and circumstance.

Chapter 24

William Longley

William 'Bill' Longley was born in Mill Creek in Austin County, Texas, in 1851, the sixth of ten children of Campbell and Sarah Longley. When he was two years old his family purchased a farm near Evergreen, Texas, in present-day Lincoln, Lee County, where he spent a large part of his childhood learning to ride and shoot. The Longley family farm was just a mile from the Camino Real, the Old Spanish royal highway that joined San Antonio and Nacogdoches, Texas.

He received an average education for the time and was just reaching adulthood when the American Civil War ended in 1865. By 1867, Texas was fully under the control of the Union Army due to the Reconstruction Act. The military acted in all capacities, including law enforcement, which caused considerable resentment throughout the state. Around this time Longley, who was around 6ft tall and of a slim build, dropped out of school and began living a wild life, drinking, and running in the company of other young delinquents.

Bill Longley's first serious contact with the law was in mid-December 1868, when he became involved in a murder and robbery accompanied by three of his friends. Three former slaves named Green Evans, Pryer Evans, and the third known only as Ned, were riding

William Preston Longley aka 'Wild Bill'.

through Evergreen, intending to visit friends further south, when they were approached by Longley and his friends and forced at gunpoint into a dry creek bed. A terrified Green Evans panicked and spurred his horse to escape. Longley shot at him several times as he rode away and killed him.

Longley and his friends then proceeded to go through the dead man's pockets, and as they did so Pryer Evans and Ned took the opportunity to escape and rode away. Although being accused of the murder, Longley later claimed that at the time he was a member of the Texas State Police and had not been the only one shooting. The fact that the Texas State Police only existed from 1870 to 1873 made this claim nonsense and exposed the true character of Bill Longley. Longley's account of this murder differs from that of his later killings, where he bragged about shooting men rather than to trying to blame others, demonstrating his deplorable character and judgement in his actions.

Now wanted by the law for murder and robbery, Longley drifted around Texas for a time, and it was during this period that he nearly lost his life. He met a young man by the name of Johnson who invited him to stay on his ranch with him and his young brother. That same night, as they were sitting in the house drinking, a posse of vigilantes suddenly surrounded the house looking for Johnson who, it turned out, was a wanted horse thief. The posse figured that Bill Longley was one Johnson's gang and within minutes the two men were being dragged out of the house. They were dragged to a clump of trees; ropes were thrown over a large branch and the two men hoisted onto the backs of horses. As the horses jerked away the two men were left swinging, but Bill Longley's rope snapped as it stretched under his struggling 200lb weight and he fell to the ground. The vigilantes had left by this time and Johnson's little brother suddenly appeared. He took the rope from Longley's neck and then untied his hands. Longley lifted the boy's brother down but it was too late, he was dead.

Some weeks later Bill Longley met up with the Cullen Baker Gang and for the next few months rode with them on a series of robberies. Then fortune shone down on Longley when the gang encountered one of the vigilantes in a bar bragging how he had strung up a couple of horse thieves. The large, imposing figure of Bill Longley, with Cullen Baker behind him, grabbed the man and took him to the same tree where they had hung Johnson and tried to hang him. After throwing a rope over the branch, he placed a noose around the man's neck and watched as the man's horse jerked forward, leaving the vigilante's body twitching convulsively as it swung around. After a few minutes Bill Longley took out his pistol and fired all six bullets into the man's body. Retribution was complete.

In 1869, Longley met up with his brother-in-law, John Wilson, and the two of them embarked on a crime spree through southern Texas. Over the next year they robbed settlers, and in one instance killed a freed slave named Paul Brice in Bastrop County, Texas, and stole his horses. They were also said to have killed a freed slave woman in Evergreen.

At the beginning of March 1870, the Union Army, who were still responsible for law and order, offered a $1,000 reward for their capture. With warrants out for his arrest and deputy US marshals on his trail, Longley left Texas and moved north to avoid the authorities and by May 1870, he had joined a gold-hunting party in Cheyenne, Wyoming. Bill Longley later claimed that John Wilson had been killed in a shoot-out with some other outlaws in Brazos County, Texas, at the end of 1870, but recent research showed that in fact John Wilson was killed in Falls County, Texas, in 1874.

The goldmining party travelled into the Black Hills of South Dakota, but were intercepted by a US Cavalry patrol and told to leave the area, as there was a treaty with the Sioux that prohibited mining. The party was forced to disband and were escorted from the area by the cavalry unit. For some unknown reason, Bill Longley then decided to enlist for a five-year engagement in the army, joining Company 'B' of the US 2nd Cavalry Regiment on 22 June 1870. His unit was stationed at Camp Stambaugh, but it soon became obvious that he was unable to adapt to the strict discipline and obey orders, so just two weeks after joining up he deserted. After being free for less than a week he was captured and returned to Camp Stambaugh where he was court-martialled. He was sentenced to two years hard labour with a ball and chain clamped to his ankle and imprisoned at Camp Stambaugh. Four months later he was released to return to his unit. One reason given for his early release was that he had exceptional marksmanship skills and was sorely needed in the regular hunting parties regularly leaving the post to get food. Needless to say he deserted once again in May 1872, only this time he was never recaptured.

For the following year Bill Longley kept a very low profile, but it is known that he returned to Texas because he was wanted for the murder of another freedman in Bastrop County in February 1873. He went to live with his father's family in Bell County, Texas, following this incident, but in the summer Sheriff Finney of Mason County arrived with deputies and arrested him for murder. He was taken to Austin,

Texas, to claim the reward from the military, but after waiting a week for the money to come through, Sheriff Finney released Bill Longley. It was rumoured that he had been bribed with a considerable amount of money by Longley's wealthy uncle, Alexander Preston Longley, who lived in California.

Bill Langley's activities were still very low key until 31 March 1875, when he was approached by one of his uncles, Caleb Longley, to kill Longley's childhood friend Wilson Anderson. The reason given was that Caleb Longley's son, Cale, had been killed and he held Wilson Anderson responsible and he wanted revenge. Bill Longley arranged a meeting with his old friend and killed him using a shotgun. Almost immediately another warrant for his arrest was issued forcing Bill Longley to go on the run, this time accompanied by his brother James Stockton Longley.

A nationwide hunt was now on, forcing Bill Longley to go from place to place, not staying anywhere long enough to be recognised. He found temporary work on a cotton farm for a while, but after a violent disagreement with a man called George Thomas in which Thomas died, another warrant for his arrest was issued and the hunt intensified. It is not known what part, if any, that James Longley took in this, but what is

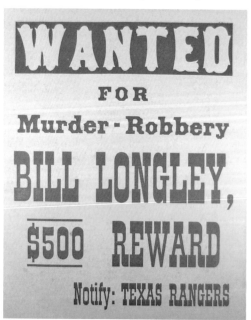

known is that he was later arrested and tried for Wilson Anderson's murder, but acquitted after it was shown that he took no part in it.

Longley's violent behaviour continued when in January 1876, in Uvaide County, Texas, in an attempt to ambush and rob a fellow outlaw, Lou Shroyer, he became involved in a gunfight with Shroyer. Shroyer shot Longley's horse from under him and in the ensuing gunfight, Longley shot Lou Shroyer dead. Once again the hunt for Longley went on and the reward money went up.

Bill Longley next appeared when he became a sharecropper in east Texas, working for a preacher by the name of William

One of the many wanted posters for Bill Longley.

Lay. All went well until he became involved with a young lady who was also involved with the preacher's nephew. A fight for the young woman's affections took place in which the nephew suffered a severe beating. Bill Longley was arrested and given a short term of imprisonment. On his release Longley rode straight to the preacher's farm and shot him dead with a shotgun, because he believed that the preacher had used his influence to get him arrested and imprisoned.

Once again on the run from the law and with another warrant having been issued for his arrest for murder, Bill Longley headed to Grayson County, Texas, where he found two of his friends, brothers Jim and Dick Sanders, languishing in the local jail. After a brief skirmish with Deputy Sheriff Matt Shelton, he broke the two bothers out of jail and the trio headed towards Louisiana. For a while Longley, now under the name of Bill Jackson, felt safe, but somehow word filtered back of his whereabouts. Then on 6 June 1877, the Nacogdoches County Sheriff Milt Mast, accompanied by two deputies, arrived and quietly, but quickly, arrested him. He was taken to the Lee County Court and, after a short trial, was convicted of the murder of Wilson Anderson and sentenced to hang. His appeal against conviction and sentence in March 1878 was denied and Bill Longley was executed in Giddings, Texas, on 11 October 1878.

Many stories concerning Bill Longley circulated after his death, among them was that his father claimed that his son was never hanged and that his death had been faked. This was disproved in 2001 after his remains had been exhumed and DNA samples taken confirming that they were the remains of William 'Bill' Longley.

Bill Longley, whilst in prison in Giddings awaiting execution, claimed that he killed more than eight black people after a horse-racing bet had gone wrong, saying that he had been brought up to believe that 'it was right to kill sassy Negroes'. William 'Bill' Longley was nothing more than a 'psychopathic racist murderer'.

Portrait shot of William Preston 'Wild Bill' Longley.

Chapter 25

'Shotgun' John Collins

Abraham Graham, also known as John Collins, was born on his grandmother's plantation in Horry County, South Carolina, on 22 November 1851. His great-grandfather, Captain Edward Connor, had served in the South Carolina Militia during the American War of Independence. His father, Hosea Graham, had married his first wife Martha Ann Graham, and whilst Abraham was just a child, the whole family moved to Texas in covered wagons in 1859.

'Shotgun' John Collins.

The family settled in Limestone County, Texas, but little is known of Abraham Graham during his early teenage years, except that he became close friends with John Wesley Hardin. Both of their families were staunch Confederates and they remained at odds with the Union throughout their lives.

Abraham Graham's first brush with the law was whilst he was in his late teens, when a warrant for his arrest for cattle rustling was issued. He immediately left Texas and headed for New Mexico ending up in White Oaks. John Collins, as he was now calling himself, found a job riding shotgun for Wells Fargo where he met Wyatt Earp and Pat Garrett, who were also working for the company. It was during this period that he acquired the nickname 'Shotgun' mainly because of the number of times he used it in shoot-outs. After leaving Wells Fargo he became a buffalo hunter and later a scout for the US Cavalry. It was while working as a scout that he became involved in the battles with Geronimo and his Apache warriors.

A chance meeting with John Wesley Hardin led him back to the wrong side of the law when he briefly rode with the Sam Bass Gang together with outlaws Johnny Ringo, Arch Clement, and Brown Bowen, rustling cattle and robbery. With the law hot on their trail, John Collins fled to Mexico to lay low until the hunt died down. Some time passed before Collins decided to return to Texas and he moved to the small town of Uvalde. It was here that he met Captain J.J.H. Patterson, who led a group of four riders called the Uvalde Minutemen, and decided to join them. They patrolled the Mexican border with a fearsome reputation, and as one resident put it, 'The Minutemen did what the Texas Rangers couldn't do'.

After several months with the Minutemen, John Collins decided to move on and went to New Mexico. He fell afoul of the law once again after he threatened to kill a man named James Smith. The circumstances are not known, but suffice it to say that he was arrested by Sheriff Whitehill of Silver City, New Mexico, and held in jail. After a few days he managed to persuade the sheriff to bail him out for $60, and promptly disappeared to Lincoln County.

This was the time of the Lincoln County War of 1878, which was a conflict between two parties; one was led by James Doolan who was the proprietor of a dry goods monopoly that controlled all the merchandise for general stores in the county. Because of this he was able to charge extortionately high prices. The other party, the two ranchers James Tunstall and Alexander McSween, opened up a rival general store with the backing of one of the most powerful ranchers in the county, John Chisum, where they sold similar goods at reasonable prices. James Doolan brought in help in the shape of the Jesse Evans gang and County Sheriff Brady amongst others. John Tunstall and Alexander McSween organised their own ranch hands into what became known as the Regulators together with their own lawmen, Town Constable Richard Brewer and Deputy US Marshal Robert Widenmann.

The killings started with the murder of John Tunstall as he was riding back to his ranch, which then escalated into a series of revenge killings by the Regulators. It was about then that John Collins met Henry McCarty, aka William Bonney (Billy the Kid), and for a time rode with him and the Regulators. The war finally came to a head after a five-day gunfight resulting in the death of Alexander McSween and many others.

Despite the war being over, resentment festered throughout the county and the appointment of Pat Garrett as County Sheriff did not help much. John Collins decided to move on, and because William Bonney was now wanted for murder in Lincoln and several other counties, it wasn't too long before they parted and went their separate ways.

John Collins moved to Old Socorro County, New Mexico, for a while then in April 1879 he was arrested for cattle rustling and horse theft and appeared in Rynerson Territory Court, New Mexico. The result of the trial is not known, but it is interesting to note that his brother-in-law John Long was the deputy sheriff at the time.

John Collins returned to Uvalde where he met and married Tabitha Cox. They had six children and at first used the name Collins, but later reverted their name back to Graham. Then in 1883 he took to drifting around again he met up with Wyatt Earp and together they went to Dodge City to support Luke Short and the Dodge City Peace Commission, which consisted of Wyatt Earp, Luke Short, Bat Masterson, Charlie Bassett, Neal Brown, M. McClain, William Harris, Johnny Millsap, Texas Jack Vermillion and Bill Tilghman. They were all participants in what later became known as the Dodge City War.

After this escapade John Collins quietly retired in to a relatively peaceful life. He was said to have died in a gunfight when at the age of 71 in El Paso, but his death certificate said it was natural causes. It is tempting to imagine that in the 'Wild West' in those days being killed in a gunfight might have been considered 'natural causes'.

'Shotgun' John Collins in his retirement years getting a haircut.

Chapter 26

Tiburcio Vasquez

Tiburcio Vasquez was born in Monterey, California, on 11 August 1835. His great-grandfather was one of California's earliest settlers and had arrived as a member of the Juan Baptista de Anza Bezerra Expedition in 1776. Tiburcio was very well educated as a child and fluent in the English language in both reading and writing. His early years were unremarkable, but this all changed at the age of 17 when he went to a local event with his older cousin, Anastacio Garcia. There had been trouble brewing for some time between two factions, the William Roachs and the Lewis Belchers, and both of them turned up at the event spoiling for trouble. A brawl started between them, which unfortunately spilled over involving almost everyone there including Tiburcio Vasquez and his cousin Anastacio Garcia. Constable William Hardmount, who had got wind of potential trouble, tried to intervene and was killed. Afraid of what was going to happen, Vasquez and Garcia left and headed for the hills where Garcia had friends. One of Garcia's friends, Jose Higuera, who was not directly involved in the brawl, stayed behind. Incensed by what had happened to the constable, a bunch of local vigilantes arrived the following morning, grabbed Higuera, accused him of being involved and unceremoniously lynched him.

Tiburcio Vasquez.

Anastacio Garcia was already well known as a local criminal, as were the friends he and his cousin sought shelter with. Within weeks Tiburcio Vasquez had learned the art of being an outlaw and within the month had joined another band of outlaws. His education and charisma shone through and he soon became the leader of gang specialising in horse rustling. For almost a year he and his gang stole hundreds of horses seemingly unchecked, but then in the beginning of 1857 it came to a sudden stop. A large posse, who had been tracking the gang, caught up with them outside Los Angeles just as they were moving a large herd of stolen horses and Vasquez was arrested.

Sentenced to five years in San Quentin prison, Vasquez managed to escape two years later but was recaptured within weeks, stealing horses once again. He was returned to San Quentin after being given an additional 12 months to his sentence and he was released in 1863. For four years he kept out of trouble with the law, but in 1867 he was caught attempting to rob a store, and was given another two-year prison sentence in San Quentin.

After his release he returned to Monterey and always something of a womanizer, took up with the wife of a man called Abelardo Salazar.

Above left: Tiburcio Vasquez.

Above right: Reward poster for Tiburcio Vasquez.

When the man found out about Tiburcio's affair with his wife there was a violent fight in which Tiburcio was badly hurt. Realising that his life was in danger, Vasquez left Monterey and headed to one of his hideouts at Cantua Creek in the Coast Range. It was some weeks before he recovered from his wounds, but having done so he joined up with some of his old gang and went back to a life of crime.

Up to this point most of Vasquez's crimes involved either stealing horses or robbing stores, but on 17 August 1871, he and two other outlaws robbed the Visala stagecoach as it was travelling between San Jose and Pacheco Pass. Within hours a posse, led by Sheriff Charles

The Hispanic gentleman outlaw Tiburcio Vasquez.

Lincoln, was on their trail. The posse caught up with the gang and in the ensuing gunfight one of the outlaws was killed and the other captured, but Vasquez, although wounded, managed to escape and returned to his hideout at Cantua Creek.

One week later he had recruited another couple of outlaws and the gang robbed Snyder's Store in Tres Pinos, San Benito County of $200 in gold. This time the robbery went horribly wrong and three innocent bystanders who happened to be in the store were killed. The senseless killing infuriated the townspeople and the state governor immediately offered a $1,000 reward for his capture.

Tiburcio Vasquez and his gang continued to carry out robberies and always appeared to be one step ahead of the law, hiding in the canyons around Tejon Pass. His favourite hiding place just north of Los Angeles was a large group of rocks now known as Vasquez Rocks.

On 26 December 1873, Vasquez's gang carried out their most audacious raid when they attacked and sacked the town of Kingston. They robbed the two stores in the town taking $2,500, but fortunately no one was killed, although townspeople were left tied up. On hearing of this audacious raid, the governor immediately increased the reward money to $3,000

Greek George, whose home was used as a hideout by Tiburcio Vasquez.

and then finally to $15,000. In an effort to apprehend the gang, the sheriffs of Fresno, Tulare, San Joaquin, Santa Clara and Monterey counties organised posses to hunt them down. Such was the intense pressure now to find and bring the gang to justice that Tiburcio Vasquez went to ground.

At the beginning of 1874, Vasquez was hiding out in the home of a man named Greek George, a former camel driver for the US Army. The house was located in a rural portion of Rancho La Brea and was an ideal hideout. Surrounded on three sides by dense, tall shrubbery and looking south, Vasquez had a clear view across the plain that stretched towards Los Angeles. Despite being the most hunted man in California, this did not stop Vasquez from continuing his life of crime. When Vasquez heard that a wealthy Italian sheep rancher nearby named Alessandro Repetto had sold his wool crop and had a lot of cash on hand, he set out with his men towards Repetto's house.

Repetto's house stood on a hilltop above a ranch where he raised sheep and goats. Vasquez entered Repetto's house by claiming that he was a sheep-shearer, but Vasquez's well-dressed appearance and un-calloused hands, showed that he was no sheep-shearer. Repetto called him out on his ruse and Vasquez admitted that he was there to rob him. He then demanded $10,000 and his men tied Repetto to a tree and threatened to hang him unless he came up with the money. Fortunately for Repetto he did not keep his money at home; instead he had it safely deposited at the Temple and Workman Bank in downtown Los Angeles. Faced with this dilemma, the gang decided that Repetto would write a cheque, and his nephew would go to the bank to collect the cash.

When Repetto's nephew arrived at the bank, he was so nervous that the banker, Francis Temple, became suspicious and contacted the sheriff. After further questioning the nephew broke down and tearfully told the sheriff was what was happening back at the ranch. The sheriff immediately started assembling a posse to capture Vasquez. Worried that now the sheriff knew what was going on and that might result in his uncle's death,

Repetto's nephew managed to persuade the banker to give him $500 in gold. The nephew returned to Repetto's house just before the posse arrived and gave the money to Vasquez. As the sheriff's posse approached Repetto's house, Vasquez and his men mounted up and started racing north. With the sheriff's posse behind them, they travelled up the Arroyo Seco, through the Devil's Gate and escaped into the mountains.

Meanwhile Vasquez's womanising was starting to create cracks in his relationship with friends and family. Whilst staying with Greek George, Vasquez caused a scandal when he had an affair with his niece, Felicita Vasquez, making her pregnant. The girl's mother was furious with Vasquez and made her feelings known to everyone including her extended family, which included Jose Jesus Lopez. Lopez's cousin, Cornelia Lopez, just happened to be Greek George's wife. It was then discovered that Lopez's sister, Modesta, had also had a sexual relationship with Tiburcio Vasquez, and she became furious when she learned that Felicita had had Vasquez's child. It is not clear exactly who informed the authorities, but it is thought that it was one of his close friends, gang member Abdon Leiva. He was also a member of the Lopez family and notified the authorities that Vasquez was hiding out at Greek George's house and agreed to turn State's evidence. The information was then passed to Los Angeles County Sheriff William Rowland to make the arrest.

Sheriff Rowland immediately assembled a posse and arranged for them to meet at a corral located near Spring and Fifth Streets

Members of the posse that captured Tiburcio Vasquez.

in downtown Los Angeles in the early hours of the morning. After Rowland had instructed the posse on how to approach the house, they quietly headed out of town towards the home of Greek George. Sheriff Rowland stayed in Los Angeles so as not to arouse the suspicion of any of Vasquez's informants. The posse approached Greek George's house in the back of a wagon, which routinely travelled by the house, and just before they reached the house, jumped out and laid themselves flat on the ground. When they were ready, they slowly approached the house on foot, and saw Vasquez sitting at a table being waited upon by a woman. The woman noticed someone outside and tried to close the door, but one of the men shoved his gun against the door and forced it open. Vasquez immediately made a break for the window, but was shot in the left arm. Despite the wound he jumped through the window and made a run towards his horse. Another member of the posse fired both barrels of his shotgun and Vasquez was hit – one shot lodged in the back of his head and the other in his right arm. When another member of the posse levelled his rifle directly at him, Vasquez threw

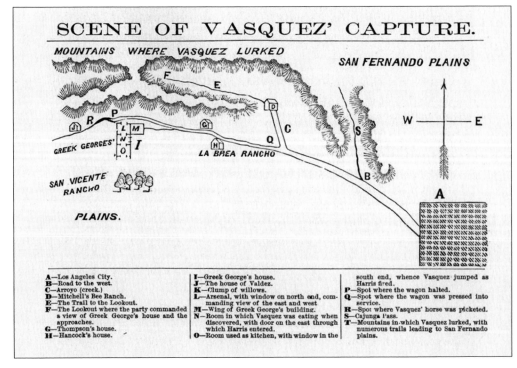

A detailed map drawn by a reporter who interviewed Tiburcio Vasquez whilst he was in prison, showing the capture of the outlaw.

up his hands and exclaimed: 'Don't shoot! I give up!' While the wagon was being prepared to take the prisoner back to town, one of the posse members offered Vasquez a drink of whiskey from his flask. Vasquez accepted saying: 'I like to drink with brave men and you are all brave, like myself.'

By the time the posse returned to town, news of his arrest had spread and large crowds waited to catch a glimpse of the notorious outlaw. After the local doctor had finished treating Tiburcio Vasquez's wounds, one of the posse offered the outlaw another drink of whiskey, which he gratefully accepted, proposing a toast the President of the United States. The arrest of Vasquez had made the headlines of almost all the major newspapers in the country and people came from miles away just to try and see him. Women in particular queued up with gifts and flowers just to speak to him. He was extremely polite at all times and admitted all his crimes, but denied emphatically that he had ever killed anyone. He sold photographs of himself from his cell window to get money to help pay for his defence. A short play was written entitled 'The Capture of Vasquez' and he even offered to lend his clothes to the actor portraying him. Within a couple of weeks Tiburcio Vasquez's wounds had healed sufficiently for him to travel to San Francisco to stand trial for robbery and murder. After a short trial he was found guilty of two counts of murder and sentenced to death by hanging. His legal team applied for clemency but Governor Romualdo Pacheco turned it down

Invitation to witness the execution of Tiburcio Vasquez.

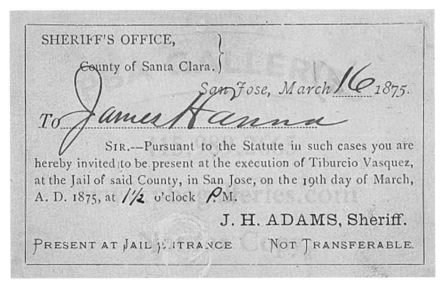

SHERIFF'S OFFICE,
County of Santa Clara.

San Jose, March 16 1875.

To James Hanna

SIR.—Pursuant to the Statute in such cases you are hereby invited to be present at the execution of Tiburcio Vasquez, at the Jail of said County, in San Jose, on the 19th day of March, A. D. 1875, at 1½ o'clock P.M.

J. H. ADAMS, Sheriff.

PRESENT AT JAIL ENTRANCE   NOT TRANSFERABLE.

Invitation by Sheriff John Adams to a James Hanna to attend the execution of Tiburcio Vasquez.

and on 19 March 1875, Sheriff John Adams of Santa Clara took Tiburcio Vasquez to the gallows and hanged him.

Writer Johnson McCulley, the creator of the character Zorro who became internationally known as a benevolent outlaw thanks to his appearance in countless movies, books and television shows, said he was inspired

by the real-life outlaw Tiburcio Vasquez, who was hunted down and eventually captured in Los Angeles. This was at a time when Los Angeles was in the midst of evolving from a Mexican village to an American city, and Vasquez served as a symbol of resistance to that change.

The gallows that hanged Tiburcio Vasquez.

Chapter 27

Dan Bogan

Dan Bogan was born in Alabama in 1860, but when he was just a boy the family moved to Hamilton County, Texas. In his mid-teens Dan Bogan began working as a cowboy, but not long after moving to Texas, his father died, and his mother quickly remarried and was to divorce twice, by the time Bogan had reached his late teens. Without much parental control, his two older brothers became involved in a series of crimes, one of which included horse theft. The result was that one of his brothers was shot and killed by the Hamilton County sheriff, whilst the other received a lengthy prison term. Up to this point Dan Bogan had avoided getting involved in any criminal activities, but at the same time he was acquiring a reputation for fighting and it seemed to many that he was always going to follow in his brothers' footsteps.

One incident happened on 2 May 1881 while he and his friend Dave Kemp, who had both been drinking heavily for most of the day, were in one of the town's saloons, when Bogan began taunting the men in the saloon, inviting anyone and everyone to fight him. Dave Kemp persuaded his friend to leave and led him to where they had left their horses tied behind W.T. Cropper's General Store.

'Dangerous' Dan Bogan.

Before they had even reached their horses, Dan Bogan came across local farmer F.A. 'Doll'

Smith, who was seated on his wagon and was in town to buy supplies. Bogan began to taunt Smith, calling him names and daring him to step down and fight him. Smith, who did not know Kemp or Bogan, ignored him, but when Bogan dragged a chair out of his wagon and began beating it on the ground, Smith became angry. Bogan then threw the chair back on the wagon, and again taunted Smith. Smith looked down at Bogan and said, 'I do not whip dogs, otherwise I'd step down and whip you'.

'Doll' Smith was a well-respected and even-tempered man, but Bogan's taunts began to wear thin. He climbed down from his wagon and headed toward Bogan and as Smith walked toward him, Bogan put his hand into his coat pocket. Smith told him that if he pulled a gun on him, he'd knock him to the ground. Bogan pulled his pistol, at which point Smith knocked him down with one punch. The two men wrestled briefly before Smith was able to take the young man's gun from him. As he did this, Dave Kemp ran over producing his own handgun, and hit Smith in the back of the head. Smith then turned, pulled out his own pistol and pulled the trigger. Fortunately for Kemp, the pistol misfired and, according to eyewitnesses, Kemp ran away leaving his friend still sprawled on the ground. With the arrival of the town Marshal, 'Doll' Smith turned Bogan's pistol over to him. After a night in the cells Dan Bogan was released with a warning.

A few days after the incident Dan Bogan left Hamilton and returned to working on ranches in and around the Texas Panhandle. In 1884, a cowboys' strike for better wages took place. Dan Bogan was one of the ringleaders, but the ranchers were too powerful and the strike ended with all those who took part being blacklisted. Finding himself unable to work in the Panhandle, Bogan rode to Wilbarger County, Texas, and joined up for a cattle drive as a drover with the Worsham R-2 Ranch. Jack Burkett, who was also working on that drive, said some years later when asked about Dan Bogan, that Bogan was a valuable hand to have around, and that one night during a fierce thunderstorm, he had stopped 600 head of cattle from stampeding all by himself. When the drive reached Dodge City, Kansas, the cowboys were paid off and commenced to drink and party. When things started to get out of hand, Town Marshal Jack Bridges and his deputies confronted them and attempted to run them out of town. A brief gunfight between the lawmen and the cowboys ensued, during which one of the cowboys, John Briley, was shot and killed. With the death of their friend, Bogan and Burkett, who were both involved in that escapade, decided to leave, with the others, but took no action in retaliation.

On returning to the Panhandle, Dan Bogan, who had changed his name to Bill Gatlin, learned that things hadn't changed but in fact had got worse for the blacklisted cowboys. He then joined up with cowboy Tom Harris, who had organised what he called the 'Get Even Cattle Company' (a new name for 'rustling'), which involved altering the brand on already-branded calves owned by the ranchers and replacing it with one of their own. Bogan registered two of the brands in his own name. The ranchers and county officials commissioned the former sheriff of Lincoln County, New Mexico, Pat Garrett, to stop the cowboys, and in doing so it was quietly suggested he 'should' or 'could', kill the ringleaders, which included Dan Bogan.

Pat Garrett and his followers rounded up thirty head of cattle that bore Dan Bogan's brand, stating they were stolen. Bogan claimed they were mavericks and approached a lawyer by the name of H.H. Wallace. He in turn demanded that Oldham County officials pay $25,000 in damages to Dan Bogan for the illegal seizure of his cattle. Fearing he might have a case, the county settled for $800, which was accepted by Dan Bogan. By the end of the year, 159 indictments had been handed down against the cowboys, Bogan being one, and Garrett and his men set out to round the cowboys up. Garrett, however, did not want trouble and made no effort to disguise the fact that he was out to arrest the cowboys. But he also made it abundantly clear that he would be more than satisfied if they just left.

In February 1885 Pat Garrett and Oldham County Sheriff Jim East together with a posse, learned that three of the cowboys on the indictment who had refused to leave the Panhandle, were among those hiding out at the Howry Cattle Company headquarters. Riding all night through a snowstorm, the posse reached the house in which the cowboys were believed to be hiding. One of the cowboys, Bob Bassett, who was outside the house gathering firewood, had spotted the posse and alerted the others. Tom Harris then yelled out to Garrett asking what his business was, to which Garrett replied that he had warrants for Woods, Bogan and Thompson, but had no issues with anyone else so they could leave. Not wanting to get involved, nine of the cowboys left the house, leaving only Thompson and Bogan inside. Woods was not present. Bogan and Thompson, however, refused to surrender, and a shoot-out started, during which Dan Bogan slipped out of the back and made his escape. Thompson was killed and three posse members were wounded during the exchange of gunfire.

By 1886, Bogan was in Wyoming working for the Vorhees Ranch, near Lusk, Wyoming. It was around this time that he got involved with the law once again, this time for the alleged murder of a dance hall proprietor who stopped Dan Bogan and his men from entering his saloon. Bogan, who was still using the name of Bill Gatlin, decided to confront the owner and forced his way into the establishment, where he met the proprietor with a rifle in his hands. Dan Bogan drew his revolver and shot him in cold blood, later claiming self-defence. Bill Calkin, who was the editor of the local newspaper, wrote that Bogan was possibly a cowboy wanted in Texas, and who had used at least two other names in the past. Bogan was infuriated, and set out looking for him, together with another cowboy, Sterling Balou. The two men went into the Cleveland Brothers Saloon, calling for Calkin and waving their pistols around, daring any of his friends to challenge them. One of the Cleveland brothers appeared carrying a sawn-off shotgun and pointed it at the two cowboys, then seconds later Constable Charles Gunn entered carrying a pistol. With two guns now pointed at them, Dan Bogan and Sterling Balou beat a hasty retreat.

Still incensed and humiliated by what had happened, Dan Bogan went back into town, after hearing that Charles Gunn was away, to remonstrate with Calkin. After causing a disturbance in the town, but unable to find Calkin, Dan Bogan left. When Charles Gunn returned he sought out Bogan and told him that if he came into town again and caused trouble he would slap him in jail in an instant. Bogan replied saying that he would do as he pleased and walked away. Charles Gunn was a former Texas Ranger and had a reputation for not backing down to anyone. He was known to have killed at least two men whilst in office. It was this reputation that Bogan feared.

Things came to a head on 14 January 1887, when Dan Bogan rode into town and headed straight for the dance hall, where he immediately got into a fight. Constable Gunn was summoned and on entering the dance hall forced Dan Bogan to back down and leave. The following morning Constable Gunn was making his normal rounds and upon entering Jim Waters' Saloon was confronted by Dan Bogan. 'Are you heeled Charlie?' shouted Bogan, meaning was he armed. 'I'm always armed', replied Gunn. Bogan then produced a pistol from behind his back and shot Gunn in the stomach. As Gunn fell to the floor, he went to pull his own weapon, but Bogan walked over to him and shot him in the head, killing him instantly. Bogan waved his pistol at the customers in the saloon in a threatening manner and then ran for the door. Once outside, he jumped on the nearest horse and started to ride out of town. Deputy Town Marshal John Owens, on hearing the gunshots, ran out of his office carrying a loaded shotgun and stood in the street blocking

Bogan's way out. Firing a warning shot over Bogan's head he ordered him to dismount. Ignoring the warning Dan Brogan rode straight at the deputy. John Owens fired a second shot, this time hitting Bogan in the shoulder and knocking him from the horse and onto the ground.

As there was no jail in Lusk at the time, Dan Bogan was placed in the back room of a local saloon, but the next day, in fact even before his shotgun wound had started to heal, he took advantage of the poor security and made an escape during a howling blizzard. Owens, knowing that Bogan was badly wounded and because of the worsening weather, believed he could not go far. Two weeks later Bogan, now burning up with fever from his infected wound, sent word to Owens that he wanted to surrender and receive medical attention. Dan Bogan met with John Owens 16 miles outside of Lusk, and told Owens that he feared a lynch mob would be waiting for him when they reached Lusk, as Gunn was extremely well liked and respected in the town. Bogan was right to be worried because as they entered town, John Owens had to face down a mob that was intent on lynching Bogan. Owens shackled Bogan in the back of the Sweeney Saloon and placed a guard on him. The following day, Owens left with Bogan en route to Cheyenne, Wyoming, and a couple of days later had him secured in the Laramie County Jail.

On 7 September 1887, after a short trial, Dan Bogan was convicted of the murder of Charles Gunn, and sentenced to death. However, Bogan still had several friends in cowboy circles, namely Tom Hall, whom detective Charlie Siringo would later identify as Tom Nicholls, a murderer from the Texas Panhandle. In a scheme to help Dan Bogan, Hall paid a professional safecracker by the name of James Jones, to commit a minor crime in Cheyenne then allow himself to be captured and placed in jail with Bogan. Concealed in his shoes, Jones had hacksaw blades, which he and Bogan used to saw through the bars and make an escape on 4 October 1887. Accompanied by two other prisoners, Charles H. LeRoy and Bill Steary, both horse thieves, they made their escape through a ventilator and onto the roof. But it wasn't long before their escape was discovered and within hours a posse was organised in one of the largest manhunts in Wyoming history.

The posse, consisting of 100 men, split into two groups of 50, and was led by Laramie County Sheriff Seth Sharpless. As an incentive, a $1,000 reward was placed on Bogan, dead or alive. Despite weeks of extensive searching Dan Bogan was not found. In an effort to find out something of his whereabouts, Charlie Siringo, acting on information he had received from various sources, went undercover and was able to gain the confidence of Hall and some of the other outlaws. He discovered

FOR:
☆ Murder of a peace officer
☆ Escape from Laramie
   County Jail

DESCRIPTION:
☆ Aged 28 years
☆ Height 5'9"
☆ Dark hair, short cut
☆ Dark brown mustache
☆ Weight 160 lbs.
☆ No. 6 boot
☆ Thin lips
☆ Bluish gray eyes
☆ Walks slightly stooped
☆ Old scar on back of neck

CIRCULAR ISSUED:
October 6, 1887

☞ REWARD:

$1,000⁰⁰

for capture or body.
Notify Laramie
County Sheriff Sharpless
at Cheyenne,
Wyoming Territory

DAN BOGAN
alias Bill McCoy

Wanted poster for Dan Bogan.

that Dan Bogan was no longer riding with them, and had made his way toward Utah. An additional advantage of Siringo's undercover work was that he was able to produce evidence for indictments against Hall and several others for their having assisted Bogan when they were later arrested.

Charlie Siringo continued to pursue Bogan, first into Utah, then into New Mexico Territory, where he came into contact with Lem Woodruff, an old Panhandle friend of Bogan. Woodruff told him that the last he heard of Bogan was that he was heading for New Orleans, Louisiana, intending on taking a ship to South America, stating he was tired of living on the run. The last factual contact with Dan Bogan was in a letter sent to Tom Hall in Cheyenne, from New Orleans, saying he was heading to Argentina.

Nothing more was ever heard of Dan Bogan, although there were a number of stories and rumours as to what happened to him. In one newspaper, the *Laramie Sentinel*, they claimed that he had been killed in a gunfight in Mexico. Then it was rumoured that he was riding with

Pinkerton detective
Charlie Siringo.

outlaws in Argentina. Charlie Siringo was convinced that Dan Bogan had slipped back into the United States under an assumed name, had married and raised a family on a small ranch. He never revealed where he had acquired this information but it was supported some years later by a former friend of Dan Bogan, a man named Campbell, who in 1931 said that Dan Bogan was alive and well living with his family on a small ranch in Texas. Everything else is just speculation.

Chapter 28

Reuben Burrow

Born in Lamar County, Alabama, on 11 December 1855, Reuben Burrow worked on the family farm until the age of 18. He then moved to Stephenville, Texas, to work on his uncle's ranch, with the intention of saving enough money to buy a ranch of his own. At the age of 25 he purchased a small spread and got married to Virginia Alvison. He and his wife had two children and Reuben settled down to farm the land. Tragedy then struck when his young wife was struck down with yellow fever and died, leaving him to care for two small children. Four years later he remarried and the family moved to Alexander, Texas. Times were hard and when his crops failed Reuben found himself almost

A young Ruben Burrow.

destitute with a wife and two children to support, and in 1886 he turned to crime with his brother Jim and it was at this point that his wife left him, taking the two children with her.

On 11 December 1886, whilst returning from a trip in the Indian Territory with his brother Jim, they unexpectedly met up with two friends, Henderson Brumley and Nep Thornton. Desperately short of money the four men decided to rob the Denver & Fort Worth Express train.

Reuben Burrow and the other men waited at the train depot at Bellevue, Texas, until the train arrived, then pointing their guns at the crew and in full view of the passengers, they entered the train. The *Fort Worth Daily Gazette* later reported the robbery, saying that the train robbers were only able to get $100 and some watches, as the passengers were able to hide most of their valuables by the time the outlaws passed through. In one of the cars, a sergeant of the Union Army's 24th Infantry Regiment accompanied by two privates, were escorting two deserters in shackles. The passengers persuaded the sergeant and the two privates not to fire at the outlaws because they did not want to be caught up in a gunfight. The gang took the sergeant and the privates' weapons and Reuben used the sergeant's Colt revolver

Ruben and Jim Burrow.

throughout his crime-ridden days. The sergeant was later accused of cowardice by his superiors following the robbery despite evidence from the passengers to the contrary. Boosted by the relative success of the robbery, Reuben Burrow had already begun planning his next hold-up.

On 9 June 1887, Reuben Burrow and his gang, now augmented by William Brock, one of Reuben's ranch hands, boarded the Texas & Pacific Express, which was heading eastbound from Benbrook. Burrow held the engineer at gunpoint and forced him to stop the train on a trestle bridge outside the town. This was done deliberately to discourage any of the passengers, who would have to 'brave the heights and the dangerous footing' in an attempt to interfere with the robbery. The proceeds of the robbery netted the robbers $1,350 and three registered letters of an unknown value were taken from the mail car. How much the Burrow gang escaped with is not clear, but it was enough for them to feel confident enough to carry out a second train robbery three months later at the same spot. News reports later estimated that the gang escaped with cash estimated between $12,000 and $30,000.

Two months later, on 9 December, Reuben and Jim Burrow and William Brock stopped the St. Louis, Arkansas & Texas Railroad express train at Genoa, Arkansas. The three men escaped with a Louisiana lottery payoff estimated to be between $10,000 and $40,000, despite the train being guarded by Southern Express guards. The Pinkerton Detective Agency then became involved because the Southern Express Company was a client of theirs. Within days Pinkerton detectives, lawmen and bounty hunters alike were alerted and the hunt was on. Within a few days, the first lead came to light when a deputy sheriff of a small town reported to two Pinkerton detectives that he had encountered three suspicious men on the day of the robbery. One of the men left behind a raincoat that was eventually traced to a store in Dublin, Texas, where the sales clerk identified the man who bought the coat as William Brock. Brock was quickly traced and arrested and once behind bars confessed to having taken part in the robbery and naming Reuben Burrow as the ringleader.

Reuben Burrow had no criminal record and the authorities had no idea what he looked like. Brock told the detectives that he did not know where Reuben Burrow was and was remanded in custody. Then came a breakthrough when the Pinkerton detectives intercepted a letter to Brock from Reuben Burrow. He had conveniently written a return address on the back of the envelope. The detectives immediately organised a posse and headed for a homestead in Lamar County, Alabama, the return address for Reuben Burrow.

On arriving at the homestead the posse surrounded the house. However, Jim Burrow had been warned of their approach after the detectives had made enquiries in a nearby town and on entering the house the posse found that Reuben Burrow and his brother Jim had escaped and were now on the run.

Just two weeks later they were spotted on a Louisville & Nashville train in southern Alabama by the train's conductor. As it arrived in Montgomery, police surrounded the train and called for the two outlaws to surrender. A gunfight then started, but then ended as quickly as it started when Jim Burrow was overpowered and captured. During the police's brief struggle with Jim Burrow, his brother Reuben managed to shoot his way out. One passenger aboard the train, a man named Neb Broy, attempted to follow Reuben Burrow but was shot in the chest. It is not known if he survived. A second posse was quickly formed and headed after Reuben Burrow, but despite wounding him, he escaped. Jim Burrow was taken first to the jail in Little Rock, Arkansas and then Texarkana. However, he died less than a year later of tuberculosis on 5 October 1888, before he could stand trial.

Reuben Burrow, now wanted by the law in several states, changed his name to Joe Jackson and joined up again with William Brock. The two men boarded the Illinois Central express train at Duck Hill, Mississippi, and attempted to rob the passengers. When the conductor became aware of what was happening, two of the passengers, Chester Hughes and John Wilkenson, grabbed their weapons and ran to the express car where Reuben Burrow was in the process of robbing the US Mail. On bursting into the express car, they pointed their weapons at Reuben Burrow who immediately opened fire, killing Chester Hughes and wounding John Wilkenson. The senseless killing of someone trying to prevent a robbery not only incensed the press and the public, but concerned the railroads, as they thought that the public would not feel safe travelling on their trains.

One might have thought that the continuing narrow escapes were beginning to worry Reuben Burrow and would have made him more cautious, but in fact it had the opposite effect as he became more reckless. In July 1889, Reuben Burrow went to the post office in Lamar County to collect a package. When the postmaster, Mose Graves, asked him to sign for the package, a violent row broke out between them after Burrow refused. Pulling out his pistol, Burrow shot the man dead in cold blood and rode away. This senseless killing angered the local people and it was made quite clear that Reuben Burrow was not welcome in the county and that he would get no assistance from any of them. Why he refused to sign is still a mystery, because the only thing in the package was a false beard that he was going to use in an attempt to disguise himself.

Reuben Burrow and William Brock had now been joined by Reuben's cousin Rube Smith and the three of them carried out train robberies seemingly relentless. The Mobile & Ohio express train was robbed near Buckattunna, Mississippi followed by the North Western Railroad train in Louisiana shortly afterwards. The Pinkerton detectives were constantly playing catch-up and at one point came close to apprehending them in Blount County, Alabama, but were forced to turn back after coming under intense gunfire in which two of their trackers, William Woodward and Harry Annertoni, were killed and three other members of the posse were wounded.

Reuben Burrow was now becoming the most wanted man in America and the subject of intense manhunts. Bounty hunters and lawmen had his name at the top of their 'wanted' lists. It was to take another two years before he was finally captured. In the meantime the three outlaws moved to Flomaton, Escambia County, but only days after arriving Rube Smith and one of his friends, James McClung, were caught trying to rob a train at Amory, Mississippi.

When it was realised that the remainder of the Burrows Gang were still in the vicinity, the hunt intensified, concentrating on the southern area of Alabama. Then came a breakthrough when a ferryman at a crossing near Milton, Florida, recognised a wanted poster for Burrow and Brock and told the detective that the two had split up after their crossing and that Burrow was working at a logging camp across the Yellow River in Santa Rosa County, Florida. A posse approached the logging camp, but once again Reuben Burrow had somehow got wind of them and had disappeared into the forest. Then news came through that William Brock had been captured travelling on a train when it stopped at the Fernbank station in Lamar County. He was taken to a prison in Memphis, Tennessee, to await trial.

After a short trial, William Brock was given a life sentence for his part in the murder of Chester Hughes and the robbery of the Illinois express, but committed suicide by leaping from the top floor of the penitentiary.

Reuben Burrow was now alone, but it didn't stop him carrying out another train robbery when he robbed the Louisville & Nashville train at Pollard. The Pinkerton detectives were now hot on his heels and they traced him back to the logging camp at Santa Rosa, but once again he slipped through their fingers and headed into the backwoods.

For the next couple of months all was quiet, although still the manhunt went on. Then just outside Demopolis in Marengo County he was recognised by a man who befriended Reuben Burrow and persuaded him to join him for dinner at his friend's house. On arriving at the house the man and his friend and a couple of others, overpowered and held him until the arrival of two of Pinkerton's detectives. The detectives bound him to a horse and took him to the jail in Linden at the Marengo County seat.

The following morning, 9 October 1890, Reuben Burrow, who was still bound hand and foot in the jail, asked that his hands could be released so that he could eat. The moment that this was done he took a hidden pistol from inside his jacket, locked the deputies in the cell and started to escape. Outside he was confronted by a local man, Jefferson Davis Carter, and opened fire with his pistol. Jefferson Carter was hit in the stomach by one of the shots, knocking him to the ground, but as he fell he fired his own pistol, hitting Ruben Burrow in the chest and killing him instantly.

Reuben Barrow's body was placed in a coffin and shipped back to Lamar County by train. Such was Burrow's notoriety that the train stopped at almost every station en route so that the public could see the body of the infamous train robber displayed. On reaching the town of Sulligent, the body was collected by his father and buried.

Body of train robber Ruben Burrow on display in his coffin.

Chapter 29

Cullen Montgomery Baker

Cullen Montgomery Baker was born in Weakley County, Tennessee, on 23 June 1835. Soon after he was born the family moved to Clarksville, Arkansas, where his father was an honest hard-working farmer, who raised cattle as well as working in the fields. As Cullen Baker matured he spent much of his time in the saloons and bars in what is now Lafayette and Miller Counties. Even as a young man Cullen Baker is said to have had a quick and violent temper, which was to become more apparent as he got older, especially when he drank heavily and often.

On 11 January 1854 in Cass County, Texas, at the age of 19, Cullen Baker married Martha Jane Petty, the daughter of Hubbard and Nancy

Cullen Baker.

Petty, and for a time he settled into normal family life. However, just eight months into his marriage and while out drinking with friends, he became involved in a violent argument with a young man called Stallcup. As the argument got more hostile, an enraged Baker grabbed a whip and beat the boy so viciously that he almost killed him. There were several witnesses to the incident, some of whom had dragged Baker away and Baker was arrested and charged with the crime. He was granted bail and allowed to return to his home, but then the following day he went to the home of one of the witnesses,

Wesley Bailey, and confronted him. After a brief but angry exchange of words Baker shot Bailey in both legs with a shotgun, then left him lying in front of his house. Despite medical attention, Wesley Bailey died a few days later. A warrant was issued for Cullen Baker's arrest, but before he could be arrested for the murder, he fled to Arkansas, where he stayed with an uncle, leaving his wife to fend for herself. On 24 May 1855, Martha Jane Baker gave birth to a baby girl, Louisa Jane. Five years later, on 2 June 1860, Martha Jane Baker died at which point Cullen Baker briefly returned to Texas, where he left his daughter with his in-laws.

Cullen Baker returned to Arkansas, but word of his violent crimes had spread, and a local woman named Beth Warthom was openly critical of him. He took a hickory switch to her house, and threatened to beat her with it, but her husband, David Warthom, fought with Baker and beat him to the ground in front of the house. At this point Beth Warthom screamed, and as her husband was distracted by her, Baker pulled out a concealed knife and stabbed David Warthom in the heart, killing him. Baker got up and ran away then fled back to Texas and again went into hiding. In July 1862, he married his second wife Martha Foster, who was completely unaware that he was wanted for murder in two states.

Although there were warrants out for his arrest, Cullen Baker managed to enlist in the Confederate Army at the beginning of the American Civil War. Supposedly he became an overseer of freemen and, it is claimed, he killed at least three black people before he had even taken the Oath of Allegiance. He was either later discharged from the army or had deserted, but it is known that he joined up with a group of men called the 'Independent Rangers' whose role was to pursue and capture deserters from the Army of the Confederacy. Supposedly aligned with the Confederate Home Guard, the Rangers were made up of some of those they were alleged to be pursuing! Because almost all eligible men were away fighting in the war, the 'Independent Rangers' used their powers to steal, rape and violently attack vulnerable people who were no match for these well-armed thugs. In one incident Cullen Baker led a party of men to intercept a wagon train carrying old men, women and children, who were heading out West away from the fighting. This was considered unpatriotic and Cullen Baker and his men caught up with the party of Arkansas settlers just as they were crossing the Saline River. Baker ordered the party to turn back, but the leader of the group refused so Cullen Baker pulled out his pistol and shot the man dead. After reassuring the remaining members of the wagon train that he would not harm anyone else, he guided them back across the river. On reaching the other side Cullen Baker and his men then started shooting, killing nine elderly men and injuring many others. This became known as the Saline Massacre.

Almost all of Arkansas was under the control of the Union Army with Captain F.S. Dodge in charge of law and order in Lafayette County. Most of the troops under his command were African-American and hated by the racist Cullen Baker. In an incident in 1864 in the small town of Spanish Bluff, Cullen Baker was in a saloon and was approached by four African-American troops, one sergeant and three privates, who asked him for his identification. Baker turned his back on the four soldiers and when asked again, turned around with a pistol in his hand and started firing. In the one-sided gunfight all four soldiers were shot dead. For some unknown reason Cullen Baker was never arrested or charged with the murder of these four soldiers.

At the end of the Civil War lawlessness increased and Cullen Baker teamed up with fellow outlaw Lee Rames to organise a gang. They operated near Bright Star, Arkansas, and carried out numerous robberies and killings, with Cullen Baker reputed to have personally killed at least thirty people including women. The truth is more likely that many of these killings were actually carried out by his gang. It is known that almost all the killings were carried out in ambushes when they outnumbered their victims or shot them in the back when they least expected it. Cullen Baker always carried a shotgun, which was his weapon of choice, as accuracy was almost guaranteed. Some residents of Arkansas regarded Baker as some sort of a hero because of his apparent opposition to the Union Army's occupation, but in fact he really didn't care about politics or loyalty to either side and would kill anyone who got in his way.

With the Union Army chasing them, the gang decided to operate between Arkansas and Texas, mainly in the Queen City and Texarkana areas. For the next two years Cullen Baker and the gang went on what can only be described as a 'killing spree'. The first of these was the killing of a man called John Salmons who had killed one of the gang members, Seth Rames, who was the brother of Lee Rames. The other was a W. Kirkman who had led a posse in a hunt for Cullen Baker. In another incident Baker entered a store in Cass County, Texas, owned by John Rowden, where he found only Mrs Rowden. Baker just took what he wanted and left without paying. When John Rowden found out he rode to where he knew Cullen Baker was and demanded payment. Baker said he would bring the money to the store the following morning. The following morning Baker stood outside the store and called Rowden out. Arming himself with a shotgun, John Rowden walked out of his store and was immediately shot dead by Baker. Cullen Baker fled back to Arkansas, but on the way back, as he boarded a ferry, a US Army sergeant and a private who recognised him and that he was wanted by the law confronted him. Baker said that his name was Johnson and then pulled his gun, shooting the sergeant dead. The private wheeled his horse and rode away to report the killing to his commanding officer, a Captain Kirkham. Immediately a troop of soldiers set off in pursuit with one purpose in mind to catch Cullen Baker dead or alive.

All the US Army forces were put on a state-wide alert and patrols were sent out specifically looking for Cullen Baker and his gang. It wasn't long before another incident with the army occurred when, whilst in New Boston, Texas, he became involved in an argument with several Union soldiers from the 20th Infantry Regiment, which resulted in guns being drawn and a shoot-out. During the exchange of gunfire one of the soldiers was killed but Cullen received a wound to his arm. The army placed a $1,000 reward for his capture – dead or alive. Once again he fled back to Arkansas and with weeks of being there was once again involved in a violent situation. This time it was when an alcohol-fuelled, racially-motivated mob, led by Cullen Baker, decided to raid the farm of a local farmer after he had hired some freed slaves. As they approached the house they came up against some fierce opposition, during which two of the farmer's daughters were injured and one of the black workers was shot and killed. After a couple of hours of shooting, in which a number of the mob were wounded, including Cullen Baker who was shot in the leg, they left to lick their wounds and sober up.

Cullen Baker's private war against the Army and law and order continued when he and his gang were involved in the deaths of a Major Andrews, Lieutenant Willis and a black soldier and the wounding of Sheriff Standel of Little Rock, Arkansas, during an incident in the town. But time was running out for Cullen Baker, as a number of the gang, including the co-leader Lee Rames, were concerned with the recklessness being shown by Baker. In a confrontation with Lee Rames, Cullen Baker backed down knowing of the man's reputation, which was equal to his own. The gang sided with Lee Rames, with the exception of a gang member called Kirby, who sided with Baker, and they went their separate ways.

Cullen Baker and Kirby then went to his in-law's home and as they walked around the side of the house they were approached by a small band of men, led by a man called Thomas Orr, who immediately opened fire on the pair of them, killing them both instantly. It appears that Thomas Orr was the local schoolteacher and had become romantically involved with Cullen Baker's wife Martha and was having an affair with her. Knowing Cullen Baker's reputation, the pair decided to kill him, which was done with the full knowledge of her family, who never approved of him.

There was another version of Cullen's death, and that was that he was killed by drinking some whiskey laced with poison. His body was then dragged outside and a number of bullets fired into it just to make sure. Whatever version is true, the fact remains that Cullen Baker met what many considered a justified violent death and Arkansas and Texas were rid of a violent murderer. The bodies of the two gang members were dragged through the town of Bloomsburg for all to see, and were then taken to the US Army fort at Jefferson where they were placed on public display before being buried in the local cemetery.

Chapter 30

Bill Posey

William Andrew Jackson Posey was born on 16 June 1846, in Talapoosa, Alabama, and was the fourteenth of fifteen children. His parents, Benjamin Franklin Posey and Eliza Berryhill, were first cousins, each one-half Creek Indian. Soon after he was born, the family moved to Nacogdoches County, Texas. His early years were unremarkable, that was until, at the age of 18, he joined the Confederate Army in the Civil War. Not long after joining up he deserted whilst stationed at Camp Hood on Padre Island in 1864.

Nothing is known of his whereabouts until the following year when he married Elizabeth Wallace. The couple settled on Tehuacana Creek, north of Waco, near her brother and sister-in-law Matt and Sarah Wallace, and the two couples went into business together driving cattle along the Chisholm Trail to Kansas to take advantage of the East's desperate hunger for beef. Buyers at the time paid $3 a head for cattle in Texas, but $15 a head at the railheads in Kansas. Bill Posey, as he now called himself, used the profits to buy 500 acres of land along the Brazos River just east of Waco. In addition he bought the 666 acres of land that was inherited by Sarah Wallace for $5,000, on the

Bill Posey.

understanding that it was payable at $1,000 a year for five years. It was during the purchase of these parcels of land that accusations of cattle rustling started to emerge concerning Bill Posey's part in the theft. Cattle displaying the brands of other ranches were spotted in amongst Posey's herds, prompting charges of theft to be filed against him.

The allegations confirmed the Wallaces' suspicions and so they decided to distance themselves from any further business dealings with him and so severed the business arrangement. Although not a lot of information about Bill Posey exists regarding the allegations and his part in them, what little can be found points to him being an arrogant and ruthless cowboy who terrorized Texas and the Indian Territory. Posey and his men rustled herds of cattle, caused mayhem in towns during violent drinking binges, tormented citizens and defied the law. A number of drunken incidents and their indiscriminate shootings left innocent victims wounded. It was rumoured that when a deputy sheriff tried to intervene in one of the towns, Posey killed him in a saloon shoot-out on the Guadalupe, and then scalped him.

Still angry about his brother-in-law's decision to end his relationship with him, he decided to seek revenge. Late one night in June 1873, he

Outlaws Matt Wallace and Bill Posey.

and some members of his gang rode up to the Wallaces' ranch and forced their way into the house. In front of Wallace's wife and two-year-old daughter, they grabbed Matt Wallace and dragged him outside. They tied his hands behind his back, lifted him on to a horse and placed a rope with a noose that one of the gang had thrown over a branch, over his head. Seconds later, in front of his distraught wife and daughter, someone slapped the horse's rump and Matt Wallace's body jerked backwards and then downwards. With his lifeless body swaying and turning in the still air, the only sounds that could be heard was the wailing of his pregnant wife as she watched horrified.

His reign of terror continued, and then in the summer of 1874, he was arrested for stealing some mules and sentenced to five years in prison. Even in prison he still continued his violence and attacked warders and prisoners alike. Despite numerous beatings from both prisoners and prison officers, Bill Posey remained a violent psychopath. He was placed on a chain gang with a 12lb ball attached to his leg in an attempt to control him. Just two years into his sentence he escaped. He attacked one of the guards, striking him down with a rock and then grabbed his gun. Seeing some horses grazing nearby he moved towards them. Keeping the horse between himself and the other guards, he quickly mounted it and rode off. He rode to his father's house where the ball and chain were removed, and he acquired fresh clothes, weapons and a horse before riding off into the Indian Territory.

Some months later he was in a temporary home in Cane Creek, when two deputy US marshals arrived with a warrant for his arrest. He invited them into the house for a meal, which they accepted. Once in the house he suddenly reached under a chair and produced a pistol and opened fire, shooting one of the deputies in the thigh and the other on the side of the head. Taking the warrant from them he destroyed it and then disarmed them. Then, in an obvious show of defiance, he allowed the two wounded deputies to leave and go back to Fort Smith and report. For the next two years, despite there being warrants for his arrest, he continued to evade the law, and such was the fear that he engendered, that there were reports that he would walk on the streets of Muscogee and Okmulkee when lawmen, who were three to his one, were afraid to attempt his arrest.

The Governor of Texas decided that enough was enough; Bill Posey was making a mockery of law and order in the state and so he approached the Chief of the Creek Nation for his help. Chief Ward Coachman agreed and ordered Captain Suntharpee of Utechee to bring Posey in dead or alive. Word reached the captain that Posey had been seen in Okmulgee and had had

Chief Ward Coachman of the Creek Indians.

a damaged finger amputated. He had then been seen riding towards the Arkansas River. With two of his officers, Captain Suntharpee picked up his trail and followed him for a couple of days. They found him on Polecat Creek, near Conchartee Town driving some stray horses, and ordered him to surrender. Showing his usual disdain for the law and in a gesture of defiance he reach for his Henry rifle. But the loss of his finger caused him to fumble for it and before he could pull it clear from its scabbard, one of the officers opened fire with a shotgun sending a load of buckshot into his right arm, breaking it and forcing him to drop the rifle. Poser then pulled his pistol from its holster and fired two shots before a second blast from a shotgun shattered his left arm. Spurring his horse Posey charged at the captain, knocking him from his horse and into the creek. Turning his horse towards the other two officers he charged at them, but they stood their ground and opened fire with their revolvers. In the meantime Captain Suntharpee had regained his feet and opened fire with his revolver. His bullet tore Posey's nose from his face and smashed through his brain, killing him instantly and sending his now-lifeless body crashing to the ground. His reign of terror was finally over.

Chapter 31

William 'Curly Bill' Brocius

Nothing is known about William 'Curly Bill' Brocius until about 1878 when he appeared with a stolen herd of cattle in the San Carlos Reservation, Arizona. He then went to work for the Cochise County Sheriff John Behan as a tax collector, which in effect was collecting revenue from other cattle rustlers. The money from these collections went to the sheriff and was added to his salary.

There are varying reports of 'Curly Bill' Brocius's description but there are no substantiated photographs. The accepted description is that he had curly black hair, was well built and had a freckled complexion. 'Curly Bill' Brocius should not be confused with that of another outlaw by the name of 'Curly Bill' Graham who was also in the same territory at the time and was later shot dead by Deputy Sheriff James Houck in a gunfight. The spelling of his name Brocius was confirmed as correct by a letter addressed to him found at his mail drop in Tombstone, Arizona.

Whilst in Cochise County he was involved in a number of drunken escapades including making a preacher 'dance' by firing pistol shots around his feet whilst he was conducting a sermon and in another incident he forced some Mexican peasants at a local dance to strip off and dance naked by threatening them with a pistol.

Brocius drifted around Texas for the next year and then

A very dapper 'Curly Bill' Brocius.

217

reappeared in Tombstone, Arizona, in October 1880, where he had his first recorded serious brush with the law. During a drunken night out with some of his friends, the party were firing their pistols into the air in a dark lot between two buildings. Town Marshal Fred White, together with Deputy Town Marshal Wyatt Earp, had been called to deal with the disturbance and approached the group. Fred White said to Brocius, 'I am an officer of the law, give me your pistol', and attempted to jerk Brocius's gun from his hand. In the tussle the gun discharged, shooting Fred White in the groin. Wyatt Earp immediately whipped out his gun and pistol-whipped Bill Brocius to the ground. Brocius was taken into custody and arrested for attempted murder, whilst Fred White was rushed to the doctors. Fred White gave a statement at the doctors saying that the shooting was not deliberate and that it was an accident. However, two days later White died of his injuries and such was the feeling of anger in the town that Bill Brocius feared that he would be dragged from the jail and lynched. The town's two deputies, Wyatt Earp and George Collins, also feared that there could be a reprisal, because Fred White was popular and well liked in the community, so it was decided to take 'Curly Bill' Brocius to Tucson to stand trial.

During the trial Wyatt Earp testified that he did not believe Brocius had shot Fred White deliberately, which supported the statement of Fred White. It was also said that Brocius's gun at the time contained six

bullets and only one had been fired. It was also discovered, during a demonstration, that the gun could be fired even with the hammer half-cocked. After Brocius spent almost two months in jail awaiting trial, the jury returned a verdict of accidental death.

Controversy was never far away from Bill Brocius and on 8 March 1881 he and his friend Johnny Ringo were in the town of Maxey, near Camp Thomas, Arizona, when he was involved in a shooting once again. A cowboy by the name of Dick Lloyd had been drinking and playing cards in two of the saloons, O'Neil's

'Curly Bill' Brocius.

and Franklins during the day and was involved in shooting one of the people he was playing with. He then appeared again in O'Neil's saloon where Brocius, Ringo and a number of other men were drinking, riding his horse and firing his gun into the air. The men in the saloon took exception to the drunken cowboy and almost all of the patrons took out their guns and shot him. During an inquest into the incident and the death of the cowboy, the owner of the saloon, John O'Neil, took the blame for the incident and was acquitted.

Wanted poster for Johnny Ringo.

'Curly Bill' Brocius left Maxey soon afterwards and went to the town of Galeyville, Arizona, in October 1881, where he met up with Deputy Town Marshal Billy Breakenridge and Jim Wallace, a 'Cowboy' who had been involved in the Lincoln County War. The two men were drinking with other 'Cowboys' when Wallace made some insulting comments about Tombstone Deputy Marshal Billy Breakenridge. Breakenridge chose to ignore the remarks, putting it down to the alcohol speaking, but Brocius took offence at the comments directed at his friend and asked Wallace to apologise. After an argument Wallace complied and apologised, but Brocius wouldn't let it go and threatened to kill Wallace, making reference to Wallace's part in the Lincoln County War. Wallace decided to leave the saloon and walked out on to the street, followed by Bill Brocius shouting that he was going to kill him anyway. With that Wallace whirled around with his gun in his hand and fired, wounding Brocius in the face and neck. At this point Billy Breakenridge arrested Wallace and took him into custody. At a later trial Jim Wallace was acquitted as the jury believed that he had acted in self-defence.

Two of 'Curly Bill' Brocius's few friends were Bill Leonard and Harry Head. It is said that when he heard that they had both been killed during an attempted robbery of a store by the owners William and Isaac Haslett, he and Johnny Ringo rode to New Mexico and killed the brothers in revenge. There were no witnesses, but it would have been typical of Brocius to do this.

On 6 January 1881 'Curly Bill' Brocius and his 'Cowboy' gang held up and robbed the Tombstone to Benson stagecoach. The following day Deputy Town Marshal Wyatt Earp put together a posse and set after the gang, but they had disappeared into the Chiricahua Mountains. A couple of months later Bill Brocius returned to Tombstone and it was whilst he was there that an inquest into the death of Morgan Earp was taking place. One of those implicated in the killing was Pete Spence, and his wife Marietta named 'Curly Bill' Brocius as being one of those involved. Justice of the Peace Wells Spicer, who was conducting the inquest, dismissed her testimony on the grounds that it was hearsay evidence and not admissible although there was a great deal of speculation that Brocius was involved.

In July 1881 a herd of Mexican cattle was ambushed by the 'Cowboys' in Skeleton Canyon and six of the Mexican vaqueros were killed. The surviving vaqueros, it was discovered later, had been tortured then killed. It was said that Brocius sold the herd to Newman Clanton, father of the known rustlers Ike and Billy Clanton who were involved in the OK Corral shoot-out. A week later Newman Clanton was taking the stolen cattle to Tombstone, when he and his companions were ambushed in Guadalupe Canyon by Mexicans bent on revenge and the return of their cattle. Although Bill Brocius was almost certainly behind the killing of the vaqueros and the theft of the cattle, no evidence could be found that would implicate him.

Nothing more was heard of 'Curly Bill' Brocius until 24 March 1882. Wyatt Earp was leading a posse in search of the 'Cowboys' and had arranged to meet a man called Charlie Smith at Iron Springs, in the Whetstone Mountains. Charlie Smith was bringing money from Tombstone to allay the expenses that the posse was incurring. As the posse approached the springs, they came across a group of men camping. They immediately recognised the men as 'Curly Bill' Brocius, Milt and Bill Hicks, Johnny Barnes, Frank Patterson, Ed and Johnny Lyle, and Bill Johnson – the 'Cowboys'. The men immediately reached for their weapons as Wyatt Earp dismounted with a shotgun in his hands. Bill Brocius was the first to open fire, aiming at Wyatt Earp. This was the man who 18 months earlier had saved him from a lynch mob and had given testimony in his defence that got him acquitted of murder. Brocius opened fire with his shotgun and missed, Wyatt Earp returned fire and did not miss, almost cutting the outlaw in half. In the ensuing gunfight some of the 'Cowboys' got away, but the posse had also suffered a number of casualties and withdrew. The remaining 'Cowboys' took Brocius's body away and buried it on the nearby ranch of Frank Patterson. The exact location has never been discovered.

In his biography, Wyatt Earp mentions that during the time he had met 'Curly Bill' Brocius he learned that he had been convicted of a robbery in El Paso, Texas in 1878 during which a man was killed. He had been convicted of the offence, but shortly after being sent to the penitentiary he had managed to escape. It is also thought that William 'Curly Bill' Brocius was in fact a man known as William 'Curly Bill' Bresnaham, who was also convicted of a robbery in El Paso in 1878 along with another man named Robert Martin, and later became the leader of a gang of rustlers that terrorised ranches in the Arizona Territory.

Chapter 32

John Larn

John Larn was born in Mobile, Alabama, on 1 March 1849. Little is known of his early years, but as a teenager he travelled to Colorado where he found work as a ranch hand. After a couple of years working on the ranch he got into an argument with his employer over the taking of a horse without permission, and killed him. With the law now looking for him, he fled to New Mexico. A few months later he became involved with the law once again when he killed a local sheriff

he thought was tracking him. Going on the run once again he moved to Texas and settled in Fort Griffin. John Larn then got a job with local rancher Bill Hayes as a trail boss, then in the summer of 1871 it was decided to mount a cattle drive to Trinidad, Colorado Territory, where beef prices were at their highest. This was a joint enterprise with other ranchers mustering some 1,700 head of cattle. John Larn had been chosen because although only 22 years old, he had been on a cattle drive to Colorado before and knew the best route, and was more than capable of handling Texas longhorns and cowboys.

John M. Larn.

The trail hands were a mixed bunch and no different to any other trial herd cowboys, a mixture of experienced trail herders, young greenhorns and a number of wanted men who were trying to keep a low profile. Among the wanted men was Delbert C. Clement, also known as Bill Bush, a self-proclaimed gunman who bragged about the notches on his gun denoting the number of men he claimed he had killed. John Larn chose 'Bush' as his right-hand man, but listened to Charlie Wilson who had been on the trail with the legendary Texas cattlemen Charles Goodnight and Oliver Loving, who both had blazed the trail to Colorado some five years earlier.

Bill Hayes went ahead of the herd to Colorado by stagecoach to negotiate the best price for the cattle before the herd arrived. It was during the cattle drive that an incident with some Mexicans took place resulting in John Larn and Bill Bush shooting dead a number of them and dumping their bodies in the Pecos River. In another incident within the camp, Bill Bush added another notch to his gun when he shot dead one of the greenhorns after a minor disagreement.

In late October, as they moved northwards through New Mexico, Bill Hayes met the herd with fresh supplies and horses, but still hadn't negotiated a price for the cattle. After taking the herd through Raton Pass they bedded the herd down just outside Trinidad to await instructions from Bill Hayes. A bored Bill Bush decided to go into Trinidad for some excitement, stole a valuable racehorse from a stable and rode it up into the mountains. After being pursued by lawmen, he returned the racehorse to the stables, and, it is said, left a note warning the lawmen not to try and arrest him or they would suffer the consequences. In another incident, some of the drovers went into the Trinidad Gambling Hall for a night out, when, during a drunken argument, shots were fired and the sheriff of Animas County, Jaun Cristobal Tafoya, was killed. A posse of deputies followed the drovers back to their camp, but were met by a row of Winchester rifles pointing at them and so left without making an arrest. This type of incident highlights the problems facing lawmen in the early years of the West where the law was ineffectual and heavily outnumbered.

Bill Hayes was having great difficulty in getting a price for his herd and the drovers were getting restless. Hayes paid some of them off and they drifted away, John Larn returned to Fort Worth clutching a 'power of attorney' letter giving him complete control over Hayes's remaining cattle in Shackleford County until the rancher returned.

After some months back in Fort Griffin, John Larn married Mary Jane Matthews, the daughter of one of Shackleford County's most prominent and well-respected citizens. Within several years John Larn himself had become one of the county's respected citizens, and the owner of a small ranch stocked with 500 head of cattle given to him as a wedding present by his father-in-law Joe Matthews. He became a member of the 'Tin Hat Brigade', a vigilante group that worked to bring rustlers and horse thieves to justice. Those who were caught were swiftly brought to justice and hanged from a tree by the river.

John Larn was an active participant in the vigilante committee and gained the respect of the other members. So much so, that in April 1876 he was elected sheriff of Fort Griffin and continued to serve on the vigilante committee. Within weeks of becoming sheriff, John Larn was involved in the hanging of a man caught stealing a horse and, as a warning to others, he was left hanging, although a pick and shovel were left underneath the tree for anyone who had the mind to cut him down and bury him. In the next few weeks six more rustlers and horse thieves were caught and hanged and two others shot and killed.

It soon became obvious to the ranchers that Sheriff John Larn was spending more time controlling the vigilantes than trying to find out who was rustling their cattle. The fact that their cattle were disappearing and those of John Larn's weren't aroused suspicion and things turned unpleasant. Just one year after accepting the job as sheriff, Larn was forced to resign, being replaced by his deputy William Cruger. But no charges were ever brought against him for rustling even though there was a great deal of speculation.

Things turned unpleasant in Shackelford County in 1878, with the return of Bill Hayes after he had managed to dispose of the herd. On his return he discovered that John Larn had mixed all his remaining cattle in with his own. Not a violent man, Bill Hayes decided to get his cattle back one way or another. He was awarded a contract to supply 1,000 head of cattle to the Indian reservation agency at Fort Still in the Indian Territory. Together with his brother John, he hired a crew of drovers with instructions to cut the herd from the ones grazing on the Shackelford County rangeland and to just ignore any other brands that might get mixed up in the round up. Heading up the crew was Bill Bush who had been John Larn's right-hand man on the Colorado drive.

On learning of Bill Hayes intentions, John Larn approached a neighbouring ranch owner, Riley Carter, who also held the post of Constable and asked for a warrant to be issued for the charge of rustling against Bill Hayes and his men. With the warrant in his hand John Larn formed a posse consisting of John Selman and his brother Thomas Selman. The posse then went to Fort Griffin to ask Lieutenant

Colonel George Buell, Commander of the Garrison there for help. Second Lieutenant Edward Turner of 'B' Troop, 10th Cavalry, was given the task accompanied by seventeen Black cavalrymen known as the 'Buffalo Soldiers'. The following is the statement by a young cowboy by the name of Drew Taylor, who witnessed the incident:

> I saw a party of men at a distance, and at first I was not sure whether they were Indians or white men. I stopped for a while and looked at them, and as they did not ride like Indians, I decided they were soldiers. I then galloped my horse around a bunch of cattle I was driving, and was riding west, when suddenly they started on a run toward me. I then stopped and waited until they came up. And as they approached, I heard one of them say, 'Oh, that's just a boy.' They rode up, and one of them asked me if I knew of any cow outfit passing through or camped in that part of the country. I replied, that only that morning I had stopped at the camp of the Hayes brothers, who were resting a trail herd about six miles away. Unhesitatingly I gave them directions, and the pursuing party rode on. 'I did not know then that I had given these inhuman brutes the information that led them to the camp where they brutally murdered unsuspecting and innocent men.
>
> These Negro soldiers, headed by two white outlaws, one by the name of John Larn and the other named John Selman . . . followed the direction I had given them and located the camp of the Hayes outfit.

As they neared the Hayes camp, members of the combined civilian-military posse dismounted and moved closer, using the banks of Bush Knob Creek as cover. There they spotted four men – Bill and John Hayes, Bill Bush and George Snow – eating their noon meal. The other four in the outfit – Jeames, Hearn, Webb and Hazlett – were tending the herd. Then, without warning, the posse opened fire on the four men in the camp; two were killed instantly the remaining two were shot trying to escape. Their bloody work finished at the camp, the deadly pursuers rode after the remaining members of the Hayes outfit. Larn, Selman and the others found Jeames, Hearn, Webb and Hazlett and arrested them without incident. Larn then directed some of his followers to turn the herd back toward Shackelford County.

That night the rest of Hayes's outfit, now under arrest, were shot and killed by the Larn and Selman party. In his official report Lieutenant Turner stated that the four men attempted to escape and had been shot down by the guards. No one in Shackleford County believed a word of their account and considered it a massacre, but the only evidence was that supplied by the Army. It became known as the Bush Knob Massacre.

John Larn continued to live in Shackleford and together with John Selman continued to rustle cattle. Then suddenly he and John Selman were appointed Deputy Hide Inspectors for Shackleford County, with responsibility for inspecting all cattle herds leaving the county, as well as supervising the butchering of the cattle. This was a heaven-sent opportunity for Larn and Selman as they were still supplying Fort Worth with cattle. As more and more cattle went missing from ranches in the county, complaints came flooding in to Sheriff Cruger. Violence erupted in the county with cattle being driven off, horses being shot, and shots being fired at ranchers' houses. Then a group of ranchers secured a warrant to search the river behind Larn's house for hides that did not belong to him. A number of hides were discovered with brands that belonged to other ranches and Larn was arrested. For some unknown reason John Larn was released without charge and the violence continued unabated.

During one incident of rustling, a rancher named Treadwell, who had originally uncovered Larn and Selman's rustling enterprise, was shot and wounded. A warrant was issued for the two men's arrest and Sheriff Cruger was tasked with executing the warrant. He managed to arrest Larn, but Selman had disappeared. Cruger placed John Larn in the local jail, and, because he still had some influential friends in Fort Worth, had him manacled to the floor by the local blacksmith to prevent them helping him to escape.

However, the 'Tin Hat Brigade', prompted by local ranchers, attacked the jail the following night with the intent of dragging John Larn out and hanging him from the tree by the river. When they burst into the jail they discovered Larn had been manacled to the floor, so they opened fire with their guns and shot him dead in his cell. On hearing that John Larn had been captured, John Selman took off and headed for Lincoln County, New Mexico, where he formed a gang called Selman's Scouts.

Chapter 33

Isom Prentice Olive
(aka Print Olive)

Print Olive was born on 7 February 1840 in Mississippi, the second son of James and Julie Brashear Olive. His early childhood was unremarkable, a member of a quiet churchgoing family. In 1861, at the outbreak of the Civil War, Print Olive joined the Confederate Army, enlisting in the 2nd Texas Infantry Regiment. He was involved in the battles of Farmington, Iuka and Shiloh, where he was wounded in action. In 1863 he was captured at Vicksburg. Three days later, because of the enormous amount of Confederate prisoners now having been captured, and still suffering from his wounds, Print Olive was paroled after signing a declaration that he would never take up arms against the United States of America.

He was returned to his regiment which was guarding the docks at Galveston, where he was assigned to supervise the unloading of ships bringing in desperately-needed supplies for the South. Here he spent the rest of the war, returning to the family ranch an embittered, hard-drinking gambler who thought nothing of getting into a fight with either fists or guns. The Reconstruction days in Texas were particularly hard as there was still the bitter taste of defeat in the mouths of many. Print realised that

Isom Prentice (Print) Olive.

he was going to have to work exceptionally hard, long hours to keep the family ranch going.

Then on 4 February 1866, he met and married Louisa Reno in Williamson County, Texas, and settled down as a family man. Over the next eight years he and his wife had four children, three boys and a girl. By this time he had formed a partnership with his brothers Jay Thomas, Bob and Ira, and between them they started to round up and brand some of the thousands of unbranded cattle in the county known as mavericks. The herds would be driven north to towns like Abilene. Wichita, Ellsworth and Dodge City, Kansas. With the assistance of his three brothers, Print quickly became one of the biggest cattle ranchers in the area. Although great fortunes could be made in the cattle industry after the Civil War, it could also be a dangerous business. Print Olive and his brothers were known to take the law into their own hands to protect their property.

On 3 July 1872, Print went into Ellsworth, which was the shipping point for cattle going to the East, to negotiate a favourable offer for the herd, whilst the herd itself was bedded down along the Smoky Hill River just south of the town. Whilst waiting for offers, Print Olive spent time in some of the gambling saloons playing poker with several local men, including James Kennedy, the son of Miflin Kennedy, an extremely wealthy cattle baron.

Jim Kelly.

The incident occurred when James Kennedy, who was unarmed, accused Print Olive of cheating. Print Olive told Kennedy, in no uncertain manner, to cash in his poker chips and leave before he killed him. Later the same evening, Print was playing a hand of poker, when Kennedy walked in, went behind the bar and came out with a handgun. He then walked across the room, pointed the gun at Print Olive, fired a shot that missed and told him to cash in his poker chips. Print Olive threw his hands in the air exclaiming 'Don't shoot', but Kennedy fired again and again. The first shot hit Print in the thigh, the second in the leg and the third in his hand. Fortunately one of Print's men, Jim Kelly, was also present and shot Kennedy in the thigh before hitting him over the head with his gun and then disarming him. Both injured men were taken into custody and then treated by doctors. Kennedy was taken to a room in a hotel under guard, but with the help of friends escaped through a window – he was never recaptured. No charges were brought against Print Olive or Jim Kelly.

The Olive brothers settled down to raising horses and cattle, but then the steady influx of settlers started to cause problems as they tried to settle on the lands where the ranchers grazed their animals. The problem was that this was in effect government land, which the ranchers considered to be theirs. The settlers of course considered the land to be available to anyone who wanted it. Inevitably violence flared between the ranchers and the homesteaders, especially when branded cattle were found in their possession. Print Olive found himself back in court in January 1867, charged with Assault with Intent to Kill or Wound after shooting a homesteader by the name of Rob Murday, who he caught driving some of his cattle. At the trial Murday never appeared to give evidence so the charges were dropped. It was discovered later that Rob Murday's wound had been patched up by Print, and Murday was now an employee of the Olives.

Print Olive was arrested again in March 1872 when he was accused of killing a man by the name of Dave Fream in a gunfight. The case was later dismissed after it was discovered that Fream had been caught rustling the Olives' cattle and had attempted to ambush and kill Bob Olive. One notorious incident in 1875 involved the murder of two suspected rustlers known as Turk Turner and James Crow. The two men were caught butchering some of the Olives' cattle and, as was the law of the day for rustling, sentenced to death. The usual way to carry out sentence was by hanging from the nearest tree, but the Olives had other ideas, they used a barbaric old Spanish method of torture, the 'death of the skins'. The two men were wrapped alive in the green wet cowhides they had butchered, placed in the sun and left to die as the skins slowly contracted, crushing them. Since the skins used had the Olive brand on them, the murders were widely believed to be done by the Olives. After a short trial the Olives were acquitted by the county court, although many people continued to believe the brothers were guilty.

The incident came back to haunt them on 1 August 1876, when a gang of men, led by Grip Crow, son of James Crow, attacked the Olives' ranch. Jay Olive was shot and killed and Print Olive was wounded in the thigh. Afterwards a watch with an inscription bearing the name of Fred Smith was found near the place of the attack, who the Olives thought was one of their friends. A couple of days later it is thought that Print Olive confronted Fred Smith and killed him. Smith's wagon was found but there was no sign of him and his body was never found. Bob Olive then shot a local rancher, Cal Nutt, who he believed was one of the men behind the attack that killed his brother.

In September the same year, two well-armed black cowboys rode up to the Olives' ranch and asked for some water. Louise Olive obliged and was then asked where her husband Print Olive was. Print Olive happened to be in the house and heard the conversation and stepped out with his rifle in his hands. Print demanded to know their business with him, and at this point one of the men, who had dismounted, jumped back on his horse and was shot dead by Print, whilst the other was whipped with a bullwhip. Print Olive believed that they had been sent to kill him, but got scared when they found themselves looking down the barrel of a Winchester rifle. Print Olive was arrested and tried for murder and assault but was acquitted.

With rustling and violence escalating, the Olive family decided it was time for a move and in 1877 they moved to the open ranges of Nebraska, taking some of their reliable ranch hands. For a year all was well, but again settlers moved into the area and rustling started to take place and all the time the Olive family were expanding. Settlers were moving onto what was essentially government land and being warned of by Olive's men, being told that this was Olive's land and to stay out. But two homesteaders that faced up to the Olives were Ami Ketchum and Luther Mitchell, both having a reputation for rustling cattle and mixing them with their own herds. In the meantime Bob Olive got himself the position of Deputy Sheriff of Buffalo County. Once in position, he got a warrant issued for the arrest of Ketchum and Mitchell on the charge of rustling. Bob Olive rode to their ranch to serve the warrant and was gunned down and killed. The two men went on the run, but two days later a posse caught up with them and turned them over to the Custer County Sheriff Barney Gillan. He then turned them over to Print Olive in exchange for the $700 reward that had been offered for their capture. Just moments after the money had changed hands and the sheriff had departed, Print Olive hanged the two men who had killed his brother. It transpired later that two local men, Bill Green and Jack Baldwin, went to where the two bodies were hanging and set fire to them.

Print Olive and his foreman Fred Fisher were arrested along with nine more of Print's men for the murder of Ami Ketchum and Luther Mitchell. The trial took place on 27 February 1879 in the Liberal Hall, Hastings, Nebraska, Olive and Fisher being tried separately from the other nine men. Both Olive and Fisher were found guilty and sentenced to life in prison. Twenty Months later Print Olive argued for a new trial, this time in his home county, and he was acquitted. What happened to Fisher and the remaining nine men is not known. One can only surmise that they too were acquitted.

The cost of the trials and the extremely hard winter that had decimated his herd left Print Olive almost broke. With what he had left, he separated his business from that of his brothers and in 1882 moved to Kansas on a range called Saw Creek just north of Dodge City and the Smokey Hill River. With what money he had left he invested in land, cattle and a meat market and within a couple of years was elected a director of the Western Kansas Stockman's Association. Slowly he started to rebuild his life and his fortune, but in 1884 his partner in the meat market absconded with all the assets of the company, leaving Print to find $10,000 owed to creditors. Just as it seemed that things could not get any worse, a severe cold front came down from the north covering the plains with ice and snow. Two more storms throughout the winter of 1885–6 almost killed off the entire cattle industry, causing the ranchers to save what could be saved by killing and skinning what remained for what they could get for the hides. Over 50 per cent of the herds were lost during that winter.

Print Olive moved to Trail City, Colorado in 1885, in the hope of rejuvenating his way of life by becoming half owner of the Longhorn Saloon and a livery business. One year later having recouped some of his losses, Print Olive decided to sell up and move back to Kansas. In the meantime he set about collect money from those who owed him. One of these was a cowboy by the name of Joe Sparrow, who had been on one of the trail herds belonging to Print Olive and who owed him the princely sum of $3.50. When he asked for the money, Sparrow told him that he had no money whatsoever, not even enough money for a meal. Print, who by this time was waving his handgun in Sparrow's face, suddenly relented, gave him a dollar to get something to eat and told him to forget about the money he owed for a while.

It would seem that Sparrow had not been impressed by Olive's 'generosity' as the following events proved. In Trail City that day was a friend of Joe Sparrow, John Stansfield. Sparrow told his friend about the argument he had had with Olive over the money he owed as they headed towards the saloon. Sparrow later said, that Stansfield said to him 'If you'll kill him I'll stand by you'. The pair were standing by the bar when Print Olive walked in with his right hand tucked into his waistband where he normally carried his gun, only this time he was unarmed. The moment Joe Sparrow saw Print Olive he pulled out his gun and fired twice, wounding Olive both times. Print fell back into the doorway, crying 'My God Joe don't murder me!' Joe Sparrow walked over to the now prostrate figure on the floor, placed his handgun against Print's head and pulled the trigger, ending his life. With that Sparrow made a run for the door but walked into a deputy sheriff who had been called to the saloon and was arrested. Stansfield, who vowed to stand beside Sparrow if he killed Print Olive, disappeared into the night and was never seen again. Joe Sparrow was taken to Las Animas, Colorado to stand trial for Print Olive's murder and was found guilty, but due to some legal irregularities he was given a retrial, only this time in Pueblo. This time the jury could not reach a unanimous decision and so a third trial was ordered in May 1888 in which the jury found him not guilty.

Print Olive had suffered an ignominious end for someone who had become a cattle baron, although some said that it was a just and fitting end for a ruthless, vicious murderer, who would stop at nothing to get what he wanted.

Chapter 34

Jim 'Deacon' Miller

Jim Miller was born in Van Buren, Arkansas, in 1861, but a few months later the family moved to Franklin, Texas. Two years later, Jim Miller's father died so his mother Cynthia Miller took the family to Evant, Texas, to live with her parents. When Jim was just eight years old, Jim Miller's grandparents were found murdered in their home and for some reason that has never been clear, young Jim Miller was arrested for their murder. However, no charges were ever brought against the eight-year-old.

Jim Miller's sister Georgia, who had married John Thomas Coop, agreed to take Jim onto their farm at Plum Creek, Gatesville for a few years, before he joined his mother and his family in Coryell County, Texas. Little is known about his activities in the next few years, but in 1884 he was arrested for murder after shooting his brother-in-law with a shotgun whilst he was asleep on his porch. It transpires that earlier that day he had had a violent argument with his brother-in-law. He was tried and convicted and sentenced to life in prison, but on appeal the conviction was deemed to be unsafe due to a legal technicality and the original conviction was overturned.

On his release Jim Miller went to work for Emanuel 'Mannen' Clements on the McCulloch County ranch. Clements was a cousin of the one

Portrait shot of Jim Miller.

Jim Miller at the gambling table.

of the most feared gunfighters at the time, Jon Wesley Hardin. One year after he started on the ranch, City Marshal Joe Townsend shot and killed Clements after an argument in a saloon in Ballinger. A couple of weeks later Joe Townsend was shot from his horse by a shotgun and, although he survived, he had to have an arm amputated. The shooting with a shotgun had all the hallmarks of Jim Miller.

Not long after the shooting of Joe Townsend, Jim Miller left and for the next couple of years travelled around the Texas-Mexico border area doing various jobs. He ran a saloon in San Seba County, became a deputy sheriff in Reeves County and for a short time was the town marshal in Pecos. His dislike for Mexicans manifested itself when he was accused of killing some Mexicans, claiming they were trying to escape from lawful custody after he had caught them rustling cattle.

After a number of years of travelling around, Jim Miller married the daughter of Mannen Clements and settled down as a deputy sheriff in Pecos. To the townspeople he was a well-respected man, always polite, a regular member of the Methodist church and had acquired the name of 'Deacon' Miller because of the long black frock coat he always wore regardless of the weather.

It is not known what the root cause was, but Jim Miller became embroiled in a feud with the sheriff of Pecos, George 'Bud' Frazer, after it was alleged that Miller was allowing criminal gangs to have a free rein in Pecos. Frazer called in Texas Ranger John Hughes to help him restore law and order to the town. Things came to a head when Frazer confronted Miller in the town's saloon and accused him of being involved in the murder of a local cattleman Con Gibson, who had been shot with a shotgun. Eyewitnesses said that before Miller could reach for his shotgun, Frazer pulled his pistol and shot Miller in his right arm. Miller then shot back using his left arm, hitting an innocent customer, but Frazer shot once again, this time hitting Miller in the groin causing him to fall to the ground. Frazer then walked up to Miller and fired four shots into his chest. Jim Miller was rushed to the doctors and it was discovered that beneath his long black frock coat he wore a metal breastplate. The injuries he suffered to his chest were just some bruising, but he had gunshot wounds to his arm and groin.

A couple of months later Jim Miller was standing outside the blacksmith's shop when Bud Frazer suddenly appeared and began shooting at him. After hitting him in the arm and the leg, Frazer rushed over and emptied his revolver into Miller's chest. Once again the metal plate on his chest saved his life. Bud Frazer was arrested and charged with attempted murder, but after a lengthy trial in El Paso it resulted in a hung jury. A new trial in Colorado City ended with Bud Frazer being acquitted. The jury were of one mind and doubtless thought that Jim Miller got what he deserved.

One year later, on 14 September 1896, Jim Miller walked into a saloon in Toyah, a small town near Pecos where Bud Frazer was at the gambling table and, without saying a word, fired two loads of buckshot into Frazer's head, killing him instantly. Jim Miller was arrested and subsequently charged and tried for murder at Eastland, but the jury couldn't agree and so a new trial date was set. At the second trial he was acquitted after a minister gave a character reference, saying that Jim Miller had conducted a prayer meeting whilst in prison on remand and was an exemplary example of a minister of the gospel. The jury acquitted him.

One of the witnesses who testified against him was Joe Earp, a distant relation to Wyatt Earp, and it was known that Jim Miller uttered threats against anybody testifying against him. A month later Joe Earp was shot dead from a shotgun blast and the blame was once again pointed at Jim Miller. But Jim Miller had an alibi: he was a hundred miles away at the time. However, it was discovered later that he ridden all night at a breakneck pace to put distance between him and the victim.

With fingers being pointed at him from all directions, Jim Miller decided to move on and, despite having had serious run-ins with the law, was accepted into the Texas Rangers operating from Memphis, Texas. The number of lawmen who had ridden on both sides of the law was quite prolific, or as one lawman put it, 'you set a thief to catch a thief'. For the next three years he rode with the Rangers carrying out his duties, which included killing three men caught rustling in neighbouring Collingsworth County.

James Brown Miller with his wife and son.

In 1900 he left the Texas Rangers and moved to Fort Worth where his wife Sallie opened a boarding house. Through various connections Jim Miller began to offer his services as 'professional killer' with varying rates depending on the person. His average charge was as little as $50 rising to $2,000 for each contract and within weeks he had completed two 'contracts'. Because one of the killings was carried out using a shotgun, Jim Miller persuaded his partner at the time, Lawrence Angel, to admit to the killing and Miller would be a witness that he acted in self-defence. It worked and Angel was acquitted.

Such was the fear that Jim Miller instilled into people around this time, that even lawmen were afraid of him. In 1904 he accepted a contract to kill a man by the name Frank Fore who was being protected by three deputy sheriffs, Jim Clark, Tom Coggins and Dee Harkey. Jim Miller followed the four men to the Westbrook Hotel in Collingsworth, and whilst the three lawmen remained in the lobby, Frank Fore went to the men's restroom. Miller followed Fore and shot him there, then went into the lobby and offered to turn himself in to the three lawmen, claiming self-defence. Dee Harker, knowing Jim Miller's reputation, walked away wanting nothing to do with it. The remaining two deputies claimed that they had witnessed the shooting and that Jim Miller had acted in self-defence.

One killing concerned a deputy US marshal and Indian policeman by the name of Ben Collins. It was thought that the killing had been ordered by a man called Port Pruit for $2,000, who had been shot and crippled by Collins when resisting arrest. Once again a shotgun was used and Jim Miller was in the frame for it. He was arrested and put on trial, but once again he managed to escape the hangman's rope by being acquitted due to insufficient evidence. A number of killings were carried out over the next few years including that of Pat Garrett, the former sheriff of Lincoln County who had killed Billy the Kid.

Casual shot of
Jim Miller.

He had been gunned down with a shotgun on a lonely stretch of road near Las Cruces and again Jim Miller was suspected. It is thought that friends of Billy the Kid had ordered the killing in revenge for what Garrett had done.

The law finally closed in on Jim Miller after the killing of former town marshal Allen 'Gus' Bobbitt. Miller had been contracted to carry out the killing by two ranchers, Jesse West and Joe Allen, who had been in dispute with Bobbitt over livestock for a number of years and blamed him for being forced to move to the Texas Panhandle. They wanted to return to the area but knew that Bobbitt would stand in their way, so they decided to remove the objection. In a letter to Tom Hope, the president of the Ada National Bank in Oklahoma who had been a close friend, Jesse West explained the problem. One of the bank's cashiers, Berry Burrell, was a friend of Jim Miller as well as being a livestock trader and sometime accomplice of Miller. Burrell carried out surveillance on Bobbitt and informed Miller when the time was right to carry out the assassination. The fee for the 'hit' was said to have been in the region of $1,700.

Around midday on 27 February 1909, Gus Bobbitt and a neighbour Bob Ferguson arrived in town with two wagons to collect cottonseed meal for their respective livestock. After loading up, the two wagons left Ada for their ranches using the Ada/Roff road. They encountered Jim Miller riding a shabby-looking brown mare with distinctive markings, but neither man recognised him, as he appeared very well dressed unlike the normal riders in those parts.

After travelling about six miles down the winding road and close to Bobbitt's ranch house, the two men approached a large oak tree at which point there were two loud bangs from a shotgun and Gus Bobbitt screamed with pain as buckshot tore into his leg and lower body. The force of the blast blew him from the wagon onto the ground, the noise frightening the team of horses, which galloped off. Miller appeared from behind the tree with a pistol in his hand and looked at his victim, who was still alive, then inexplicably turned, ran to his horse and galloped away, throwing his shotgun into a nearby stream. Both Bobbitt and Ferguson recognised Jim Miller at once, but Ferguson's main concern was for his friend Gus Bobbitt and after catching up with the wagon went to his friend's ranch to seek help.

Gus Bobbitt's wife, Tennessee, had heard the shots and came out and ran to her husband's side. In the meantime Ferguson had telephoned for a doctor and the law. Gus Bobbitt told his wife that Jesse West and Joe Allen were responsible for the 'hit', but he died before a doctor could get to him. The law immediately put out a warrant for the arrest of Jim Miller after Bob Ferguson's description and the fact that they recovered the shotgun and wire cutters used by Miller at the scene. Berry Burrell, a known associate of Miller, had purchased the cutters some days earlier. The law then traced the shabby brown mare to John Williamson, Miller's nephew who lived in Francis a few miles north-east of Ada. After questioning, Williamson admitted that he had loaned the mare to his uncle, who on returning told him that he had just killed Gus Bobbitt.

One month later Texas Rangers arrested Berry Burrell in Fort Worth and one week later Jim Miller. Jesse West was in Texas at the time of the murder, but evidence by way of a statement from a former employee, said that West had told him during a discussion about Gus Bobbitt that: 'He wouldn't work again until one of us was in the grave, and I have kept my promise.' Jesse West met Joe Allen in Oklahoma and both were promptly arrested. When told they were being taken to Ada to stand trial for the murder of Gus Bobbitt, they both insisted that if they were returned to Ada they would be lynched. The four men were taken to the town jail and placed in custody. Mutterings throughout the town started and became increasingly vociferous. Gus Bobbitt had been a popular man and the townspeople had had enough of the reign of terror that had been created by Jim Miller and his cronies. They were also deeply mistrustful of the law after Miller had got away with a

Jim Miller and three of his gang, Joe West, Berry Burrell and Jesse West, hanging in a barn next to the jail having been lynched by a mob.

number of murders due to lack of evidence or witnesses who were too frightened to testify.

On 18 April, close to midnight, a large mob descended on the jail and forced their way in, disarming the deputy sheriffs and the jailer. The four men were unceremoniously dragged from their cells and taken to a barn next door. Just minutes later their four bodies were swinging on the end of ropes hanging from the beams. The reign of terror brought about by Jim Miller was over.

Chapter 35

William 'Billy' Thompson

William 'Billy' Thompson was born in Knottingley, Yorkshire, England in 1845, the brother of Ben Thompson. The family moved to America in 1852 and settled in Texas. Little is known about his early years other than he was known to have a quick and sometimes violent temper. During the American Civil War both the brothers joined the Confederate Army and served with distinction. After the war, with the taste of defeat still in the mouths of the Southerners, and with Reconstruction under

Billy Thompson, brother of gunfighter Ben Thompson.

way in the South, times were hard and it wasn't long before Billy Thompson found himself in trouble.

His first serious encounter with the law came on 31 March 1868 whilst watching a fistfight between a white US soldier and an African-American. The townspeople were supporting the black man, mainly because the soldier was part of the occupying army and this angered another US soldier named William Burke, who was also watching. Billy Thompson, who was standing close to Burke, was shouting loudly along with the townspeople, which annoyed the soldier, who then began to berate Billy verbally. A violent argument followed, but later Burke apologised and invited Billy for a drink, which he accepted. After a couple of hours of drinking the two men went to a brothel, still having minor but friendly bickering. Billy went upstairs with one of the prostitutes, whilst Burke stayed downstairs drinking. Then, fired up by drink, William Burke got to his feet shouting threats against Billy Thompson and drawing a pistol from its holster, marched upstairs to the room in which Billy was with the girl. On reaching the room, Burke kicked in the door and fired shots at Billy but missed. Billy Thompson returned fire and shot Burke, seriously wounding him. William Burke died the following day. Despite being the innocent party and having a witness, Billy Thompson panicked and decided that as the man was a US soldier, he probably wouldn't get a fair trial and would end up being hanged. That morning he left town and headed out of the county.

Billy Thompson contacted his brother Ben and told him what had happened, asking him for some money. Ben obliged, but told him to keep his head down and try and not get into any more trouble. Two months later Billy rode into Rockport, Texas, and took his horse to the livery stable. The 18-year-old stable hand, Remus Smith, took Billy's horse and was leading it to a stable when the horse put its nose into some feed. The young man slapped Billy's horse hard on the rump to get him away from the feed, at which point Billy Thompson shouted at the boy threatening to do the same to him. The boy shouted back, telling him to take off his gun belts and come and try. Without a moment's hesitation Billy Thompson pulled out his pistol and shot the boy twice, killing him. Remus Smith was a well-liked and popular young man in the town and almost immediately a large posse was formed to hunt down his killer. Billy Thompson's life was being mapped out for him. He now thought he would be wanted for two killings, but unknown to him there was no warrant out for his arrest for the killing of the US soldier, as it was considered to have been carried out in self-defence.

For the next five years, supported financially by his brother, Billy Thompson travelled around the state and kept out of trouble, although he was still on the run for the murder of Remus Smith. On 18 April 1873 he checked into the Grand Central Hotel in Ellsworth, Kansas to wait for his brother. Ben Thompson arrived two months later and the pair of them became house gamblers in Joe Brennan's Saloon. The sheriff of Ellsworth, Chauncey Whitney, kept a very tight grip on the town and was extremely well liked throughout the county. The two brothers got on well with the sheriff, despite their reputations, but not so well with the town constable John Morco. Morco was always bragging about the number of men he had killed in the line of duty as if to warn everyone that he was not someone to tangle with.

Sheriff Chauncey Whitney.

Things started to go wrong for Billy Thompson on 30 June when John Morco arrested him for carrying a weapon within the town limits. Although very angry, Billy paid the fine, keeping his fiery temper under control. But it was obvious that John Morco was out to get Billy Thompson one way or another. His chance came on 15 August when, after he had been drinking heavily, Billy Thompson started shouting threats against John Morco. In the meantime Sheriff Chancey Whitney had been ready to leave town with his family, but decided to postpone it until things quietened down. Ben Thompson in the meantime had introduced a man by the name of John Sterling into a high-stakes poker game, on the understanding that he would get a percentage of any winnings Sterling might acquire. After winning $1,000, Sterling left to go to another game in a rival saloon, without honouring his arrangement with Ben Thompson. On entering the rival saloon, Ben Thompson found Sterling drinking with John Morco and confronted him demanding his share of the winnings. Sterling just laughed and then, realising that Ben Thompson was unarmed, slapped him hard across the face. As he did so, John Morco pulled out his pistol and forced Ben Thompson out of the saloon. A little while later Sterling and Morco stood outside Joe Brennan's saloon shouting for Ben Thompson to come out and fight them. On hearing that his brother was in trouble, Billy Thompson ran to help and the two brothers armed themselves and walked out into the street. Sheriff Whitney, on hearing the shouting and threats, ran out into the street unarmed and confronted the Thompsons. He managed to persuade them to join him for a drink and let things calm down, to which they agreed. Sterling and Morco had other ideas however, and as the three men made their way to Brennan's saloon, they moved to intercept them. As they did so, a warning shout from a friend of Ben's, Neil Cain, caused Ben Thompson to whirl round and fire a shot at Sterling and Morco. At the same time he heard his brother's shotgun go off and saw their friend Sheriff Whitney fall to the ground. Billy Thompson looked aghast as his friend hit the ground, Ben Thompson said, 'My god Billy, you have just shot your best friend'.

Billy replied, 'It was an accident.' Sheriff Whitney lay on the ground and looking up, was heard to say, 'He did not intend to do it, it was an accident, please send for my family.' Witnesses later testified that Billy Thompson was not looking at Whitney at the time, as the sheriff was at his side and the shotgun, which was cocked, just suddenly went off.

Ben Thompson realised that his brother could be lynched if he stayed around, such was the popularity of Sheriff Whitney, and told his brother to get out of town immediately. Billy Thompson jumped on his horse and left town before anyone could react. Whitney died of his wounds three days later and a $500 reward was placed on Billy's head. Neil Cain was ordered to leave town at gunpoint by John Morco, who then had a warrant issued for the arrest of Ben Thompson for assault. The following day the town council sacked John Morco after deciding that he had instigated the incident that had brought about Sheriff Whitney's death. Deputy Sheriff Ed Hogue, a crony of John Morco became sheriff but only for a short time as the town council dismissed the entire police force and replaced it with all-new personnel.

The new town marshal, Ed Crawford, caused another problem when he arrested a cowboy by the name of Cad Pierce. Texan cowboys had been causing a few problems in the town during large cattle drives and the town council ordered the marshal to keep a lid on the activities of the drovers when they came to town. During the arrest of Cad Pierce, he was shot and then clubbed to death with a pistol butt. Trouble flared up immediately, which prompted the townspeople to organise vigilante groups to roam the streets looking for Texan cowboys causing trouble.

John Morco remained in Ellsworth and continued boasting how he had killed twelve men in a gunfight, but then got involved in a drunken, heated argument with a cowboy and pulled a pistol on the unarmed man. A newly-appointed police officer, John Brown, ordered him to put the gun away, but when Morco refused and waved the gun in his direction, he shot Morco dead. A couple of weeks later Town Marshal Ed Crawford was shot dead, it was thought by friends of Cad Pierce in revenge for the death of their friend. With all the killings going on, former Deputy Sheriff Ed Hogue decided that it was time that he moved on and left town.

Over the next few years Billy Thompson was on the run from the law and from bounty hunters. Warrants for his arrest were being regularly sent out across the state for the murder of Remus Smith but not for the other two killings in which he was concerned, because the first one was considered to be self-defence and the second an accident.

In September 1874 he was arrested in Mountain City, Texas, for a minor offence, but quickly escaped to San Antonio before they realised who he was. Within days of arriving in San Antonio he was in trouble again, when he entered the Long Horse brothel and hit one of the prostitutes after a row about money. After being chased by two of San Antonio's police he managed to escape. But in October 1876 his luck ran out whilst he was working on the Neal Cain Ranch in Travis County, Texas. Captain John Sparks was leading a detachment of Texas Rangers that was looking for Neal Cain in connection with some rustling, when they recognised Billy Thompson from a wanted poster they were carrying. He was immediately arrested and preparations made to take him to Ellsworth to stand trial. Ben Thompson was contacted and he in turn notified Aransas County in the hope that they would apply to have him extradited there to stand trial rather than in Kansas.

Then it was discovered that a number of Ben Thompson's friends were travelling to Ellsworth to support him, so the decision was taken to send him to the prison at Fort Leavenworth, Kansas.

The trial of Billy Thompson for the murder of Sheriff Chancey Whitney lasted nine days at the end of which he was acquitted as it was proven to be an accident. Despite representations from Aransas County for Billy Thompson to be held until he could be extradited to stand trial for the murder of Remus Smith, he was released and he promptly disappeared.

Nothing was heard of Billy Thompson for three years, and then out of the blue he was arrested for assault with intent to kill. He was in the town of Ogallala, Nebraska and had become involved with a prostitute by the name of 'Big Alice' who was working for a saloon owner by the name of Bill Tucker. Tucker resented the affection Billy Thompson was showing Big Alice and told him so in no uncertain manner. On 21 June 1880 a drunk Billy Thompson stood outside the saloon waving his shotgun in the air and shouting threats against Bill Tucker. Then suddenly he opened fire, sending two loads of buckshot into the saloon, and then reloading, fired another two shots into the saloon, only this time he hit Bill Tucker in the hand, severing one finger and damaging others. Tucker grabbed a shotgun from behind the bar and ran outside only to see Bill Thompson running down the road. He opened fire and hit Thompson in the back, sending him crashing to the floor. Thompson was arrested and, because of his injuries, he was allowed to stay in the Ogallala House Hotel to recover, but under heavy guard.

On hearing of his brother's arrest, and of the heavy guard placed over him, Ben Thompson decided against going to the town himself, but asked his friend Bat Masterson to intervene. Masterson met with Billy Thompson, then went to see Bill Tucker, who after a long conversation, agreed to drop the charges against Billy for a sum of money. It is not known how much was asked for, but Ben Thompson was unable to raise it, so after distracting the guards Bat Masterson was able to sneak Billy out of the hotel and on to a train taking them south. A grand jury later indicted Bill Thompson for the charge of assault with intent to kill but the charges were eventually dropped.

Aransas County in Texas were still sending out arrest posters for Billy Thompson in respect of the murder of Remus Smith and on 28 October 1882, he was arrested in El Paso by Captain George Baylor of the Texas Rangers. He immediately handed him over to the county sheriff, who in turn gave the responsibility of his custody to his deputy Frank Manning. For reasons best only known to himself, Deputy Manning was persuaded by Billy Thompson to be allowed a night on the town, promising to return the following morning. It was to take another six months before he was finally tracked down by Deputy Sheriff Court from Aransas and returned to Aransas to stand trial.

The problem now facing the authorities in Aransas was that over 15 years had passed since the murder, witnesses had left town, and the lawmen at the time had either moved on or died. The prosecution had almost no evidence to produce to the court and failed to prove their case, so Billy Thompson was acquitted of the one blatant murder that he was entirely responsible for.

The following year his brother Ben Thompson was killed in San Antonio, Texas after being ambushed in the Vaudeville theatre there. Speculation was rife that Billy Thompson would be looking for his brother's killers but he never did. He spent the remaining years of his life making a living out from gambling in Houston and Galveston, Texas. He died alone on 6 September 1897 in Houston, Texas at the age of 52.

Chapter 36

The Rogers Brothers

Amongst the more obscure, but nevertheless very violent, outlaws were the Rogers Brothers. The three brothers, Bob, Sam and Jim, who were one-quarter Cherokee, had moved with their father, Frank Rogers, from Arkansas to the Cherokee nation in Oklahoma in the mid-1870s. The family settled on Big Creek, near Horseshoe Mound, just south of Coffeyville, Kansas. At the age of seventeen Bob Rogers took up a job as a cowboy working on a ranch near Nowata. He was a headstrong and violent young man and was soon in trouble with the law when on 10 November 1891 he attacked another cowboy, and was arrested and charged with 'Assault With Intent to Kill'. He was just 18 years old. Taken to Fort Smith, Arkansas, he was released on bond two days later and immediately left for Oklahoma.

Outlaw Bob Rogers, leader of the Rogers Gang.

Whilst in custody he had heard tales of the Dalton Gang and their exploits and became fascinated by them. On his return to Oklahoma he put together his own gang with the intention of emulating his 'heroes'. In the summer of 1892, together with Willis Brown, 'Dynamite Jack' Turner, his brother 'Kiowa' Turner and Bob Stiteler, they started rustling horses in the Cherokee Nation and taking them to Arkansas to sell. The inept young gang were soon traced by Deputy US Marshal Hickman 'Heck'

Bruner and his posse and arrested. They were taken to Fort Smith to appear in front of the dreaded Judge Isaac Parker. Bob Rogers was immediately recognised as the leader of the gang and was initially sentenced to the Federal reformatory, but because of his age Judge Parker placed him on probation and said to him, 'This is your first offence lad, if you continue on this path of life, death may be the next penalty'. For some unknown reason the earlier charge of 'Assault with Intent to Kill' seemed to either have been forgotten by the authorities or dismissed. The lenient sentence seemed to have the opposite effect on Rogers, because as soon as he

Deputy US Marshal Eli Hickman 'Heck' Bruner.

got back home he continued in his ways, petty stealing and rustling.

Just three months later, on 3 November 1892, Bob Rogers was in a pool hall in Catoosa, Oklahoma, when he got into an argument with a Cherokee Indian Police deputy by the name of Jess Elliott. Both of them had been drinking and the alcohol-fuelled argument descended into a violent struggle in which Elliott was knocked to the floor. Bob Rogers began to mercilessly beat the almost unconscious figure on the floor and was pulled away by some of the men in the hall. They then forced Bob Rogers out of the pool hall, but kept the deputy there until they decided he was fit to leave. Later Jess Elliott got on his horse and rode out of town, but just on the outskirts Bob Rogers, who had followed him, knocked him off his horse and slashed his throat with a knife. Some minutes later a passer-by found Jess Elliott propped up against a post with blood gushing from his throat. A number of other people came to try and help, when suddenly Bob Rogers appeared on his horse, scattered the people and then began to trample the now lifeless body under the hoofs of his horse. He then got off the horse and went through the deputy's pockets, removing a number of documents. In the meantime someone had gone to fetch Deputy Town Marshal John Taylor, but by the time he got there Rogers had gone.

The deputy town marshal trailed Bob Rogers to the small town of Sapulpa where he found out that Rogers had had his horse re-shod, telling everybody he was heading west. Six months later Bob Rogers re-appeared with a new gang consisting of his two younger brothers, Jim and Sam, and a man called Ralph Halleck. The gang rode to the railway station at Chelsea, Oklahoma, and forced the stationmaster to open the safe, stealing just $418. Two days later the gang robbed the Frisco Railway at their depot at Bluejacket, Oklahoma, forcing the stationmaster there to open the safe. Two weeks later on 13 July 1893, the gang held up the Mound Valley Bank at Labette, Kansas, and stole just $800.

The sudden train station robberies became a cause for concern and Judge Isaac Parker ordered Deputy US Marshal 'Heck' Bruner to track down the Bob Rogers Gang and bring them before him. Two weeks later Bruner and his posse caught up with two of the gang, Sam Rogers and Ralph Halleck, at a farm just outside of Vinita, Oklahoma. When challenged to give themselves up the two outlaws opened fire on the posse, but within minutes Halleck was dead and Sam Rogers badly wounded. Sam Rogers was later to live with his father, crippled for the rest of his life.

Bob Rogers teamed up with members of his old gang, Willis Brown, 'Dynamite Jack' Turner, his brother 'Kiowa' Turner and Bob Stitele, and just before Christmas 1893, attempted to rob the Missouri, Kansas & Texas train at Kelso, Oklahoma, but the quick thinking of the engineer prevented this by diverting the train through a siding. One of the train's crew, however, was shot and badly wounded in the attempt. Two days later the gang struck again at Seminole, Oklahoma, when they stopped the Arkansas Valley passenger train, stole money from the express car and then robbed the passengers. The gang split up and went their separate ways, but on 8 January Deputy US Marshal William Smith was told that one of the outlaws, Bob Stiteler, was hiding out at the home of a Henry Daniels who was Bob Rogers' brother-in-law. Stiteler was arrested and taken into custody. It was discovered much later that Bob Rogers had turned Stiteler in for the reward money. It was never disclosed how he was going to collect the reward, considering there was also a reward out for him.

Two weeks later Deputy US Marshal 'Heck' Bruner and his posse, still on the trail of the remaining members of the Bob Rogers Gang, discovered that three of the gang were hiding out a ranch at Big Creek just outside Centralia, Oklahoma. The posse surrounded the house in which the gang were holed up and called for them to surrender. A gunfight followed in which Kiowa Turner and Willis Brown were killed and 'Dynamite Jack' Turner was captured.

With his gang decimated, Bob Rogers went to ground and went to live with his father and crippled brother Sam at his father's house near Horseshoe Mound. His younger brother Jim had joined up with another gang and was involved in rustling horses. Then on the morning of 17 March 1894, Deputy US Marshal Jim Mays and a large posse surrounded the house with rifles and shotguns covering every window and door. Also in the house at the time was a man called Charlie Collier and his wife, who were employed by Frank Rogers. Deputy Mays knocked on the door of the house and spoke to Bob's father, telling him that he was there to arrest Bob Rogers and that a well-armed posse had the house surrounded. Charlie Collier and his wife, still in their nightclothes, fled the house and went to stay with a neighbour nearby. After ascertaining that Bob Rogers was in the house, Deputy Mays called out for him to give himself up. 'Come and get me' was the response. Three deputies, McWilliam, Daniels and Smith, offered to go and with Daniels and McWilliam leading and Smith, with Frank Rogers behind, they started up the stairs. Bob Rogers confronted them at the top with a pistol in each hand. On being ordered to put down his weapons Bob Rogers opened fire. The first shot hit McWilliam in the heart, killing him instantly, the second tore through Daniels' arm sending him tumbling back down the stairs, causing him to crash into Smith and Frank Rogers, all of them ending up in a heap on the floor. The three men stumbled out of the door and with that Mays ordered the posse to open fire. It was reckoned that over 300 bullets were fired into the house and remarkably not one of them hit Bob Rogers. Mays ordered a ceasefire and called for Bob Rogers to give himself up. Rogers replied that he would as long as he could bring his gun. When the door opened and Bob Rogers stepped out with his gun in his hand, he was told to point the gun downwards. For some unknown reason Bob Rogers asked Deputy US Marshal Mays if he had a warrant for his arrest, and when Mays replied with a wry smile that he didn't need one, Rogers started to raise his gun. Seconds later he was slammed back against the wall of the house as a volley of shots hit him. Bob's younger brother Jim Rogers was arrested in 1901 by members of the Anti-Horse Thief Association and sent to Federal prison for ten years.

Chapter 37

Ann Bassett

Ann Bassett was born near Browns Park, Colorado, in 1872, but soon after her birth the family moved to Utah. Her sister, Josie, was born in 1874 and in their early years both girls were sent to boarding schools back East, as their mother, Elizabeth Bassett, wanted them to have a good education. Whilst the girls were away, their parents moved back to Browns Park, where their father, Herb Bassett, became a successful rancher. The ranch unusually straddled the borders of Utah, Wyoming and Colorado. The area known as Browns Park was a notorious area for outlaw hideouts and it wasn't long before Herb Bassett became involved

Ann Bassett.

with such outlaws as Butch Cassidy, 'Black Jack' Ketchum and Harvey Logan (Kid Curry) selling them beef and horses, and allowing them to run rustled cattle and horses through his land. In return they never touched any of his cattle or horses.

The two girls returned from their education, both in their late teens and very attractive. They were intelligent and articulate but preferred life on the ranch to that of the city. Their father had taught them to ride and to shoot with pistol and rifle and both were excellent shots. Their presence on the ranch soon attracted the attention of the outlaws who started to make more

Ann Bassett's ranch.

visits. It wasn't long before Ann became romantically involved with Butch Cassidy, whilst her sister became involved with a man called William Ellsworth 'Elzy' Lay. But the girls shared their affections with other members of the Wild Bunch, Ben Kilpatrick and Will Carver.

The two girls' romantic associations with the outlaws were to prove very helpful when some of the wealthy cattle barons started to put pressure on the family to sell their ranch. When the Bassetts refused to sell, some of their cattle started disappearing and it was obvious who was doing it. So in turn the girls started rustling cattle from the other ranchers in the area, helped no doubt by their outlaw friends. In desperation the ranchers called in a Pinkerton detective turned professional killer by the name of Tom Horn to deal with the problem. He caught two of the outlaw rustlers, who were both known to the Bassetts, Isom Dart and Matt Rush, and killed them. However, he never once approached the Bassett family. Maybe it was their close connection with members of the 'Wild Bunch' that deterred him. Tom Horn was later convicted of murder and hanged.

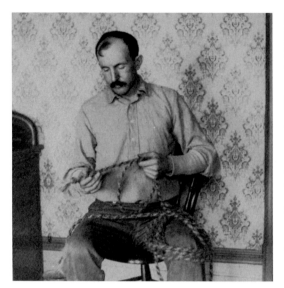

Above left: Killer Tom Horn awaiting trial.

Above right: Tom Horn awaiting execution after being found guilty of murder.

Josie Bassett was becoming heavily involved romantically with 'Elzy' Lay, who was Butch Cassidy's closest friend, but this didn't stop her becoming involved with Butch Cassidy too after he was released from prison. Ann Bassett was still involved with Ben Kilpatrick, but when 'Elzy' Lay began a new relationship with another woman by the name of Maude Davis, Josie took up with Will Carver. Ann Bassett then restarted a relationship with Butch Cassidy and despite the romantic exchanges between the outlaws there appears to be no animosity from either side.

The Bassetts continued to supply the outlaws with beef and fresh horses and the outlaws in turn made it known that the Bassetts were under their protection. This deterred any cowboys brought in by the wealthy ranchers to harass the family, as they knew it would bring down the wrath of the outlaws upon them. In one report, when it was heard that some cowboys had been paid to cause the Bassett family some problems, Kid Curry, who was the most feared member of the gang, met up with them and warned them of the consequences of their actions if they were to carry them out. The Bassett family occasionally had a few minor problems with the other ranchers, but they were never seriously approached again.

Over the next few years the two young women continued their merry-go-round relationships with members of the Wild Bunch, but by the beginning of the 1900s most of the gang were either dead or in prison. Then in 1903 Ann Bassett married a rancher by the name of Hyrum Henry Bernard and settled down. One year later Ann was arrested for cattle rustling and put on trial, but after a short trial she was acquitted. The marriage lasted just six years, but Bernard and Ann remained friends, with Ann returning to the family ranch. Ann and Josie were now running the ranch, as their father was now too old to manage. Fortunately for the sisters, Ann's ex-husband Hyrum helped them to maintain the property. Outlaws still occasionally dropped by for beef and fresh horses, ensuring that the cattle on the ranch were left alone. In 1928 Ann Bassett remarried, to rancher Frank Willis, and moved to Utah where she remained for the rest of her life.

One mystery has always surrounded Ann Bassett and that was if she was also known as Etta Place, the girlfriend of the Sundance Kid. There is a certain amount of evidence to say that she was the same person. She dated Butch Cassidy as Ann Bassett and dated the Sundance Kid as Etta Place. There are reports that say that the descriptions of both women are almost identical and that both women were well educated and very articulate. They both could ride well and were very capable of handling guns. The two women were never seen together. When the Sundance Kid was killed, Etta Place just vanished and was never seen again. On the other side of the argument Ann Bassett was known to have been in custody charged with rustling, when it is said that Etta Place was in South America with Harry Longabaugh.

In her memoirs Ann Bassett never claimed to have been Etta Place, although there must have been a time, if they had been two separate people who were romantically involved with the same men that they would have met. It is a matter for conjecture, and certainly enhances an intriguing romantic story whether it is true or not.

Chapter 38

Morris 'Railroad Bill' Slater

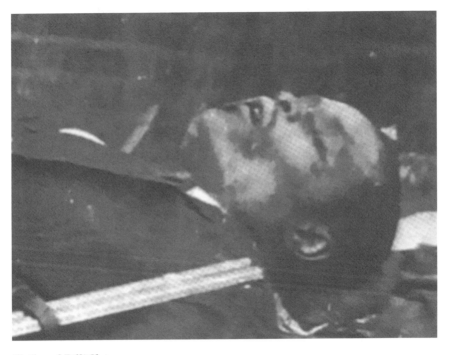

'Railroad Bill' Slater.

One of the most feared train robbers of the West was a man who came to be known as 'Railroad Bill'. His real name is not known, but some think he was Morris Slater who was born to slaves in Alabama. He left home at an early age and worked with a travelling circus, becoming a very adept showman and magician.

Tiring of the travelling, Morris Slater went to work for a turpentine company in South Carolina, and then, when the company moved to

Baldwin County, Alabama, and then to Bluff Springs, Florida, he moved with them. He was a very energetic worker and highly regarded by the company. He was well liked by all who worked with him, but it was a quirk of his that he always carried a Winchester rifle and when working, had it stuffed down one of his trouser legs.

His life changed when he was caught hitching a ride aboard the Louisville and Nashville (L&N) Railroad by the brakeman, who threw him off the moving train. Upon hitting the ground, Morris Slater, badly shaken and bruised, pulled out his rifle and fired a shot at the brakeman, fortunately missing him. The railroad company, when told of the incident, immediately dispatched a railroad detective to investigate, offering a reward of $350 for his capture. As the detective did not know the name of the assailant he simply called him 'Railroad Bill'. When Morris Slater discovered that he had been given that name he was delighted and vowed to live up to it in his vendetta against the railroad.

He came to the attention of the law again, when he was stopped by a deputy sheriff for carrying a repeating rifle without a permit, which was against the law in Florida. Morris Slater immediately threatened the lawman and a gunfight ensued. The deputy's shotgun was no match for the rifle and he was wounded, fortunately not seriously, but enough to make Morris Slater a wanted man in Florida.

Now on the run from the law, Slater organised a gang to rob the freight trains of the L&N. The plan was simple; they would place one of their men in one of the freight trucks at night just before the train left the station and, at a prearranged spot where the train slowed down, the man would throw the freight out onto the track where members of the gang collected it. It is assumed that he followed soon afterwards. Rumour had it that 'Railroad Bill' gave a lot of the stolen freight to the poor, but the truth was that he sold most of it to his contacts in the turpentine camps.

On 6 March 1895 'Railroad Bill's' luck nearly ran out when he was discovered fast asleep behind a water tank close to the Bay Minette railway station. The crew of the freight train, who found him, took his rifle and pistol and then woke him up. A startled 'Railroad Bill' immediately jumped to his feet and ran off down the track, drawing a second pistol from beneath his shirt. He then engaged in a gunfight with the crew of the freight train, who immediately ran and took shelter in a small section hut. Minutes later they were enforced by some of the bridge crew armed with shotguns. They decided to go after 'Railroad Bill' and walked slowly towards him, firing as they did so. Just then a second freight train arrived and 'Bill', who had suffered a minor gunshot wound, jumped on the footplate and forced the engineer to drive it out of the station. As the train moved off, 'Bill' fired at the other train crewmembers, who did not fire back in case they hit the engineer. After travelling about 300 yards, 'Railroad Bill' clambered down from the footplate and started to walk back along the track towards the men. The gunfight lasted a few more minutes before 'Bill' ran out of ammunition and deciding that discretion was the better part of valour, he headed into the swamp area and escaped.

One month later 'Railroad Bill' was spotted on a back road near Bay Minette, Alabama, by two railroad men. A gunfight erupted and the two men headed for town and informed the law. A posse was quickly formed and a hunt for the wanted man started. After trailing him for several miles, 'Railroad Bill' was discovered hiding in a barn. The posse surrounded the barn and opened fire, but in the ensuing gunfight one of the posse, Deputy Sheriff James Stewart, was killed. In the confusion that followed 'Railroad Bill' escaped.

Now began a state-wide search for the outlaw and the reward was raised to $500, Sheriff Edward McMillan of Escambia County, Alabama, who was familiar with 'Railroad Bill's' ways, vowed to catch him. Railroad Superintendent McKinnie, also desperate to catch the outlaw, recruited a known associate of his, Mark Stinson, as an undercover agent. One week later information came back that 'Railroad Bill' was

Sheriff Edward McMillan.

going to carry out a robbery in Pollard, Alabama, so armed with the information a posse set out. On reaching the town they discovered that 'Railroad Bill' had attacked the Pollard armoury, stolen rifles and ammunition and then disappeared. Stinson got word to the posse that 'Railroad Bill' had arranged to meet him two nights later at a remote cabin alongside the railroad track in Mount Vernon, Alabama. On the arranged night the posse crept up on the cabin and then attacked. They mistook Mark Stinson for 'Railroad Bill' in the confusion and shot him dead.

They discovered later that somehow 'Railroad Bill' had learned of the plan and was nowhere in the vicinity.

Sheriff Edward McMillan, who was still trailing the outlaw, learned that he was in Bluff Springs, Florida. The fact that he was an Alabama sheriff wasn't a problem, because he had been deputised as an officer of the law for Florida. Quickly organising a posse they crossed the state line and, after some hours of hard riding, they approached where they had been told he was hiding. As they neared the hideout, they came under fire from the outlaw who had been warned of their approach. After a short, but intense gunfight, 'Railroad Bill' escaped, leaving behind several wounded men and one dead Sheriff McMillan.

Despite the loss of Sheriff McMillan, the chase continued with the size of the posse increasing. Word then reached the posse that 'Bill's' trail had been picked up in Escambia County, Alabama, heading into the swamplands of Murder Creek. Then came a message from a storeowner in Atmore, Alabama, saying that 'Railroad Bill' was coming into his store that evening. On reaching the store that same afternoon, the posse concealed itself and awaited a prearranged signal from the storeowner. The hidden posse watched as 'Railroad Bill' arrived just before the store closed and waited until he went inside. At that moment a two-man posse, who had also been trailing 'Railroad Bill', arrived, and one of them went into the store. Constable Leonard McGowin entered

Railroad Bill on the coolin' board

Body of Morris 'Railroad Bill' Slater stretched out on a board.

the store and saw 'Railroad Bill' seated with his back to him talking to the owner. He immediately raised his rifle and fired at point-blank range at the outlaw. The impact of the bullets sent the outlaw staggering forward and he desperately tried to claw his pistols from their holsters. By this time two other lawmen had entered the store and 'Railroad Bill' fell dead under a fusillade of shots. The state-wide manhunt for 'Railroad Bill' was over.

'Railroad Bill's' body was taken to Montgomery, Alabama, where it was embalmed. The body was then officially identified, so that the reward for his capture dead or alive could be sanctioned. But such was the public interest when they discovered that the body was in Montgomery, that the local people clamoured to see it. The local police officers, seeing an opportunity to make some money, put it on display for 25 cents per person to see the body. The local authorities were horrified and demanded that the body be taken elsewhere. It was then sent to Pensacola, Florida, for further reward identification, where once again it was placed on display for a fee. Once again the local authorities ordered the practice stopped and the body of Railroad Bill was taken back to Birmingham, Alabama. At first it was decided to 'petrify' the body and put it on display at carnivals and the suchlike, but in the end it was taken back to Pensacola and given a proper burial.

Conclusion

The Wild West was in fact not as wild as some people tried to make it out to be. Some of the so-called gunfighters never killed anywhere near the number of people they themselves claimed – or their biographers claimed they did. One good example of this was Bat Masterson, the famed gunfighter, who when asked to sell the gun he used in his gunfights, went and bought a second-hand Colt .45 from a pawn shop in New York, cut twenty-two notches on the handle and sold it to a collector. When asked if these were the number of men he had killed, he replied that he didn't count Indians and Chinamen, but neither did he confirm or deny it. In truth Bat Masterson killed only three men for certain and another three probably.

Of the know recorded killings by the various outlaws and gunfighters, Billy the Kid only killed four men, not the twenty that fiction writers attributed to him and this applied to a number of gunfighters. John Wesley Hardin, a notorious gunfighter, was said to have killed twenty-seven men, but was only charged with one murder. Wild Bill Hickok killed three men, two of them in Abilene whilst he was City Marshal and one in Springfield, Missouri, for which he was tried and found not guilty, whilst Clay Allison, however, was thought to have killed at least fifteen men in his time as a gunfighter.

Several of these gunfighters were influenced by difficult home circumstances and had early violent experiences during the Civil War, but some of them just seemed to be inherently bad despite education and a good upbringing. Today many lawbreakers are much more sophisticated, using computers and banking methods to line their pockets. There are however still some unsophisticated common criminals who demonstrate uncontrollable violence with little or no consideration for life or property. It seems that now, as then, outlaws continue to attract our fascination.

The days of the Wild West and the legends it produced gradually came to an end, as communication, transport and technology improved and spread its control over the Wild West, its deserts, mountains and plains.

Bibliography

Burton, Aft T., *Black Gun, Silver Star*, University of Nebraska Press, 2006.

Cunningham, Eugene, *Triggernometry*, Barnes & Noble, 1996.

Marks, Paula Mitchell, *And Die in the West*, William Morrow & Company, 1989.

Metz, Leon Claire, *The Shooters*, Berkley Publishing, 1976.

Shirley, Glen, *Law West of Fort Smith* Bison Books, 1968.

Index

Sallee, Reverend Robert 15
Salmons, John 210
Salt Lake City, Utah 2
Sampson, Sam 134, 138
San Antonio, Texas 79–80, 87, 179, 244, 245
San Benito County, California 189
San Carlos Reservation 217
San Francisco, California 126, 193
San Jose, California 189
San Joaquin, California 190
San Miguel Valley Bank 55
San Quentin Prison, California 82, 126, 188
San Seba County, Texas 234
Sanders, Dick 183
Sanders, Jim 183
Santa Clara, California 190
Santa Fe, New Mexico 74, 94, 99
Santa Fe Cattleman's Association 96
Santa Rosa County, Florida 206
Sapulpa, Oklahoma 247
Saw Creek, Kansas 231
Sayles, Bill 58, 64
Scaggs, Larkin 13
Scales, Clint 119–20
Sceyene, Texas 44
Schufeldt's Store 119
Scott, Fernando 15
Scraper, Jennie 169
Seamen, Carey 156
Sedailia, Missouri 143
Sehlbrede, Judge 114
Selman, John 224–6
Selman, Thomas 224–5
Seminole, Oklahoma 248
Seminole Nation, the 116
Shackleford County, Texas 223, 226
Shadley, Deputy US Marshal Lafe 31, 32

Sharpless, County Sheriff Seth 199
Shawnee, Kansas 13
Shell, Nancy Old Lady 169–70, 171
Shelton, Deputy Sheriff Matt 183
Shiloh, Battle of 227
Shine, John 124
Shirley, Myra Belle see Belle Starr
Short, Luke 186
Shroyer, Lou 182
Silver Bow, Montana 124
Silver City, New Mexico 94–5, 151, 185
Simmons, Dell 31
Simms, Billy 79
Sioux, the 181
Siringo, Charles A. 58, 59, 143, 199–201
Skagway, Alaska 108–14
Skagway Military Company, the 110
Skeleton Canyon, Arizona 220
Slater, Morris 'Railroad Bill' 254–8
Smiley, Kentucky 8
Smith, Bascomb 104, 107–8
Smith, Charlie 220
Smith, F.A. 'Doll' 195–6
Smith, Fred 230
Smith, James 185
Smith, Jefferson Snr 102
Smith, Jefferson Randolph 'Soapy' 102–14
Smith, Remus 241, 243, 244, 245
Smith, Rube 205
Smith, Deputy US Marshal W.C. 119
Smith, Deputy US Marshal William 121, 248–9
Smith's Parlour 108
Smoky Hill River, South Dakota 228
Snow, George 225
Snyder's Store 189
Sohn, Alf 29